Shell Game

Corporate

America's

Agenda

for Schools

Clinton E. Boutwell

PHI DELTA KAPPA
EDUCATIONAL FOUNDATION
Bloomington, Indiana
U.S.A.

Cover design by
Victoria Voelker

Cover illustration
by John Berry
Copyright ©1997

Library of Congress Catalog Card Number 97-67352
ISBN 0-87367-499-5

Table of Contents

Introduction

American education has experienced a continuous tug-of-war between two contending forces. One of those forces, called here "utilitarian," attempts to direct education toward specific, pragmatic ends. Business has been one of the major advocates of the utilitarian, insisting at various times that educators produce more scientists, more engineers, more college graduates, or currently, a "world-class workforce." At various times parents also have been utilitarians, especially when stirred by the media railing against some educational deficiency. Then parents worry that their sons and daughters will not have the educational advantage they need to advance in the world of work, and they demand that the schools adopt the "basic skills" programs that the parents feel they experienced in school.

The other contending force, awkwardly called the "educationalist" view, develops from within the profession and focuses on the development and growth of individual children. The heroes of that view are John Dewey, Jean Piaget, Lev Vygotsky, and similar philosophers and cognitive scientists. They laid out the precept that the target of education was *individual* development without reference to society's demands or parents' needs. It was the developing child and adolescent who needed to be the focus of pedagogical efforts. That view has driven education research until modern times. As more insight was gained about how children learned, how they obtained and used knowledge, it was translated by mid-level scholars and educators into practical teaching strategies, curricula, and school organization patterns.

During the 20th century, each of these forces has gained temporary sway over the schools. When the utilitarians' pragmatic demands were not shrill, educationalists were able to go about their business in peace and quiet, developing ideas and implementing programs congruent with the state-of-the-art understandings about cognition and learning. The voices of the utilitarians periodically broke through that calm, demanding solutions to whatever problem had emerged to rile them. Thus when the Soviets put an object in space before the United States did, pundits and government officials alike castigated educators for letting that happen. The federal government began to pour millions into teacher training to make sure the Commies never got the advantage again. However, life for educationalists soon returned to its normal, benign neglect as business and government turned their attentions elsewhere.

That "red scare" stirred other pundits, who soon were on the utilitarian bandwagon. Johnny can't read, or do math, or write a decent letter, or whatever, became the hue and cry. Those attacks lasted for a time, but again settled down to occasional bleats until business again found itself in dire straits. Competitors in Japan and Germany were beating American corporations, and profits were falling rapidly. As the reader will find, America's top executives were responsible for that situation. But since they were unwilling to admit their mistakes, they made education the scapegoat. This time the ruckus was heated. Charge after charge was made, all directed at the educationalists' position: Students need rigor, standards, tougher courses, harder teachers, real grades, longer hours and years. If we don't get a world-class workforce, we will become a second-class economic power.

Those charges were threatening to middle-class families, so parents began to clamor for something to be done about the schools. Schools needed to become "effective," like the Japanese schools were; they needed better management, like in business. On and on the utilitarian argument went. Education reeled under the onslaught and tried its best to accommodate the utilitarians' demands. The schools never did get up to the level that business pundits thought they should. But, strange to say, those same businesses, once they did what good businesses always do — invest in technology, re-engineer management processes, and rationalize their workforce — became super-profitable.

2

In the meantime, the socioeconomic conditions for both the utilitarian and educationalist positions changed. Corporations put in technology, re-engineered, automated, laid off millions, increased the quality requirements for the jobs that remained, and made money. Educators were off the hook. Or were they? Under the twin demands coming from business and parents, by the end of the 1980s schools were immersed in reform and restructuring, trying successfully to tool up to meet utilitarian demands. For those tracked into vocational education, there was more school-to-work, more tech-prep, more career academies. For those tracked in college-bound courses, there were more honors courses, more homework, more "rigor," more of everything.

But there was a problem. The American economy was about to be inundated with qualified workers and highly qualified college graduates in numbers never before dreamed. At the same time, the *number* of American job opportunities was dropping because of a combination of downsizing and technological replacement of workers. Neither Corporate America nor educators had ever had that situation before. It was a paradox: lots of well-qualified graduates coming out of high schools and colleges, and too few jobs to go around. That is the *jobs dilemma*.

In this book I take that dilemma as a starting point and explore a number of questions: With too few decent job opportunities, how can education be an advantage? Is the whole push for greater numbers of "high-tech, high-skill" workers a fraud? What will happen to all those highly qualified workers and college graduates who are not lucky enough to get one of the few jobs for which they are qualified? What are the consequences for the country if millions more highly qualified graduates have to take substandard jobs? Must we delude students into thinking that good times await them? Are there ways to increase the number of high-tech, knowledge jobs in order to expand opportunities and avoid those consequences? What is education's role in all this? Shall we stop producing high numbers of qualified graduates? How could we do that and be true to the ethic that the centrality of each individual child's education is inviolate? In an economy that increasingly focuses on global markets and international competition, is there any extraordinary educational potential that will help American students cope with the challenges and threats of the 21st century, including getting a good job?

I also suggest answers to all those questions. In the end, the reader will see that John Dewey was right, that all we had to do was be patient. In his *Experience and Education*, Dewey argues that there is no necessary duality between the desires of the utilitarians and what the educationalists want. For educationalists that became true only when cognitive research taught us specifically what kinds of instruction, programs, and school organization worked best for humans. And it became true for Corporate America only as executives realized the full impact of computer-based and information systems technology. Cognitive research told us that education needed to focus on the development of higher-order thinking and problem-solving processes. Modern corporate enterprise demanded a qualitatively different workforce, one that could think and solve problems and be creative and innovative. That is just what educationalists had been saying all along!

However, the confluence of the utilitarian and educationalists views has come at a time when the schools are not really ready. There exists, especially in the high schools, too much emphasis on the "transmission of the end-results" of academic disciplines, on the students as receptors; and there is not enough emphasis on exploration, student activity, problem solving, and other aspects of authentic learning. Schools have to do more than restructure; their practices are so inconsistent with cognitive learning theory — and so far away from the knowledge and habits of mind needed by modern business — that they are unable to break the hold of inertia without completing more radical and fundamental changes. To meet new standards of performance and expectations, high schools will need a complete metamorphosis, what is called here a *transformation*. That issue will be important in whether we are to avoid a debilitating job dilemma crisis in America.

Each of these questions and issues is addressed in the chapters that follow. In Chapter 1 I discuss the causes of the jobs dilemma and analyze projections of future workforce needs.

4

Then, in Chapter 2 I describe the consequences that will result if the economy continues to blindly follow its current path. It will use figures from the Labor Department and other sources to describe a two-tiered workforce, with a few very well-paid employees at the top and a huge number of poor at the bottom. It will share the predictions economists and sociologists make for such an America and the implications of those predictions for educators.

In Chapter 3 I tackle the issue of blame. Even though it is fashionable, now that Corporate America has re-established its economic primacy in the global marketplace, to eschew laying blame, it is necessary to set the record straight for educators, especially since we have carried a lot of guilt for such a long time. We will see, again from the economists, what really went wrong with the economy and how America's education system has always been a strength in its economy, not a weakness.

In Chapter 4 I discuss the possibility of expanding the number of decent job opportunities for school and college graduates beyond the limited numbers now projected by the Labor Department. I present the solutions posed by economists and describe where and how those job-expansion ideas are being put in place — unfortunately, not here in the United States, but by our chief economic rivals in the European Union. The chapter ends with my questions regarding whether our corporations can afford to implement job-expansion practices.

Chapter 5 answers that question in the affirmative. I describe the relationship between productivity, profits, and job expansion, and point out that the traditional formula still is in effect: increased productivity means more jobs. But I also make it clear that neither wages nor jobs have benefited from the technology-driven productivity now being experienced by America's corporations. The new wealth being created is going almost exclusively to top executives' and shareholders, and it is coming out of the pockets of workers who have seen no wage or income increase for a decade. But at least the point is made: If they wanted to, America's corporations could afford to expand job opportunities for more Americans.

In Chapter 6 I show how they could do that. The chapter describes high-performance work organizations and their different approaches to employees. High-performance firms are dedicated to the rapid expansion of technology and automation. Their secret lies not only in technology, but also in management's relationship with workers. The executives in high-performance companies know full well that their highly trained workers add value to the products they sell and that valuable employees are the key to corporate success. I offer examples of the basic strategies being used right now by America's best corporations, practices that easily could be extended to make job expansion affordable and profitable in other firms. What is needed is more diffusion of high-performance processes and values to more firms. That and a thrust to increase productivity to expand job opportunities will be the contribution of business to the resolution of the jobs dilemma.

That puts the ball back in the educators' court. Thus in Chapter 7 I ask whether the schools are ready to provide the kind of high-tech, knowledge workers an expanded job market will demand. Right now, with business downsizing and reducing the demand, it is relatively easy to provide a quality workforce for business without modifying a single thing in the schools. But as we move closer to the 21st century, the backlog of well-qualified graduates will surely grow, especially as corporations continue to cut excess workers through automation. By not changing a thing, schools are going to experience the fallout from downsizing. More students will be prepared for good jobs but will be forced to take jobs for which they are overqualified, because the good jobs have been taken. Thus educators again will take the rap.

In Chapter 8 I describe what could and should be done to get high schools and community colleges up to speed. Getting "up to speed" means simultaneously meeting the educationalists' goal of preparing young people for life and the utilitarians' goal of preparing students for the world of work. Exemplary high schools and educational practices are discussed, showing the way things could be for both students and schools. We are not too far from a solution, but there are a number of encumbrances along the way.

6

Finally, in Chapter 9 I discuss those encumbrances and sound a call for more sophisticated professional development programs, with special emphasis on professional development schools. It will be argued that a teacher cadre ready to use constructivist and responsive teaching practices, the principles of emergent curriculum organization, and the infusion of technology, will meet the needs of individual students, as well as those of industry. I also discuss how corporate executives have come around to the educationalists' insight that changing the schools is a long-term, collaborative process in which blame and vitriol are out of place.

This book closes on a happy note. All that will be needed is the political will of our representatives and the economic acumen of our top business executives. They must realize that if they do not tend to the needs and aspirations of the American people, if they cast those needs aside for some mythical global market, then the only recourse for America is a choice that no one wants — political disequilibrium.

As a practicing educator for many years, I came to realize the discrepancy between what I saw was a good education for kids and what business demanded. As a superintendent, I found that business people do not realize that their needs are easily met by the schools if we work together. However, all educators need to understand where business executives are coming from, what they see as the bottom lines. We need that insight in order to convince them that we can help in their endeavor if they accept a partnership, rather than a dominant relationship. Thus as educators read this book, they will find an unsentimental view of businesses that are acting in a predatory way; but they also will find that those businesses that care about people, their workers, and their customers will soon be the dominant force in American economic life. The more educators understand and support the efforts of those businesses, the better off education will be.

Chapter One

Profits Without People

Louis V. Gerstner Jr. had a busy year in 1993. He was recruited from RJR Nabisco to become the CEO at IBM. He also was the principal author of a book that berated American schools and teachers.[1] He held educators accountable for not increasing America's supply of world-class workers — those with high-tech skills and problem-solving abilities — that he claimed the corporations sorely needed.

Gerstner's recruitment to IBM turned out very propitious for him, though not for IBM's world-class employees. First, Gerstner was paid a bonus of $4,924,596 just to sign as CEO. Then he was given a stock package worth $10,820,880. That, plus some incidental incentives, brought Gerstner's total package to more than $21 million.[2] For that kind of money, one would think that Gerstner might just take care of IBM's business and let educators take care of their own, especially when Gerstner's advice to educators was wrong-headed and disingenuously misleading.

Gerstner's own executive behavior belied the message of his book. IBM made its reputation, and huge profits, by employing the high-tech researchers, engineers, and technical developers who represented the finest products of American schools, indeed, the very kind of graduates that Gerstner claimed schools are not supplying for business. Yet, in line with IBM's new "lean and mean" management strategy, Gerstner fired 90,000 of those highly trained employees, just about one third of IBM's 270,000 employees. That was in addition to the other 183,000 quality employees that IBM fired before Gerstner arrived.[3]

Gerstner's actions were driven by the current conventional wisdom held by business executives regarding the new global economy, to wit: Systemic restructuring of the world's industrial economies is proceeding rapidly, and corporations have to capitalize on the power of technology and use more sophisticated production processes to become more efficient. They need to build what the executives stylishly call a *New Economy*. Gerstner, along with most other corporate executives, believed that American business had better get on the bandwagon or be left behind. These corporate executives had dilly-dallied and had managed to *lose* America's competitive advantage through a series of ill-advised and inept decisions. The effects of those poor decisions were accelerated by a series of unwise governmental actions, especially certain tax policies and a military expansion.[4]

For at least two decades, the United States did little to protect its manufacturing base against intrusion from foreign competitors. But by 1980, America's core corporations finally had recognized the steady loss of competitive advantage to businesses in other countries, Japan and Germany in particular. In their panicky reaction to the new global economic challenge, those core corporations initiated a number of piecemeal actions.

America's business executives could have responded more effectively to changes occurring in the global economy. They could have cultivated new ideas and approaches to make the American economy competitive again. But they did not. Instead, they adopted simple-minded downsizing.

First, the core corporations and their subsidiaries began to shift factories and routine manufacturing work to low-wage areas within the United States. When they ran out of American places to move, routine manufacturing companies began moving to Mexico, Malaysia, Ireland, and other low-wage foreign countries. Based on what one writer calls a "post-industrial fantasy," many thriving high-skill industries, such as textiles, electronics, autos and auto parts, and hundreds of home consumer products — VCRs, televisions, and the like — were allowed either to move overseas or to come under the domain of other advanced industrial countries — Japan, Germany, The Netherlands, France, and others.[5]

Step-by-step, American executives began to dismantle the workable, tacit compact they had with their workers and the American public, thereby undermining much goodwill between themselves and their employees and customers. From 1947 through 1979 that compact had assured better job security, wages, and fair prices for most American workers and the public. To justify ending that compact, industry apologists and pundits argued that America was moving from an industry-based economy to an information-based economy. The policy-elite argued that America's "information age" would generate high-wage, high-tech jobs to replace those lost manufacturing jobs. Thus the country witnessed a decline from 31 million manufacturing jobs in 1980 to 16.6 million jobs in 1993, including the loss of tens of thousands of high-skill, high-quality jobs.[6]

When shipping the jobs to foreign countries did not solve the problem of competition, the next set of executive decisions was to slash wages and lay off workers — a practice euphemistically referred to as "downsizing" and "right-sizing." But foreign competitors met those actions with further price reductions. Thus, in the 1980s, America's core corporations began to merge, hoping to gain advantage from greater economies of scale. But computer-based manufacturing methods reduced the cost advantage of mass-produced goods, and foreign competitors continued to eat away at America's advantage. Corporate executives appeared to have run out of piecemeal solutions; all that was left was a complete abrogation of the social compact and the beginning of a serious restructuring of the American economy, a process that still is continuing.

Restructuring America's economy to make it lean and competitive involves four basic elements. First is the relentless application of technological innovation in the workplace to replace or

11

deskill workers. Second is the radical modification of managerial processes — loosely grouped under the rubric, "re-engineering" — in order to organize the functions of employees and managers to maximize the efficiency of technological innovations. Third is the internationalization of economic interests, investments, and ownership.

Fourth, and most germane to our purposes, is the increasing internationalization of intellectual talent and ideas. Knowledge workers — including those from newly industrializing countries — and the intellectual products they create can be imported and exported by any country, including the United States. Being a knowledge worker gives one the capability of moving anywhere in the world where one's intelligence, talent, and services are needed; it also means that one can command handsome salaries and perks. America's corporations are capitalizing on that worldwide intellectual potential to hire the best minds in the world or, at least, to snap up and control the intellectual products of those minds and, in that sense, to reduce the work options for Americans.

Implementing those four restructuring elements has made it possible for America's major corporations to regain much of the competitive advantage they had lost to businesses in other advanced industrial countries. However, in regaining that competitive advantage, American corporations became not only lean but also mean.

America's corporate executives, like IBM's Gerstner, discovered that they did not need a huge world-class workforce. Therefore, the bottom line of corporate restructuring for America's people was the massive shedding of workers, a reduction in future job opportunities, and a concomitant plunge in income, benefits, and living standards for millions of households. For example, Xerox, AT&T, Bank of America, United Technologies, General Motors, and other Fortune 500 companies consigned more than 583,000 high-tech, high-skill workers to the unemployment lines in 1993. The steel industry shed 208,000 high-skill employees since the late 1980s.[7] In 1994 there was another round of cuts by powerful firms, those that typically employ high-skilled, high-quality workers; for example, General Motors fired an additional 74,000 workers, AT&T fired 83,500, Sears fired 50,000, and GTE fired 32,150. AT&T cut another 77,800 employees in 1995, more than half its 151,000 managers; and it eliminated another 40,000 high-tech and managerial jobs in 1996.[8] On top of that, the telecommunication industry overall plans to lop off another 100,000 high-skill employees by the year 2000.[9]

Managers are not immune from the downsizing frenzy. Many managers report that, between mass firings and coping with the mound of work still remaining, job stress is pervasive. A recent survey of managers by the American Management Association found widespread erosion of morale at companies with job cuts. "Millions of white-collar supervisors and mid-level managers are joining blue-collar production workers in a common category, frayed-collar workers in gold-plated times," said Robert Reich, Labor Secretary in the Clinton Administration.[10]

Table 1.1: Declining jobs (in thousands).

Occupational Area	Lost Jobs
Word Processors	212
Bookkeeping/Audit Clerks	178
Bank Tellers	152
Sewing Machine Operators	140
Cleaners/Servants	108
Computer Operators	98
Calculating Machine Operators	64
Office Machine Operators	56
Textile Workers	47
File Clerks	42
Material Movers	36
Farm Workers	36
Machine Tool Operators	34
Central Office Operators	24
PBX Installers & Repairers	33
Servants/Electronic Assembly	30
Telephone Installers/Repairers	26
Personnel Clerks	26
Data Entry Keyers	25

Adapted from "Why That Sheepskin Is Worth So Much," *Los Angeles Times Special Careers Supplement*, 14 June 1996, pp. 14-15. Farm jobs actually were the big losers at 273,000, but were not included in this table because they constitute less than 2% of the workforce and thus have a negligible overall effect.

Large numbers of high-performance workers who received their pink slips have been forced into low-wage, temporary, and contingent jobs. In 1994 two-thirds of all new jobs created in the United States were low-wage, non-benefit jobs.[11] The Conference Board, the corporations' major research alliance, notes that the number of "contingent workers," — temporary hires, part-timers, independent contractors — was at an all time high in 1995, constituting at least one-tenth of the workforce. That is almost double the proportion of contingent workers in 1990.[12] Contingent workers get pay comparable to that of full-time staff, but without the benefits that typically add 40% to labor costs. A contingent workforce also is more flexible: When business sags, the temps go first.

Many of the new jobs being "created" are actually temporary jobs. In fact, at least a quarter of those employed today are temporary, part-time, or contract workers. The number of Americans working part-time grew by 2.2 million from 1973 to 1996, reaching a total of 6.2 million. This growth was entirely a function of involuntary part-timers, those who would rather work full time. Moreover, hundreds of big companies have outsourced non-core functions — such as legal, assembly, maintenance, repair, customer services, audit, cafeteria, and mailroom operations — to outside companies.[13]

The total *number* of high-tech, high-skill jobs is shrinking as America builds its New Economy. The Bureau of Labor Statistics' projections up through the year 2005, the most authoritative figures available, show clearly that high-skill, high-tech jobs will be at a premium while low-tech, low-wage jobs become abundant.[14] One business magazine concluded:

> The country that invented mass production can no longer compete for routine manufacturing jobs. . . . [But] the hot industries of the 1980s — computers, finance, retailing, and defense — [also] are shedding workers at a furious pace.[15]

All Dressed Up and Nowhere to Go

Newspapers and the publications of professional organizations are filled with reports bemoaning the decline in good jobs. However, universities continue to produce large numbers of high-quality professional graduates. As Daniel Greenberg, publisher of the influential *Science and Government Newsletter*, reports, "The Ph.D. production system is so obviously out of whack with the needs of the economy."[16] Both the National Science Foundation and the Bureau of Labor Statistics report that the number of scientists in the United States increased 12.6% between 1987 and 1992. Unfortunately, that growth produced such an unabsorbable glut that many science graduates end up with jobs for which their education overqualifies them. The lack of science and engineering jobs is forcing many Ph.D.s to become "migratory workers," moving from one low-paying technician's job to another.[17]

The pharmaceutical industry has cut more than 3,000 science jobs, and the chemical industry cut 16,000 science jobs.[18] Yet in 1993 American universities awarded a record 39,754 doctorates, up 2.3% from the previous high in 1992. This caused one critic to comment sarcastically: "The university system has never been particularly permeable to logic. . . . The university version [of featherbedding] will expire when the money runs out."[19]

A RAND report concluded that new doctoral degrees in science and engineering average 25% *above* employment opportunities. RAND charged that universities are oblivious to the job market, especially one that has no place for so many expensively trained graduates.[20] One investigator summarized the problem: "These bright, energetic scholars are all facing the same problem. Our universities are turning out more scientists with advanced degrees than our culture can absorb."[21] The problem is so severe that many experts recommend that requirements for doctoral degrees be broadened to provide graduates with training in business, education, and other fields that might enable them to switch careers.[22]

More than scientists and engineers are caught in the supply/demand bind produced by corporate restructuring. Thousands from other professions face the same bind. Even graduates of America's most prestigious *business* schools, for example, are finding no guarantee of a job. MIT's Sloan, one of the top two business schools in the United States, had 4% of its graduates unable to find jobs after graduation; Northwestern University's Kellogg had 4.5% unemployed; Dartmouth's Amos Tuck, 11%; and an amazing 16% of the MBA graduates from Stanford University were unable to find jobs. Less prestigious business schools fared even worse: 40% of Ohio State's business school graduates could not find jobs; Georgia, 30%; Texas at Austin, 24%; and Tulane, 24%.[23]

As the American economy continues to restructure, all indicators show clearly that the demand for high-performance and high-skill workers will never reach what was needed by the old economy. In other words, millions of graduates will find *no* jobs awaiting them or will have to accept *substandard* jobs, ones for which they will be overqualified. Educators working to help high school and college students "prepare for the world of high-tech, high-skill work" have a quandary: How can educators' efforts to prepare an American world-class workforce be reconciled with the increasingly obvious decline in world-class job opportunities?

Even with the glut of college graduates and high-tech, high-skill workers, America's high schools continue to push students to take more academically challenging classes. They do so with the rationale that such classes will prepare them for tomorrow's workforce. Enrollment has increased dramatically in those subjects. For example, by the middle of the 1980s, almost every state had *increased* the number of math and science credits required for graduation. The Council of Chief State School Officers reported that students taking math and science courses increased dramatically between 1982 and 1994. By the early 1990s, enrollment in upper-level math and science courses went up in more than half the states. At the same time, there was a commensurate enrollment decline in lower-level math and science courses, as students were convinced that such low-level classes were dead-ends.[24]

A comparison of what students took in science over a decade ago with more recent data reveals how efforts to entice them into knowledge-worker precollegiate courses has paid off. The percent of students taking three years of science — biology, physics, and chemistry — doubled from 9.8% in 1982 to 21.6% in 1993, and that growth is expected to continue into the 21st century. The percent taking both biology and chemistry almost doubled, from 28.6% in 1982 to 53.9% in 1993. Each of the sciences saw dramatic gains in enrollment between 1982 and 1983; physics increased from 13.5% of students to 24.7%, chemistry from 31.6% to 55.5%, and biology from 78.7% to 98%.[25]

And the trend continued after 1993. In 1994, for example, 60% of high school graduates had completed three years of math, up from the 37% in 1982. Much of that increase was from students taking academically challenging math courses. The percentage in algebra and geometry, for instance, went from 29% in 1982 to 50% in 1994. Participation in calculus classes more than doubled, from 4% in 1982 to 10% in 1994. Contrary to what some critics have averred, these courses were not watered down, a conclusion affirmed by an on-site study conducted by the Wisconsin Center for Education Research at the University of Wisconsin.[26] Perhaps that helps to explain why, on a scale of 200 to 800, the average SAT math scores went up three points to 482 and why, with girls taking more advanced math/science than ever before, the gap between girls' and boys' scores has all but disappeared.[27]

Not only are high school students taking more challenging classes, they also are entering college in record numbers — rising from 49.9% of the males and 43.4% of the females in 1970 to 58.7% of the males and 64% of the females in 1993. As usual, 68% of seniors from the wealthiest families (the top economic quartile) were in college-prep courses. However, as more students became aware that one needed a college education to earn decent wages, enrollment in college prep courses increased dramatically, including a 21.8% increase of high school seniors from the lowest economic quartile.[28] All of those young men and women who are entering and finishing college in record numbers are expecting to get quality jobs when they graduate, but they will be disappointed.

The lack of demand for high-skill workers has lead to a continuous decline in wages since 1973. In the early 1970s, 25.9% of the workforce aged 25-64 had more than 12 years of schooling

rary jobs have been created, jobs paying only $7.74 per hour even though the average wage is almost $12 per hour. Eighty-six percent of all companies now farm out work they used to do. Those downsized workers who manage to find a new job also find themselves making at least 10% less than in their old job. With such a large pool of qualified workers, is it any wonder that fully 79% of currently employed workers say they are worried about their jobs?[35] On the other hand, the Department of Labor's projections, reflected in Table 1.3, show very few opportunities in the better job areas

Table 1.2: Where the jobs are (in thousands).

Occupational Area	Number
Cashiers	562
Janitors/Cleaners	559
Salespersons Retail	532
Waiters/Waitresses	479
Registered Nurses	473
Top Managers/Executives	466
Systems Analysts	445
Home Care Aides	428
Guards	415
Nursing Aides/Orderlies	387
Secondary Teachers	386
Marketing/Sales Supervisors	380
Teacher Aides	364
Receptionists/Info Clerks	318
Truck Drivers	271
Secretaries Nonmedical/Legal	267
Clerical Supervisors	261
Childcare Workers	248
Maintenance Repairers	231
Elementary Teachers	220

Adapted from "Why That Sheepskin Is Worth So Much," *Los Angeles Times Special Careers Supplement*, 14 June 1996, pp. 14-15.

It is apparent that millions of routine production jobs are gone and that low-paying service jobs are on the rise. In fact, the number of jobs that demand a better education are diminishing in number, as Table 1.3 shows.

Table 1.3: Number of new jobs created relative to education demand (in thousands).

Education Level Required	Number of Jobs
Less Than One Year on the Job Training	7,377
Work Experience Plus BA or Higher	3,764
Work Experience	1,331
Bachelors Degree	1,303
Long-Term On-the-Job Training	1,229
Associate Degree (2 Years)	963
Postsecondary Vocational Training	743
Master's Degree	427
Lawyer/Dentist/Physician's Degree	374
Doctorate for Adademic Work	180

Adapted from "Why That Sheepskin Is Worth So Much," *Los Angeles Times Special Careers Supplement*, 14 June 1996, pp. 14-15.

Indeed, in the inexorable process of building a New Economy, corporations in the United States have created a critical problem for the American people and the education system. With encouragement from opportunist business executives, anxious educators failed to heed the warnings implicit in a fundamental principle of economics: the law of supply and demand. Business thought, "If educators provide a huge increase in the supply of qualified workers, even though we have a need for only a handful of them, then we will have a large field to choose from and even be able to control wages. Workers are more passive when they know they can be replaced easily." Educators thought: "Here is our chance to get business support."

Using an oversimplified but not inaccurate example, the problem can be illustrated this way: If 100 workers are needed (*demand*) and educators produce 100 qualified workers (*supply*), there is a balance between demand and supply. However, if business finds ways to eliminate the need for half those 100 workers — for example, through technological innovation — and education continues to produce a supply of 100 qualified workers, an *imbalance* occurs. That is the situation developing nationwide in the United States.

The American economy now has far fewer decent jobs than ever before and, worse still, fewer challenging job opportunities for future graduates.[36] As Corporate America became lean, through cor-

21

porate re-engineering, downsizing, and the use of labor-saving technology, it simultaneously reduced the overall *demand* for quality workers. At the same time the number of jobs in quality occupations was declining severely, millions of new temporary, contingent, and contract jobs were being created with low wages and few benefits.[37] That is not a situation in which having an education is an advantage.

However, Corporate America has been insistent in its demand that the education system produce a world-class workforce. With help from business-oriented media, corporate executives have aroused the concerns of parents about the schools; and parents have become restive regarding their children's future. As a result, America's school and university educators have been scrambling to produce that world-class workforce. Universities are redesigning curricula to skew them toward technical training and professional applications. In addition, high schools are trying to redefine how they prepare students for the future by setting new standards, reforming, restructuring, and reinventing. Thus the education system is developing an ever-growing *supply* of workers with high-performance abilities. But that supply of well-qualified graduates (along with those employees displaced from their current jobs) will overwhelm the available demand for decent jobs. Millions of American college and high school students are being prepared for high-performance jobs that may never exist.[38] There is a glut of high-quality workers about to hit the U.S. economy.[39]

The Need for Low-Skill Workers

The reduction of quality job opportunities is structural, not cyclical. Thus it is not a question of just waiting it out. Cyclical problems are associated with the typical ups and downs of a free-market economy, in which recession is soon followed by a period of growth. Structural change results from a fundamental, long-term transformation of an economy. Structural changes are more profound and permanent. America experienced such a transformation when its basic economy shifted from agriculture to industry beginning shortly after the Civil War.

The current dilemma arises because the world in general, and the United States in particular, is experiencing an even more profound transformation, one in which the shift is from an economy based on mass production to a *techno-informational* economy. The techno-informational economy (often referred to as the "Information Age" or the "post-industrial economy") rests on the development of computer-based manufacturing and information systems technology. These developments allow businesses to reduce their dependence on human resources.

At first, the profound structural changes occurring in the economy appeared to promise lots of interesting, high-wage, high-skill jobs, as well as an easier life. All around there were tangible signs of the benefits of the techno-information revolution: computers, cellular telephones, autos with computer chips, the Internet, faxes, high-definition television, organ transplants, rockets to the moon. Who could doubt that we had truly entered a new age? For educators, it was pretty heady stuff. We wanted and needed to get on the technology bandwagon, both in terms of automating schoolrooms and implementing 21st century curricula. The promise was that by getting more and better education, especially technologically focused education, the lives of most American high school and university graduates would be better. That promise may never be kept.

As it turns out, the need for a greater supply of high-quality workers is a myth perpetuated by businesses' vested interest. Rather than a greater need for high-quality workers, the need for greater numbers of low-skill, low-wage workers will grow higher than ever before. Every caring educator believed the myth. But that myth soon will be exposed when 80% of America's graduates, regardless of their high-tech training, will have to resign themselves to menial, routine, dead-end jobs.[40]

Why is it that so many Americans continue to believe the myth and ignore the growing jobs dilemma?

One reason is that the jobs dilemma is *not* an issue of the total number of jobs and employment rates. The United States economy is known throughout the world as a "jobs machine," meaning that American businesses hire lots of people and the country's unemployment rate is low in comparison with most other advanced industrial nations.[41] As Table 1.4 shows, the official unemployment rate is low, averaging below 6% in 1994.

Table 1.4: US unemployment rate by category, 1994.

Category	Rate
Men	5.2
Women	5.4
Whites	5.2
Blacks	11.5
Hispanic	9.5
All Teens	18.3
Black Teens	36.5

From "Labor Markets Hit a Slow Boil But Inflation Keeps Its Cool," *Business Week*, 22 August 1994, p. 21.

Almost two million workers were hired in 1994, mostly in low-wage jobs.[42] The only group that *increased* in unemployment was black teenagers, the last hired and first fired of all groups. However, these official figures convey an incomplete statistical view of employment in the United States. One of the reasons the United States can claim that it has produced a lot of new jobs is the way it determines who is and who is not employed. In almost every other advanced industrialized country, anyone who wants a full-time job and is forced to work part time is counted as unemployed. In the United States, a person working part time is counted as employed, which reduces the overall unemployment numbers. If the United States counted as the other industrial countries counted the unemployed, we would have 4.5 million more people unemployed and an unemployment rate equal to or higher than the 11% rate in Europe.[43]

Be that as it may, the average monthly growth in new jobs was 247,000 in 1994, which totals almost three million jobs in one year. That number was up another million by 1995 and reached a total of 4.8 million by 1996.[44] The Bureau of Labor Statistics projects that total employment will increase from 121.1 million in 1992 to 147.5 million by 2005.[45] That projected 22% rate of employment growth is slightly higher than the increase attained during the previous 13-year period, from 1979 to 1992.[46] So, *absolute* job growth is not causing the jobs dilemma. However, growth in *quality* jobs is.

The number of workers employed in any occupation depends in large part on the demand for the goods and services provided by those workers. Over the last decade or so, for example, increased use of computers by businesses, schools, scientific organizations, and government agencies has contributed to large increases in the number of systems analysts, programmers, and computer repair technicians. However, even if the demand for goods and services provided by a group of workers rises, employment still may not increase because of changes in the way those goods are produced and services are provided. In fact, some changes in technology and business practice cause employment to decline despite increased demand for those goods and services.[47]

Another issue central to the jobs dilemma is the difference between the *rate* or *percent* of employment growth and the *numerical* employment growth in an occupation. Thus the rate of growth tells us only what occupations are growing quickly or slowly, not how many jobs are involved. To know how many jobs are involved, we need to know the current *size* of the occupational base; the bigger the base, the more apt the occupation will demand replacement workers. In those occupations, replacing retired workers will have a great effect on the structure of future employment by slowing the *rate* of growth but not the *number* of jobs.[48] While occupations that require a bachelor's degree or other postsecondary education or training are projected to have faster than average *percent* of employment growth, the occupations that are projected to have above-average *numerical* growth are those that require less formal education or training, and which thus are low-pay, low-skill jobs. Therefore the real issue is the not the quantity of jobs available but the limited number of quality job opportunities being generated by America's businesses.

As Table 1.5 shows, in 1992 when much of the American economy's restructuring was proceeding apace, most jobs (62.2%) were in low-wage, low-skill occupational areas and one-third

(34.9%) were in high-wage occupations (shown in bold type in Figure 1.6). By 2005, when today's fourth-graders will graduate from high school, there will be little change in the proportions of low-skill and high-skill jobs, according to the BLS projections. Low-skill jobs still will constitute 61.2% of all jobs, while high-wage, skilled jobs and other knowledge work jobs will constitute only 36.2% of all jobs. (The remaining 2.5% are in agriculture and related occupations.) However, because the total number of jobs is expected to increase by more than 26 million, the *number* of low-paying jobs will increase much more than the number of high-paying jobs.

Table 1.5: Employment by major occupation groups, 1992 and projected 2005, and percent change 1979-92, 1992-2005 (number in thousands).

Occupation	1992 Number	1992 Percent	2005 Number	2005 Percent	%Change 79-92	92-05
All	121,009	100.00	147,482	100.00	19.0	21.8
Executive Administrator, Managerial	12,066	10.0	15,195	10.3	50.4	25.9
Professional Specialty	16,592	13.7	22,801	15.5	43.0	37.4
Technicians, Related Support	4,282	3.5	5,664	3.8	57.6	32.2
Marketing, Sales	12,993	10.7	15,664	10.6	30.7	20.6
Administrator Support, Clerical	22,949	18.5	25,406	17.2	15.0	13.7
Service	19,358	16.0	25,820	17.5	24.6	33.4
Agriculture, Related Jobs	3,530	2.9	3,650	2.5	-5.2	3.4
Precision Production, Craftspeople	13,580	11.2	15,380	10.4	4.3	13.3
Operators, Fabricators, Laborers	16,349	13.5	17,902	12.1	-10.3	9.5

From U.S. Department of Labor, *The American Workforce, 1992-2005* (Washington, D.C.: Bureau of Labor Statistics, April 1994, p. 57. Boldface items are the knowledge worker, symbolic analyst occupations.

Most employment growth will be in service-producing industries. As a result:

> occupations concentrated in those industries will experience rapid employment growth, compared with occupations in goods producing industries. Of the 26.4 million projected increase in total employment over the 1992-2005 period, more than 25 million jobs are projected for service-producing industries and fewer than a million jobs are expected in the goods-producing industries.[49]

It is important to note here that the term, "service industry," is misleading. The service sector actually is two unequal occupational areas: 1) high service, which includes such high-income jobs as professionals, computer engineers, and systems analysts, and 2) low service, which includes such low-wage jobs as health aides, waiters, and gardeners, who provide in-person personal services. That distinction is needed when looking at job projections. The service occupations that require little education or training are expected to add a significant number of jobs because of their large employment bases. Service occupations with higher educational requirements will experience a rate increase but, numerically, will provide fewer job opportunities than other occupations. Thus, while the economy is projected to continue to generate jobs for workers from the lowest to the highest levels of education and training, the high-skill, challenging job opportunities will decline as a portion of that overall growth.[50]

Tables 1.6 and 1.7 better illustrate the difference between the *rate* of growth and the actual *size* of the increase in the number of job opportunities.

Note that of all the groups listed among the "fastest growing occupations" in Table 1.6, only a few (in bold) can be classified as high-quality occupations: psychologists, computer engineers and scientists, systems analysts, teachers, creative entertainment, pathologists, therapists, and operations analysts. Most other fast-growing jobs demand little education, and only a few need any special training (for example, paralegals, travel agents). However, compare those "fastest growing" occupations with the jobs that will have the *largest growth* by 2005, as shown in Table 1.7.

Table 1.6: Fastest growing occupations, 1992-2005 (numbers in thousands).

Occupation	Employment 1992	Employment 2005	Numerical Change	Percent Change
Home Health Aides	347	827	479	138
Human Service Workers	189	445	256	136
Personal/Home Care Aides	127	293	156	130
Computer Engineer/Scientist	211	447	236	112
Systems Analysts	455	956	501	110
Physical Therapy Aides	61	118	57	93
Physical Therapists	90	170	79	83
Paralegals	95	176	81	86
Special Education Teachers	358	625	267	74
Medical Assistants	181	308	128	71
Private Detectives	59	100	41	70
Correction Officers	282	479	197	70
Childcare Workers	684	1,135	460	66
Travel Agents	115	191	76	66
Radiological Technicians	162	264	102	63
Nursery Workers	72	116	44	62
Medical Records Technicians	76	123	47	61
Operation Research Analysts	45	72	27	61
Occupational Therapists	40	64	24	60
Legal Secretaries	280	439	160	57
Teachers Preschool & K	434	669	236	54
Manicurists	35	55	19	54
Creative Entertainment*	129	198	69	54
Speech-Language Pathologists	73	110	37	51
Flight Attendants	93	140	47	51
Guards	803	1,211	408	51
Insurance Adjusters/Agents	147	220	72	49
Respiratory Therapists	74	109	36	48
Psychologists	143	212	69	48
Paving Equipment Operators	72	107	35	48

From U.S. Department of Labor, *The American Workforce, 1992-2005* (Washington, D.C.: Bureau of Labor Statistics, April 1994), p. 72.

*Includes producers, directors, actors, and entertainers.

Table 1.7: Occupations with the largest job growth, 1992-2005 (numbers in thousands).

Occupational	Employment		Numerical	Percent
	1992	2005	Change	Change
Salesperson, Retail	3,660	4,446	786	21
Registered Nurses	1,835	3,417	765	42
Cashiers	2,747	3,417	670	24
General Office Clerks	2,688	3,342	654	24
Truck Drivers	2,991	3,309	648	27
Waiters/Waitresses	1,756	2,394	637	36
Nursing Aides/Orderly	1,308	1,903	594	45
Janitors, Maids	2,862	3,410	548	19
Food Preparation	1,223	1,748	524	43
Systems Analysts	455	956	501	110
Home Health Aides	347	827	279	138
Secondary Teachers	1,263	1,724	460	66
Childcare Workers	684	1,135	450	66
Guards	803	1,211	408	51
Marketing/Sales Supervisors	2,036	2,443	407	20
Teacher Aides	885	1,266	381	43
Top Executives, General Managers	2,871	3,251	380	13
Maintenance, Repairers	1,145	1,464	319	28
Gardeners	884	1,195	311	35
Teachers, Elementary	1,456	1,767	311	21
Food Counter Workers	1,564	1,872	308	20
Receptionists	904	1,210	305	34
Accountants, Auditors	939	1,243	304	32
Clerical Supervisors	1,267	1,568	301	24
Restaurant Cooks	602	879	276	46
Teachers, Special Education	358	625	267	74
Practical Nurses	659	920	261	40
Fast Food Cooks	714	971	257	36
Human Service Worker	189	445	256	136
Computer Engineers, Scientists	211	447	236	112

From Bureau of Labor Statistics.

Disregarding teacher groups for the moment, the numbers of high-skill, high-wage, knowledge-worker occupations (in bold) are modest. Note that while two of these occupations (systems analysts and computer engineers/scientists) show a high rate of growth, they start and end with the smallest number of positions (except for health aides and human service workers). There are no high-wage craft jobs, the kind that demand high-tech, precision skills for computer-based manufacturing. As a matter of fact, most of the largest job areas in 1992 — mostly the low-skill, low-wage occupations — also will constitute the overwhelming number of jobs by 2005.

The message is clear: Much of the growth in high-quality jobs already took place between 1983 and 1993, the major period of economic restructuring in the United States.[51] And during that time, the American economy still produced more low-quality than high-quality jobs.[52]

Moreover, the growth in projected new high-quality jobs between 1992 and 2005 is overstated, because it miscalculates the "replacement effects" for retirees and others. Judging by the miscalculations of the previous decade (1983-93), the effect of replacing retirees will be an important factor when calculating how many available jobs require high educational attainment. The statistics show that during the 1983-93 period, there was a percentage increase (21.1% to 28.3%) for jobs with "high educational requirements" and an actual drop (47.3 % to 45.4%) in those with "low educational requirements." But when the replacement effects are included in the calculations, jobs with low educational requirements accounted for 47.1% of all job openings, while those with high educational requirements accounted for merely 20.7%.[53] Thus:

> Employment growth from 1983-1993 indicated that occupations requiring the most education had a larger share of growth than their share of employment. But in terms of replacement needs, *jobs that require the least amount of training* account for a greater share of replacement needs than their share of employment. [Emphasis added][54]

The U.S. economy is effective as a "jobs machine" only because it has huge numbers of low-wage, routine manufacturing jobs and low-level, low-wage service jobs to soak up new graduates, as well as those who have been laid off through corporate downsizing. Moreover, the overall employment rate underestimates the true extent of *underemployment*. Underemployment — highly trained workers toiling at jobs that require few of the skills they possess and employees working in part-time or temporary positions that pay considerably less than they once made — is increasing along with unemployment. While growth has created almost five million new jobs, thus far, at least half of them are "soft jobs," that is, part-time, temporary, and contingent jobs that pay low wages and offer limited benefits to workers.[55]

Solutions must be explored to resolve the jobs dilemma. These solutions might include the smarter use of technology-driven productivity gains, more participation of labor in decisions, changes in social welfare programs, and a more efficient investment structure to replace the one that now tends to reward only stockholders and executives for productivity gains and short-changes workers.[56] Those ideas and others like them will be explored in later chapters.

Hardship in Good Times

The focus of economic restructuring in the United States is getting along with fewer employees. Businesses are able to do that by getting more work out of every worker (including increased overtime), slashing costs, and getting rid of as many workers as possible.

> I'm one of the thousands downsized by IBM. . . . I did not have a great deal of trouble getting another job . . . [when IBM laid me off] but it pays half what I was paid before and absolutely no benefits. Who am I working for? IBM . . . [who said] we need you but not the salary you were earning after 21 years.[57]

Overall, profits for the top 500 companies went up 13.8% in 1995.[58] But just as profits are soaring, wages continue to go down or stagnate. The average wage for working people dropped from $7.73 in 1987 to just $7.41 in 1995.[59] In just one year, from 1994 to 1995, wages declined from $479 per week to $475 per week.[60] In 1979, the average weekly wage was $498, adjusted for inflation.[61] Real wages have fallen for 80% of the workforce.[62] Clearly, most Americans are experiencing a decline in their standard of living as a result of Corporate America's economic changes.

Though U.S. workers are the most productive in the world, their wages are among the lowest for workers in advanced industrial nations (AIN). That is true even when health insurance and other benefits paid by employers are included. The hourly wages in other advanced industrial nations do not include health benefits because those countries have national health plans supported by taxes that spread the costs among the entire population, thus increasing the workers' buying power. Table 1.8 compares wages in typical, high-tech, advanced industrial nations.

Table 1.8: Wage comparison, industrial nations, 1995.

High-Tech Country	Hourly Wages
Germany	$25.71
Switzerland	22.63
Belgium	21.21
Austria	20.27
Japan	19.01
Average AIN	21.76
U.S.A.	16.73*

From Bureau of Labor Statistics.

*Includes employee health benefits in addition to straight pay.

American productivity, measured as hourly output per worker, has zoomed to an all-time high, rising 19% between 1980 and 1995; and corporate profits doubled during that time. Indeed, from 1993 to 1995 the American economy contributed twice as much to world growth as did the other six major industrial nations combined.[63] Profits for American companies rose by almost 14% in 1993 and were higher in 1995. By midterm 1995, when the latest figures were available, corporations reported increased first-quarter earnings of 30% compared to the previous year, and then an additional 19% advance in the second quarter! At the same time they had extraordinarily low unit labor costs, a minuscule .06% increase overall. Costs were actually *falling* in key manufacturing sectors while prices were rising about 3%. Falling costs plus rising prices meant huge profits. American workers, however, did not benefit from those great productivity gains and the economy's growth.[64]

The drive to lay off employees did not slow in a period of booming profits. For example, even after six continuous years of record-breaking profits, the world's largest toy-maker, Mattel, decided to eliminate 5% of its workforce — not because it needed to, but just because in today's business climate, it could.[65] Downsizing fever had changed the meaning of "America, the land of opportunity."

Though the pundits tell us that the economy is going strong, things are not so fine for the typical American family. The reality experienced by the average American does not square with the expressions of optimism coming from pundits and the business media. Wages, benefits, and living standards continue to slide, even though many workers are putting in more hours. A steady erosion of family income has continued unabated since the 1980s. Though both spouses work in many families, median household income is at its lowest level in a decade, down more than 7% from its 1989 peak. In spite of the business boom, 1.3 million Americans have dropped into poverty in 1994 alone, putting the total poor at an astounding 39.3 million people.[66]

Many Americans feel that they are working harder but taking less home. By 1993, U.S. workers were working more overtime hours than in any year since 1970. There were more than 6.2 million employees — about one in every 20 workers — who had part-time jobs while they were hoping to find full-time work. And the number of Americans with employer-provided health insurance fell from 62% in 1988 to 57% in 1993.[67] As one economist put it:

> There is a squeeze on American workers. We've got what looks like the healthiest economy in decades, but that doesn't sound good if you are working two or three jobs without benefits, your wife is working and you are just keeping even with where you used to be, and you don't have much leisure time or time with your family.[68]

Thus it should not be surprising that a national poll in 1995, three years after the official recovery from the 1989-92 recession, revealed that American families are terribly stressed by the economic anxieties they face. Even though the economy had produced 4.8 million new jobs by 1995 and unemployment had dropped from 7.9% to 5.6%, only 20% of those surveyed believed that the employment situation was improving.[69] The anxieties of these Americans are grounded in reality.

Pundits and business spokespersons vaunt the new computer-based workplace as "liberating" workers from boring jobs and empowering them as decision makers, and that is true for a few workers. But there is the bleak underside of the new workplace: For every empowered employee, there is at least one other who is cowering in his or her office, putting in longer hours to keep up with a job that used to keep two people busy. For every highly skilled worker moving up the ladder, there is another who is marginalized, struggling to make ends meet.

What Lies Ahead

Unless there is a fundamental change in policy, millions of American university and high school graduates will be unable to find decent, challenging, well-paying work. A large part of this problem is the result of the American education system's misguided commitment to producing world-class graduates without a commitment from Corporate America to make quality jobs available. The vested interests of the business establishment and the historic mission of America's education institutions seem to be working at cross purposes.

Some economists argue fatalistically that a high-quality labor supply will always exceed demand, especially given the current and projected technological capability of American businesses. Few scholars see any turning back from the economic restructuring taking place in America.

But what are the consequences of passive acquiescence to radical economic restructuring? To understand the implications of capitulation to "inexorable forces," rather than making political and economic decisions that might mitigate those "forces," the American public, and especially America's educators, need look no further than the dire predictions made about America's society as it moves into the 21st century.

Ending the jobs dilemma will demand creative solutions and a push for *more* technologically driven economic growth. Growth will allow our economy to absorb a larger number of qualified graduates of universities and community colleges, as well as graduates of sophisticated school-to-work and apprenticeship programs. The challenge is to find *structural* ways to increase the number of employment opportunities, job openings, for high-skill, high-tech craftworkers, as well as other knowledge workers.

There is an advantage to education. It is reflected in the higher incomes and challenging occupations found with the elite American craftworkers and other knowledge workers. The question is how to expand those job opportunities.

Notes

1. Louis V. Gerstner Jr., Roger D. Semerad, Denis Philip Doyle, and William B. Johnston, *Reinventing Education* (New York: Dutton, 1994).
2. "The Big Picture: Out There, the Percent of U.S. Corporate R&D Spent Overseas," *Business Week*, 18 April 1994, p. 8; and *Business Week*, 31 October 1994, p. 6.
3. "Big Blue's White-Elephant Sale," *Business Week*, 20 February 1994, p. 36; and *Forbes*, 25 April 1994, p. 13.
4. For details see Michael A. Bernstein and David E. Adler, eds., *Understanding American Economic Decline* (New York: Cambridge University Press, 1994).
5. David Friedman, "Why the Big Apple Is No Economic Model for LA," *Los Angeles Times*, 12 June 1994, p. M1.
6. Robert E. Kutscher, "Historical Trends, 1950-92 and Current Uncertainties," *Monthly Labor Review* (November 1993): 7.
7. "Downsizing Continues," *Business Week*, 19 January 1993, p. 26.
8. "For a Pink Slip, Press 2," *Business Week*, 27 November 1995, p. 48; and "AT&T Offers Buyouts to More than Half Its Managers," *Los Angeles Times*, 16 November 1995, p. D1. These were primarily managerial, professional, and white-collar positions being cut. That represents a savings of $50,000 per job. Upon hearing the

announcement, Wall Street investors pushed the price of AT&T's shares $1.25 to $64.50.

9. "AT&T Split into 3 Firms to Cost 40,000 Jobs," *Los Angeles Times*, 3 January 1996, pp. A1, A9; and "The Bloodletting at AT&T Is Just Beginning," *Business Week*, 15 January 1996, p. 30.

10. Tom Petruno, "Merger Frenzy Adds to Angst of Wage-Earners," *Los Angeles Times*, 4 September 1995, pp. A1, A20.

11. "Strong Employment Gains Spur Inflation Worries," *Washington Post*, 17 May 1994, pp. A1, A9.

12. "Use of Contingent Workers Rising, Report Says," *Los Angeles Times*, 15 September 1995, p. D4.

13. Sometimes outsourcing work can be deadly. The ValuJet airline crash that killed more than a hundred people had its airplanes maintained by outside contractors, who apparently failed to do quality work. The airline company shut down after the Federal Aviation Administration questioned its maintenance quality control. See "FAA Shake-Up Is Scheduled, Hinson Says," *Los Angeles Times*, 18 June 1996, p. A15.

14. George T. Silvestri, "Occupational Employment: Wide Variations in Growth," *Monthly Labor Review* 116 (November 1993): 58-84. Entry-level jobs, the least skilled of all, also may soon be in short supply. The BLS forecast suggests that as the new welfare law forces recipients to get jobs after two years on welfare, there may not be any jobs for them to get, regardless of how hard they try. See "Welfare Bill May Deplete Job Supply," *USA Today*, 28 July 1996, p. 27.

15. "Downsizing Continues," *Business Week*, 19 January 1993, p. 26.

16. Daniel S. Greenberg, "So Many PhDs," *Washington Post Weekly National Edition*, 5-12 June 1995, p. 24.

17. Ibid.

18. Boyce Rensberger, "No Help Wanted, Young Scientists Go Begging," *Washington Post National Weekly Edition*, 9-15 January 1995, pp. 5, 7.

19. Greenberg, op. cit.

20. Lee Dye, "Blame Federal Grant System for America's Ph.D. Glut," *Los Angeles Times*, 29 March 1995, p. D4.

21. Ibid.

22. Jerry Glasser, "Nascent MBAs Take Their Show on the Road," *Business Week*, 5 September 1994, p. 8.

23. Ibid.

24. "Upper-Level Math, Science Enrollment Is Up, Study Says," *Education Week*, 11 October 1995, p. 10.

25. "By the Numbers: Science Enrollment Soars," *Education Week*, 12 October 1994, p. 48.

26. "Studies Chart Big Boost in Course Taking," *Education Week*, 30 September 1995, pp. 1, 16.

27. "More Take Science, Math in High School," *Los Angeles Times*, 9 October 1995, p. 4.

28. "Moving Ahead," *Education Week*, 13 September 1994, p. 4.

29. U.S. Departments of Labor and Commerce, *Commission on the Future of Worker-Management Relations: Fact Finding Report* (May 1994), pp. 12, 17. Hereinafter referred to as "The Dunlop Report." These figures are for male workers. The 17% drop in wages was partially offset by the entrance of women into the workforce in great numbers. Women's wages went up from $21,530 in 1971 to $23,161 in 1990.

30. Dean Baker and Lawrence Mishel, "Profits Up, Wages Down," Briefing Paper (Washington, D.C.: Economic Policy Institute, September 1995), p. 5.

31. Stanley Aronowitz and William DiFazio, *The Jobless Future* (Minneapolis: University of Minnesota Press, 1994), pp. 325-27.

32. "Job Market Jitters," *Education Week*, 10 November 1993, p. 3. A more recent study, which indicated a tiny 1.1% increase in hiring new college graduates, states that the increase was the lowest in 14 months and came nowhere near making up for the huge loss of job opportunities reported by the Census Bureau. See "Downsizing Slows But Sheepskin Set Is Still Scrambling," *Business Week*, 22 August 1994, p. 20.

33. Mary McClellan, *Why Blame the Schools?* Research Bulletin No. 12 (Bloomington, Ind.: Phi Delta Kappa Center for Evaluation, Development, and Research, March 1994), pp. 1-6.

34. *Business Week*, 24 June 1996, p. 36.

35. Ibid.

36. Neal H. Rosenthal, "The Nature of Occupational Employment Growth, 1983-1993," *Monthly Labor Review* 118 (June 1995): 45-54.

37. Ibid.

38. Stanley Aronowitz and William DiFazio, op. cit., pp. 325-27.

39. Jeremy Rifkin, *The End of Work: The Decline of the Global Labor-Force and the Dawn of the PostMarket Era* (New York: Tarcher/Putnam Books, 1995), pp. 3-15 and *passim*.

40. Ibid.

41. Alfred Herrhausen Society, *Work in the Future, The Future of Work*, the Second Annual Colloquium of the Alfred Herrhausen Society for International Dialog (Stuttgart, Germany: Schaffer-Poeschel Verlag, 1994), p. 4; see also the Organisation for Economic Cooperation and Development, *Employment Outlook* (Paris: OECD, July 1994), Chapter 2.

42. "Labor Markets Hit a Slow Boil But Inflation Keeps Its Cool," *Business Week*, 22 August 1994, p. 21. The high-growth jobs were in such service areas as personal supply, health care, and the retail trade, while the juicy jobs in finance and manufacturing were slight.

43. Lester C. Thurow, "America Reverts to the 19th Century," *Los Angeles Times*, 29 January 1996, p. B9.

44. The year 1992 is used here because that is the base year the Bureau of Labor Statistics established for its very precise projection of employment opportunities through the year 2005.

45. Silvestri, op. cit., pp. 52-53.

46. George T. Silvestri, "Occupational Employment: Wide Variations in Growth," *Monthly Labor Review* (April 1994): 52-53.

47. Bureau of Labor Statistics, *The 1995-2005 Jobs Outlook in Brief* (Washington, D.C.: U.S. Department of Labor, 1994), p. 2.

48. Silvestri, op. cit., pp. 56-57.

49. Ibid., p. 58.

50. Ibid., pp. 58-86.

51. Rosenthal, op. cit., pp. 45-54

52. Ibid.

53. Ibid., p. 50.

54. Ibid.

55. The assertion that millions of jobs, even though low-wage and unskilled, are being produced in the United States has rarely been questioned, and yet some analysts point out discrepancies between Bureau of Labor data and household surveys. The latter show less job creation, even fewer lousy jobs, than the BLS estimates. See, for example, "Why U.S. Employment Numbers Can Be Hard to Read," *Business Week*, 26 September 1994, p. 24.

56. Eileen Applebaum and Rosemary Batt, *The New American Workplace: Transforming Work Systems in the United States* (Ithaca, N.Y.: ILR Press, 1994), pp. 123-45.

57. Raymond Kent, "Letter to the Editor," *Business Week*, 14 August 1995, p. 10.

58. "Profits Are Up, Jobs Are Down, Magazine Says," *Los Angeles Times*, 4 April 1994, p. D2.

59. Robert Reich, "Meet the Frayed Collar Workers Getting the Boot," *Los Angeles Times*, 4 September 1995, p. B4.

60. Weekly wages are a more accurate indicator of income than are hourly wages, because weekly wages reflect overtime pay.

61. Reich, op. cit., p. B5.

62. Lester C. Thurow, "America Reverts to the 19th Century," *Los Angeles Times*, 29 January 1996, p. B9.

63. "Riding High: Corporate America Now Has an Edge Over Its Global Rivals," *Business Week*, 9 October 1995, p. 134-46.

64. Dean Baker and Lawrence Mishel, "Profits Up, Wages Down: Workers Losses Yield Big Gains for Business," Briefing Paper (Washington, D.C.: Economic Policy Institute, 1995).

65. Ray Delgardo, "Despite Record Sales, Mattel Says It Will Cut 1,000 Workers," *Los Angeles Times*, 29 December 1994, p. D11.

66. Sam Fulwood and Melissa Healy, "1.3 Million More Drop into Poverty," *Los Angeles Times*, 7 October 1994, p. A22.

67. James Risen, "Voters Reluctant to Credit Clinton for Recovery," *Los Angeles Times*, 24 October 1993, p. A9, quoting Allen Sisnai, chief economist of Lehman Brothers Global Economies in New York.

68. Ibid. For the effects on the economy of women working, see Karen Nussbaum, *Working Women Count: A Report to the Nation* (Washington, D.C.: U.S. Department of Labor, Women's Bureau, 1994).

69. Risen, op. cit., p. A9.

Chapter Two

Winners and Losers

With lousy jobs and poor incomes, millions of Americans see their standard of living dropping rapidly. However, the elite are getting fabulously wealthy. In the last two decades, America has become the most economically stratified of all the advanced industrial nations. The growing inequality of wealth in America is fast making this nation a two-tiered society.

In 1992, at the end of the last recession, millions of Americans did *not* go back to work. There were no jobs for them.[1] High-quality jobs were especially hard hit in the decade of downsizing. And without the number of high-quality jobs found in the past, or even the potential of increased high-quality jobs in the future, the United States faces the most dramatic downward mobility that it has experienced in its history.[2]

Increasingly, a mere handful of Americans — 20% of the workforce, or roughly 25 million adults — will hold high-performance, high-skill, high-income jobs. The rest of the workforce will have low-paying, de-skilled manufacturing and personal-service jobs. And, as we have seen, only a very limited number of American school and college graduates will be able to get the good jobs — not because the rest are not properly educated, but because the jobs will not be there. The restructuring of the American economy saw to that.

Nevertheless, the New Economy is a knowledge-based economy and does value highly educated people more than did the old economy. However, knowledge is not the exclusive domain of the United States; and with an increase in the number of symbolic analysts throughout the world, heightened global competition is inevitable for America's businesses. That competition will be tough and vigorous. Capital, raw materials, and land were the sources of strength in the old economy. In the New Economy, knowledge is strength. And knowledge is accessible to everyone, enabling every country to create businesses that can be potential competitors.

Research and development efforts are central to knowledge expansion, and thus decline awaits the country that lives off past research and neglects education. The White House Council of Economic Advisors declared that 50% of U.S. economic growth since WWII has come from investment in R&D. That is why the best-paying jobs are those in the professional and symbolic-analyst categories. And the more education a worker has, the better his or her potential for getting a high-quality job. Education is particularly essential in high-tech states. In California and Massachusetts, for example, 60% of the decent jobs currently require at least a community college degree or advanced vocational training, whereas in 1976 only 30% of the decent jobs demanded that level of education.[3]

As noted in Chapter 1, the largest absolute numerical growth will be in occupations that require little education or training. But though occupations that require professional and college degrees will experience smaller growth, they will constitute most of the high-quality jobs.

There are four factors affecting future occupations, all of which depend on the level of education and training a person has: 1) an increased demand for professional and technical workers, 2) the proliferation of new occupations with a technical or scientific core, 3) the infusion of analytical and technical content into jobs that have not traditionally been considered technical in nature, and 4) declining employment among the ranks of the semiskilled and unskilled workers.[4]

Thus education is the critical factor for getting and keeping a decent job. But even a fine education will not guarantee a decent job, since job opportunities will be severely constrained. If current corporate and government policies continue, the essential condition in America's 21st century economy will be a two-tier workforce, with a vast divergence in wealth between those Americans who hold high-performance, high-skill jobs and those who do not. The consequence of that two-tier job structure will be a small group of educated economic winners and a huge group of educated economic losers.

The Winners Are Those Who Know

The major shareholders of America's corporations and their top executives, about 1% of all Americans, are the obvious winners in our country. But typically, they are not thought of as part of the workforce. The most powerful of them had very wealthy parents and were brought up in a protected social milieu. They had special educational opportunities in exclusive private schools and a privileged college education. Some were just plain lucky.

For the rest of us, there are two additional categories that will include the winners in the workforce: symbolic analysts and craftworkers.[5] Symbolic analysts and craftworkers constitute the most highly educated and highly trained occupational categories. But more than that, symbolic analysts and craftworkers have skills and talents that span occupational categories; thus they can command high wages.[6]

Former Secretary of Labor Robert Reich described symbolic analysts as those whose work involves the "manipulation of symbols — data, words, oral and visual representations. . . . The manipulations are done with analytic tools, sharpened by experience. The tools may be mathematical algorithms, legal documents, financial gimmicks, scientific principles, psychological insights . . . or any other set of techniques for doing conceptual puzzles."[7]

Reich's examples of symbolic analyst jobs include research scientists, design engineers, public relations executives, investment bankers, lawyers, real estate developers, financial consultants, architectural consultants, management information specialists, systems analysts, cinematographers, film editors, publishers, and other occupations demanding high levels of creative thinking in addition to basic professional techniques.[8]

Symbolic analyst jobs are divided into two subcategories: *professionals* and *creative technicians.* Professionals have specialized knowledge and skills that set them apart from other workers. Few outside their occupation have more than a trivial understanding of the professional's knowledge. Professionals are university educated and are constantly upgrading their knowledge. Most of their work is mental and analytic, and entry into the professions is highly restricted through certification and licensing processes.

Creative technicians also have specialized knowledge, but usually it is quite technical in nature and oriented toward specific operations, creative applications, innovation, and processes. They also have college educations, usually within a narrow specialization (finance, computer science, film directing, financial planning, and the like). The extent of "on the job training" for them is simply figuring out what products are expected from the job. Most of their work is mental, but in some areas it also requires much hands-on work. A greater reliance on experience than on additional study is one of the attributes that separates creative technicians from professionals. Gaining entry to a creative technicians occupation generally is competitive; it depends on the possession of skills, but it also sometimes depends on "who you know" referral networks.

Since the New Economy is based increasingly on brain power, technical knowledge, and innovation, symbolic analysts are in great demand. Thus they generally command very good salaries, and most of them are in the top 20% income bracket.[9] They have the education and skills necessary to take advantage of modern technology and global markets. Sometimes symbolic analysts work alone, but most work in small teams; and they almost always are connected to a large corporation or one of its worldwide satellites. They control financial assets, and the value of those assets has increased markedly. Together, those two qualities — education and financial control — have created enormous incomes for symbolic analysts. In addition, their talents are exportable and can be used by companies throughout the world. Indeed, the stronger the cadre of symbolic analysts in a country, the stronger that country's competitive position.

All symbolic analysts are university graduates, and most hold advanced degrees. But for many symbolic analysts who hold high positions in major businesses and corporations, the professional-managerial elite, their training began in relatively privileged schools and continued throughout their university careers. The social cohesion of the professional-managerial elites is strengthened by the quality of the public schools in their communities and their university experiences. As Reich puts it, their:

> teachers and professors are attentive to their academic needs. They have access to state-of-the-art science laboratories, interactive computers and video systems in the classroom, language laboratories, and high-tech libraries. Their classes are relatively small; their peers are intellectually stimulating. Their parents take them to museums and cultural events, expose them to foreign travel, and give them music lessons. At home are educational books, educational toys, educational videotapes, microscopes, telescopes, and personal computers with the latest educational software.[10]

The education of symbolic analysts emphasizes four basic skills: abstraction, systems thinking, experimentation, and collaboration.[11] These privileged young people are exposed to curricula that emphasize inquiry, problem solving, and creativity. When they graduate from high school, they attend the best universities in the country and the world. There they "overcome the provincial folkways that impede creative thought" and develop skeptical, curious, and creative minds, capable of solving any problem and equal to any challenge. When they enter the world of work, they embrace it enthusiastically, loving the challenge of experimentation, creativity, and lifelong learning that their work provides them.[12]

The second major category of well-paying jobs is that of *craftworker*. Craftworkers are educated people with high-tech, high-skill

45

training that gives them special, but job-specific, expertise. Many of the jobs identified by the Bureau of Labor Statistics (BLS) as "precision production" occupations fall within this category, but so do the jobs that demand education beyond high school, usually community college or advanced vocational training.

Craftworkers often:

> wear white collars, carry briefcases, conduct relatively scientific and mathematical analyses, and speak with an educated flair. Yet [craftworkers] use tools and instruments, work with their hands, make objects, repair equipment, and . . . get dirty.[13]

Craftworkers' skills and abilities do not depend on a specific company's product. For craftworkers, on-the-job training is merely learning the procedures that are expected by a particular employer, rather than learning how to apply their skills.[14] Thus, even when they work in a multilayered organization, craftworkers have considerable autonomy, much as managers do.

Craftworkers are highly paid because their high-tech skills and experiences enable them to add value to the products and services on which they work. Because they have a good high school education, usually complemented by community college or well-designed apprentice programs, these workers can use technology effectively and intelligently. As we shall see in later chapters, craftworkers today and in the future will be required to have excellent literacy, numeracy, and problem-solving skills to enable them to deal efficiently with technological applications in their workplaces. Part of their responsibility also will include practicing good teamwork skills.

In a high-tech society, workers with such technical and artisan skills are in high demand; and those same skills will allow them to fill the limited number of high-quality jobs that will become available in the future.[15] While some craftworker jobs will be eliminated or deskilled as computer-based machines and processes take over, there are many new craftwork occupations being created by that same technology. Thus a large number of craftworker jobs is projected by the BLS into the year 2005. However, there will not be as many jobs for craftworkers as *could* be available, as we shall see.[16]

Today, many forward-looking vocational programs focus on training for craftworker jobs. In those programs, people receive the knowledge needed to master new and emerging computer-based technology, as well as numeracy and problem-solving skills. That education is especially important for gaining work in high-performance work organizations, such as the Saturn, Mercedes, and BMW automobile factories that have recently been built in the United States or in the aircraft, electric, and other goods-producing firms that rely on high-tech processes.

Currently, highly skilled craftworkers constitute an elite workforce able to demand good wages and benefits and are included in the second 25% of American incomes. Unfortunately, in the absence of certain job-expansion policies, the future demand for highly skilled craftworkers will be very limited, as more businesses incorporate computer-based technology and innovative managerial and processing techniques. Interestingly, in spite of the declining number of craftworker jobs, most education policy recommendations focus on preparing this type of worker; and the technical education, apprentice, and school-to-work programs of schools and colleges also concentrate on preparing craftworkers.

The Rest of the Workforce

Two other classifications of occupations in the workforce — "routine production services" (RPS) and "in-person services" (IPS) — require neither high-tech skills nor unique attributes that would be difficult to replace. Routine production services are those performed by workers in high-volume businesses where they are responsible for assembling finished products — for example, automobiles, television sets, or even computers. RPSs include not only the frontline-workers in factories but also such routine supervisorial people and mid-level managers as foremen, line managers, clerical supervisors, and section chiefs, those responsible for checking on and evaluating the work of other RPS workers.

RPS workers have only job-specific skills — often learned on the job — and therefore are interchangeable with any other able-bodied person. Because they depend more on physical expenditure of labor than on technical skills, as individuals they add little value to products and thus do not command good wages — most RPS workers find themselves in the third quartile of incomes — unless they are unionized.[17] To get around unions, many RPS jobs have been contracted out by major corporations, leaving millions of workers not only with low pay, but also with no benefits or pension plans.

RPS jobs constituted one-quarter of America's workforce in 1990, but that number declined quickly as Corporate America's downsizing gathered momentum. RPS jobs declined by three million in 1992; and by 2005, another 518,000 RPS jobs are expected to disappear and never return. Another 454,000 operator, fabricator, and laborer jobs also will disappear to technological innovation between now and 2005. Today, RPS jobs constitute, at best, 16% of the workforce; and by 2005 the percentage of RPS jobs will be even smaller.[18]

The next category of worker in Reich's schema provide "in-person services." Workers who provide in-person services "are in direct contact with the customer who benefits from the service-worker's" ministrations, rather than indirectly through "streams of metal, fabric, or data." IPS jobs include retail workers, waiters, hotel workers, cashiers, hospital attendants and aides, health care cadres, flight attendants, paralegals, physical therapists, security guards, and others performing similar personal tasks. IPS jobs usually have high school diplomas and perhaps some community college or vocational training, but they seldom have jobs that need other than low-level technical skills.

In 1990 IPS jobs constituted 30% of the workforce. However, IPS as a percent of the workforce is projected to increase rapidly. By 2005, there are projected to be well over three million *additional* IPS jobs, not including 389,000 more jobs in transportation, 403,000 in the retail trade, and 252,000 in construction, numbers that far overshadow the number of RPS jobs. Half of all American workers will perform either RPS or IPS with private businesses, within governmental agencies, as contract/contingent temporary workers, or they will be connected to agricultural occupations. Most of them will earn incomes that, on the upper end, are classified as the third quartile of all American incomes; those not so qualified will be in the bottom quartile of income. Of course, many will be among the chronically unemployed.

Most of this four-way categorization of the workforce rests on a single criterion: education. The division running through today's workforce is based on the amount of education and computer-based skills a person acquires: the higher the skill level, the higher the earnings, making education and technological literacy essential requirements. The computer revolution has obviously deepened existing divisions within the workforce. Two-thirds of college graduates use computers at work compared to only one-third of high school graduates and fewer than one in ten high school dropouts. Well-educated and skilled craftworkers are prospering. RPS workers who are not computer literate and do not possess other advanced skills are walled off from the advances in the economy.

In 1979 a male college graduate earned 49% more than a male with only a high school diploma. By 1992 that gap had grown to 83%. However, those with skills that are out of date or out of sync with the industrial demands of the New Economy are worried and anxious about their prospects.[19] Older Americans also are feeling the pinch of unemployment. Many lose good-paying jobs and are forced to take similar jobs at less pay. Even though self-help networks are established, little hope is offered those laid-off employees.[20] The educational and technological demands of the new American workplace are driving a wedge between the haves and the have-nots in the economy.[21]

Schools and the Workforce

Typical RPS and IPS workers do not have schools of the same quality as those provided to children destined to become the privileged elite, symbolic analysts, or even craftworkers.[22]

The RPS and IPS workers tend to live in urban communities, the working-class suburbs of America's largest cities, and remote rural areas. Those in the working-class suburbs live in modest houses; the families own two cars because both parents work, but one of the cars is definitely older. Those who live in the central city areas live in what used to be called tenements and usually depend on public transportation; their children also depend on public transportation to go to school. The major difference between workers in these communities is the wage levels. People in the suburbs make an average of $35,000 to $60,000, while those in the central city have average incomes of $14,000 to $30,000; the rural poor make even less.

The children in these communities have at least one thing in common: Their communities provide little opportunity for experiences beyond their immediate neighborhoods. There are movies, a few affordable rock concerts, Little League and soccer, high school dances and other extracurricular events, church-sponsored activities, and, most of all, unorganized, informal interactions. Typically, these children do not develop cosmopolitan worldviews. Their experiences reinforce a narrow frame of references that often leads to an acceptance of "givens as givens" and attitudes intolerant of diversity.[23]

There are differences in the physical conditions of the schools that distinguish the suburbs from the central cities. In the suburbs, schools tend to have been built within the last 15 or 20 years; and while there have been attempts to keep them up despite cutbacks and tax revolts, the schools tend to look shabby. In the central city and poor rural areas, some schools were built 50 or 60 years ago. In those communities, the facilities often have a grimy, broken-down appearance. The schools often are covered with graffiti; and broken windows, doors, lockers, and other things go unrepaired, lending to the appearance of dilapidation. Technology and access to the information highway are, for all intents, nonexistent in poor schools.

However, the curriculum and instruction in these schools is similar in all these communities. The curriculum is the typical lock-step by grade level and subject. The emphasis in teaching is on rote, the basics, and covering the content. Few opportunities arise for inquiry, exploration of uncertainty, problem solving, or moving beyond the strictures of the textbook and similar materials. Schools that attempt to break that mold find themselves vilified by parents ("get back to the basics") or are directed by politically motivated school boards to include parochial content in the curriculum ("Hispanic studies," "creationism"). These schools contrast sharply with those provided for symbolic analysts and craftworkers, described earlier in this chapter.

When children graduate from those schools, which most do, some try to enter the world of work; but increasingly they are entering community colleges or four-year colleges, most often state institutions. There they receive similar straightjacketed instruction in large classes attended by 50 to 300 other students. There is little time for creativity and broadening of experience, the kind that may have been able to counteract some of the parochialism developed in their neighborhoods, because most must work to pay tuition and support themselves. The result typically is a college graduate with an education *unsuited* for the challenges of the New Economy. Many of those graduates end up in substandard jobs — given their education credentials — and many of them find themselves forced to return home to their parents because they are unable to afford places of their own.

Growing Inequality

When we look at the earning power of the four major occupational types, we see vast differences in income and wealth. Symbolic analysts are earning huge incomes, and craftworkers are earning decent wages. However, low-skilled Routine Production Service workers and In-Person Service workers are sinking into debt and poverty. That slippage is becoming increasingly apparent in a comparison of wage/income differentials between those in the top quartile of income and the rest of us, as Table 2.1 shows.

Table 2.1: Inequality in growth in U.S.A., 1980-1992.

A. Income Share by Quartile

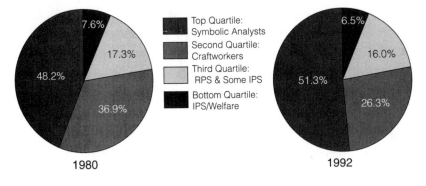

1980   1992

B. Average Income by Quartile

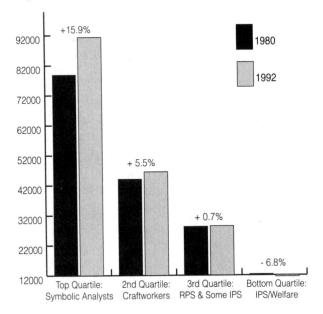

Adapted from Lawrence Mishel and Jared Berstein, *The State of Working America, 1994-1995* (Washington, D.C.: Economic Policy Institute, 1995), pp. 35-40.

Another way to look at the differences in income is to view them as a ratio between the top 10% and bottom 10% of incomes. The higher the number, the higher the difference between the lowest and highest paid workers. Table 2.2 provides that ratio for the United States and four other advanced industrial nations.

Table 2.2: Ratio of average hourly pay of top 10% of wage earners with wage earners in the bottom 10% in selected advanced industrial nations (AIN), 1984-1992.

AIN Country	1984	1992
Germany	2.9	2.7
France	3.3	3.2
Japan	2.6	2.8
Britain	2.5	3.4
U.S.A.	4.8	5.6

Adapted from Keith Iradshie, "Gap in Wealth in U.S. Called Widest in West," *Los Angeles Times*, 17 April 1995, pp. A1, A4.

The trend toward inequality in the United States began at the end of the 1970s and accelerated during the 1980s. Researchers at the University of Michigan who followed 5,000 specific families for two decades beginning in 1967 confirm that fact. The data reported by the researchers reveal the slow but continuous growth of wage and class division. (All data were averaged and adjusted for inflation.) They found that wages for low-wealth workers began to decline at the end of the 1970s and that all incomes began a sharp divergence toward inequality starting in the 1980s. The study found that wages for both white and black American workers declined in those two decades, though the wages of blacks declined more severely than did those of whites.[24]

As Americans began to realize the importance of education for earning better salaries, their graduation rates increased at all levels. But that increased education did not prevent further erosion of wages for ordinary Americans, since incomes grew for only those in the top 20th percentile. Thus there was an increase in the number of families in which both spouses worked to make ends meet, changing forever the stereotypical image of the 1950s nuclear family. However, even with both spouses working, things did not improve for long. The Michigan study found that all groups except the top 5% experienced declining incomes as America entered the

1980s. The middle class slipped from 61% of families ($15,000 to $50,000 in today's dollars) in 1980 to barely 50% in 1992.[25]

A clear indication of the emerging inequality in the United States is to contrast it with what is happening in other nations. Reversing its historical role as the egalitarian leader of the world, upward mobility is more difficult now in the United States than in other advanced industrial nations. For example, when averaged over a decade, the contrast of how many people were able to work their way up out of poverty within a year in industrial nations shows the United States far behind.

Table 2.3: Percentage of people able to move out of poverty within a year.

Country	Percent
The Netherlands	44%
Sweden	37%
France	28%
Germany	26%
Ireland	25%
U.S.A.	13%

Adapted from "Is America Becoming More of a Class Society?" *Business Week*, 26 February 1996, pp. 86-91. The percentage is the average of all years from 1980 to 1990.

Aside from the raw numbers, two recent studies investigating the growing concentration of American wealth and income challenge the notion that "America is the land of opportunity." Both studies demonstrate that, rather than being an egalitarian society, since the 1970s the United States has become the most economically stratified of the advanced industrial nations.[26] Today, the top 20% of American households controls more than 93% percent of the country's *financial wealth*, a figure higher than that in any other industrial nation. Federal Reserve figures, using the most recent information, show that the wealthiest 1% of American households, the major shareholders and top executives (those with an average net worth of about $2.3 million each), owns nearly 46% percent of the nation's wealth.[27] The next 19% percent of American households owns another 49.4% of the country's wealth. That leaves the remaining 5% of the wealth for America's other 80%.

Compare that spread with a couple of other industrial countries. The wealthiest 1% of the United Kingdom's population, which also has a wide gap, owns about 18% of the wealth. By contrast, in Finland, a nation with an exceptionally even distribution of income, the lowest-earning 20% receives 10.8% of such income.[28]

Wealth and income are more concentrated in the United States than in Japan or Germany, America's chief economic rivals. Most data show wealth being more equitably distributed in Japan, though the Japanese government does not publish enough detailed information regarding income inequality to make exact statistical comparisons with the United States. Data from the Organisation for Economic Cooperation and Development (OECD) clearly indicate that both Japan and Germany have much more equal distribution of income than does the United States.[29] No other advanced industrial country has anywhere near the wealth-gap found in the United States. Much of that equity has to do with how their governments control inequality impulses.

A study by Lynn A. Karoly of RAND, an exhaustive analysis of the distribution of income and wealth between 1963 and 1989, pinpoints the rising inequality in wealth for American families and workers.[30] With her data, it is possible to identify the effects of the uneven distribution between symbolic analysts and other occupations (for example, RPS and IPS workers). She begins with this general statement:

> One of the basic beliefs of the American Dream has been that the standard of living for Americans has improved since the Second World War and that *relative* well-being among individuals has remained stable. Thus, while the income of day laborers and corporate executive officers might differ in absolute terms, all would be borne equally by the rising tide of prosperity. . . . [However, recent investigations show] that the level of inequality in family income had reached a post-war high in 1989.[31]

Karoly draws the same conclusions as do other economists studying wage and income over the past three decades. She says that income inequality has been increasing in the last three decades among families, individuals, and workers.[32] Between 1967 and 1973, the income of families and individuals at all levels of income distribution remained fairly stable, relative to each other. However, between 1973 and 1979, real incomes below the median failed to grow as fast as did incomes above the median. That trend accelerated in the 1980s.[33] Between 1979 and 1987, real income for families in the 10th percentile (the lowest income group) *declined* 6%, while real income *increased* 14% for those in the 90th percentile. By 1987, the income level of a family at the 90th percentile was almost nine times greater than the income of a family at the 10th percentile. It was a historic case of the rich getting richer, the poor getting poorer.

There are variations in that larger generalization. Families with children showed greater inequality. If there were two children, a family in the 10th percentile showed a 22% decline from 1973 to 1989, while families with two children in the 90th percentile had a huge increase of 23%. Black and Hispanic families suffered even greater declines in those years. Male workers, in particular, have seen dramatic decreases in their incomes that have resulted in ever-growing inequality over the last 25 years. Men in the 10th and 25th percentiles saw their income fall 13% and 10%, respectively. Between 1963 and 1989, the inequality in weekly wages between male workers in the 10th and 90th percentiles grew more than 35%.[34] Women's wages historically have equaled 75% of those paid to men; but women's incomes have not declined as much as males' incomes, so it is the *decrease* in men's incomes that has reduced the gap between men's and women's incomes.

The increasing inequality in income and wages did not slow down even during the so-called booming 1980s. It was during that period, as we saw above, that America's businesses were restructuring, using technological innovations and automation to shed their employees, while those who remained employed felt powerless to demand wage increases, fearing that they would be the next victims. Income from 1989 to 1995 continued its inexorable decline. The poorest fifth of working families received only 4.6% of the total income, while the richest fifth received 44.6%. The historical progression in the growth of those inequalities can be seen in Table 2.4.

Table 2.4: Percentage change in family income by quintile percentiles, 1967-1989.

Time Period	10th	25th	50th	75th	90th
1967-73	21.9	12.4	17.3	20.6	21.8
1973-76	-1.2	0.2	3.5	5.0	6.2
1979-87	-8.7	-1.4	2.4	7.7	10.1

Adapted from Lynn A. Karoly, *The Trend in Inequality Among Families, Individuals, and Workers in the United States* (Santa Monica: Rand, 1992).

However one looks at it, the data are clear: Income for families and individuals at the bottom of the heap lost ground, while those already above the median gained. Growth was greater the higher the level of income. The subtle message revealed by these figures is that as the rich got richer and the poor got poorer, the middle class was slowly beginning to disappear. A few increased their income high enough to join classes in higher percentiles, but most dropped into lower income percentiles because of falling incomes.

The U.S. Census Bureau recently updated Karoly's analysis and found that not only has the gap between the affluent and the rest of us widened further, but in the past few years the rich have increased their wealth faster than ever. Those earning in the top 20% saw their income rise 44% since 1968, while those in the bottom 20% saw their income stagnate in that same period.[35]

Men have experienced the greatest inequality in income. Among men, the decline in real wages is found almost exclusively in the bottom half of the distribution. In contrast, the incomes of men in the 75th and 90th percentiles grew faster in every period. Overall, the gap between men at the 10th and 90th percentiles grew about 35% since 1967, with most of that accounted for by sharp declines in real wages at the bottom and modest gains at the top.[36] As a consequence, even with women workers in the family, those in the lower percentiles were *worse* off in 1987 than they were in 1975.[37] Karoly summarizes the analysis this way:

There is no doubt that inequality has increased in the United States. . . . Furthermore, this is not strictly a recent phenomenon. The economic status of families at the bottom of the distribution has been declining since the 1970s. The relative gains of the rich, however, are primarily the product of the 1980s. Inequality among men has accelerated in recent times. . . . [T]he data through 1989, the last full year of the expansion, gave no indication that inequality has begun to decline significantly. . . . Instead, the growth in inequality appears to be indicative of more fundamental changes in both the *structure of the economy* and the composition of families and workers. [Emphasis added][38]

Other economists have confirmed the work on income inequality done by Karoly. A more recent study by Edward Wolff took a slightly different approach than that of Karoly. While Karoly focused her study on wages and income, Wolff's study focused on family *wealth*. Wolff defines "financial wealth" as the total of "bank accounts, stocks, bonds, life insurance, savings, mutual fund shares — plus houses, unincorporated businesses; consumer durables like cars and major appliances; and the value of pension rights, minus consumer debt, mortgage and other outstanding debt."[39]

Using wealth as the criterion for analyzing inequality revealed even greater diversity than using income only. Again, as with income, there was a trend toward equalization between 1930 and 1970; but that trend was reversed from the 1980s onward. The gap now is wider than it has been since the depression of 1929.

The most obvious indicator of growing inequality in America is the concentration of wealth and income in the top 1% of families. Wolff's data confirm that, during the 1980s, those who already had financial advantages benefited most by the Reagan Revolution. During that time, the rich used their money to rapidly accumulate more tangible assets — bank accounts, stocks and bonds, pension funds, and other financial resources. Financial wealth surged for the top 1% and remained high for the next 19% of Americans. The other 80% experienced declining wealth.[40] Table

2.5 summarizes the percent share of total net worth (assets minus liabilities), income, and wealth for the top 1% and the affluent 19% (less than 2.5 million people) in comparison with the income and wealth of the rest of us.

Table 2.5: Total income and wealth in percentiles, 1983-1989.

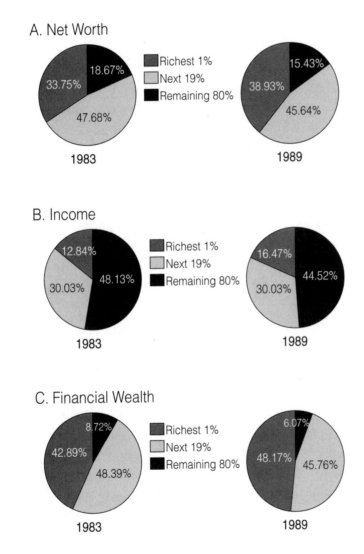

Adapted from Edward N. Wolff, *Top Heavy: A Study of Increasing Inequality of Wealth in America* (New York: Twentieth Century Fund Press, 1995).

The top 1% controlled more than 48% of *all* the financial wealth, while the next richest 19% dropped about three percentage points. Even after deducting liabilities, the top 1% still has 39% of all wealth. Together, the top 20% control more than 90% of the nation's financial wealth. In the 1983-89 period, the remaining 80% actually lost financial wealth. For blacks and other nonwhite minorities, the situation was even worse. Between 1983 and 1989, the median white family had eleven times the wealth of the median nonwhite family. Today, one-third of all nonwhite households have *no* positive wealth at all, in contrast to one in eight white households who have no positive wealth.

The best comparative indicator of the concentration of wealth among the top 20% of American families is the *Gini coefficient*. The Gini coefficient is used by statisticians to determine the inequality of anything of value. It ranges from zero, which would indicate exact equality, to 1.00, which would mean that only one person owns everything. Thus the *higher* the Gini coefficient, the higher the level of concentration of wealth and income in the control of a few families. In 1989 the Gini coefficient for the United States was .34, indicating that the country now has the highest concentration of wealth and the greatest degree of inequality since 1929. In addition, when compared with other rich industrial nations, the United States has the highest concentration of wealth in fewer hands than ever before. The Gini comparisons with other advanced industrial nations are shown in Table 2.6.[41]

Table 2.6: Extremes of rich and poor in selected industrial nations, 1995.

Country	Rank	Position
U.S.A.	0.34	1
Italy	0.31	2
Canada	0.29	3
Germany	0.25	4
France	0.25	5
Finland	0.21	6

Adapted from Keith Iradshie, "Gap in Wealth Called Widest in West," *New York Times*, 17 April 1994, pp. A1, D4.

What explains these huge inequities in the distribution of the economy's benefits? Traditionally, wage growth moves in step with productivity gains. Because productivity stems from an efficient workforce, productive businesses are more profitable and have more money to pass back to their workers. But the equitable distribution pattern has been tossed out in the United States. The United States has the most productive workforce in the world, and it is not only the most productive country but also the wealthiest of all countries in the world. Yet the average compensation for all U.S. workers has fallen 12% in the last two decades, while in the same period of time corporate executives got a 21% increase in compensation. There was a further 3% drop in worker wages in 1994, the largest decline since the Labor Department began keeping track of the data.[42] On top of that, the bureau also reported that average U.S. wages suffered still another decline in 1995, even as the productivity of American businesses surged 2.7% in the same year. As a matter of fact, productivity has outstripped wage growth for eight straight years. As it stands now, wages for routine manufacturing workers and ordinary low-level service workers (non-government) have declined from a high of $7.73 in 1987 to $7.41 in 1995.[43]

Pro-business media attempted to mask the stagnation of ordinary Americans' wages by claiming that prices dropped over the past few years, so that, in effect, was a "wage increase, a statement most Americans don't even find remotely amusing."[44] All of the objective data clearly indicate that the "trickle-down" theory of economics, called "supply side economics," is still a myth. Increasing productivity has meant more wealth only for the super-rich and the top 20% of Americans, not for the rest of us. Here is how Robert Reich summarizes the situation:

> Since the beginning of the recovery, employers have done everything they could to prevent workers from achieving higher wages. . . . Employers have been able to do so because of new technologies coming on quickly, and because of the continued loss of bargaining power by organized labor. Combined with a relentless determination by Wall Street to de-

mand short-term profits, all of this has conspired to force wages down. No wonder [the stock market] is setting new records. . . . The consequence is that we have seen a substantial redistribution of income from people who work to people who own the financial assets of this country, most of whom are quite wealthy.[45]

When even *Business Week*, a pro-business magazine, finally admits that American income disparities are creating a new class structure, it is not surprising that most Americans already knew that. The world of the wealthy 5% of the population is where fortunes are made and kept. All the rest of us are running in place or losing ground. The workforce now has 25% earning only $15,000 or less. The working poor make even lower wages, averaging $4.25 to $6.00 an hour, while 10% of the potential workforce is made up of discouraged workers, those who have given up looking for work and have joined the growing underclass that does not work at all. That is 35% of the population making substandard or no income.

Poor Americans often tolerated low wages because they thought their children would do better. But most studies now indicate that after the 1980s, upward mobility probably became a thing of the past.[46] Most likely, given the reduction of job opportunities, those workers now at the bottom will stay there. Only for high-end professionals, college-educated workers who specialize in technical specialties — computer science, systems analysis, and the like — and craftworkers who have developed artisan-level, high-tech skills is there a chance for mobility and decent incomes. But getting the education and degree to do even that often is a function of who you are, not what you can do.

> Those born in families and neighborhoods that provide the money and motivation to help them complete college are more likely to get ahead. . . . [Those] who lack the access . . . are increasingly likely to sink, no matter how much they hustle.[47]

The middle class has shouldered most of the pain of downsizing and corporate restructuring. Gains in productivity are not benefiting either the middle class or workers; rather, they are going into corporate profits. Those same corporations may find that their unwillingness to share in productivity gains will turn out badly for them in the long run. As Reich puts it, "Workers are also consumers and at some point American workers won't have enough money in their pockets to buy all the goods and services [corporations] are producing."[48] Indeed, with poverty becoming an increasing feature of American life, one wonders how long such inequities will be tolerated before a huge political backlash occurs. The signs point only downward.

Creeping Poverty: A Sign of the Times

As the wealthiest 20% of American families see their wealth increase even further, the other Americans are faced with growing impoverishment. Indeed, if this trend is allowed to continue without public intervention, America's people will be divided between winners and losers, making what Kevin Phillips and others call a two-tier society.[49] That trend could result in social and economic conditions that Americans have never before experienced.

The 20% of Americans in the top tier will live the good life. They will hold interesting jobs and will work in teams with others of their class. Conspicuous consumption will be their style. They will drive expensive cars, eat in fine restaurants, vacation in exotic places, and have other fine amenities. They will live in wealthy, isolated, gated, guarded, rich-ghettoes, removed from the harsh reality of the "other world."

The top tier's benefits will not be only luxuries. While others scramble to find decent medical services, the top tier's medical care will be complete.[50] Even now there are, for example, 339 primary-care physicians per 100,000 people in the wealthy Beverly Hills/Santa Monica, California, communities and only eight per 100,000 in poverty-stricken Central Los Angeles.[51]

In the bottom tier will be the vast majority of Americans: routine production workers, low-skill in-person service providers, gray-market workers, and the unemployed underclass. Hanging on for a time in the declining middle will be the high-skill, educated craftworkers and government professional employees. The middle class already has started to decline; a small portion of them have acquired sufficient education and experience to propel themselves into the upper 25% of incomes and wealth, while the remainder find themselves slipping into the ranks of the near-poor.[52] Some in the middle class who now operate their own small businesses will, if they are lucky, be gobbled up by megafirms; if unlucky, they may find their goods and services produced more cheaply and efficiently by megafirms, just as the Home Depots and McDonalds are eliminating mom-and-pop hardware stores and restaurants. In the absence of public intervention, a tiny remnant of craftworkers will be all that remains of the middle class; and American democracy will change.

Eighty percent of America's people will work in temporary, part-time jobs that have been deskilled. They will not have the medical coverage and retirement funds they had in the past. They will be unable to afford a college education for their children. They even will lack the public services that now are available to the poor, because taxes will be so restricted that the government can no longer afford to fund such services — including government-sponsored clinics, libraries, social services, mental hospitals, and other agencies only the poor turn to now. The affluent will organize politically to defeat any attempt to raise taxes so the "others" should benefit.[53]

A growing underclass, which was once largely made up of ethnic minorities and is today just over 6% of the population, will become bloated with ex-middle-class whites; and it will tax government resources.[54] Divorces will accelerate, which will further impoverish single parents and their children. In today's dollars, the average family monthly income drops from $2,435 to only $1,711 just 16 months after parents separate, and that will get worse as both bread-winners make only marginal wages.[55] Children who once lived in bucolic suburban communities will fall into poverty.[56] Malnutrition, disease, homelessness, and hunger will grow.[57] Crime will increase, which will produce irrational fears among the affluent, motivating them to gate their communities and demand more stringent police activity and stiffer sentences. The

United States of the 21st century may resemble a Third World country, much like Luttwak describes:

> That poverty should mark Third-Worldization is obvious enough. But as any visitor to those countries can readily see, a special kind of wealth is also one of the traits of Third-Worldization. At the end of a dirt road lined with shacks along which barefoot children play, there is a fenced mansion with manicured gardens, illegally obtained antiques, private zoo . . . modern art, satellite dish, and all the latest Japanese entertainment machines — although garden, house and kitchen need no labor-saving appliances given the abundance of gardeners, servants, cooks, and maids.
>
> The charming host and hostess, recently back from their latest shopping trip to Paris or [Tokyo], well educated . . . are happy to entertain at length, often offering to escort the visitor to the local attractions in gratitude for the diversion that can occupy their ample time.
>
> But do not ask them why the children along the way are not in school, or why the road is unpaved. . . . Usually that special kind of wealth is disconnected from any real work, and your hosts are thus profoundly uninterested in improving public education, for that would require "new" taxes, while they employ only gardeners, servants, cooks, and maids, the less educated, the more pliant the better. Paved roads would be convenient, sparing the Mercedes or Range Rover, but they are not worth "new" taxes either. . . . Actually there are no public improvements at all your hosts are willing to pay for with their taxes.[58]

Those who believe that such projections are far-fetched need to consider the evidence of creeping impoverishment that already is developing in the United States. And they should remember that the poverty level in our country is defined officially as $15,335 a year, that is $1,278 per month for a family of four.

- The poverty rate of 15% in 1993 was the highest rate recorded since 1983.
- Children make up 40% of the nation's poor. Families with children make up four-fifths of all poor families.

- The poverty rate was 33.3% of black children, 29.3% of Hispanic children, 12.5% of Asian-American children, and 11.6% of white children; by 2010, those rates will increase to 22% of white children, 51% of black children, and 40% of Hispanic children living in poverty.
- The poverty rates for children under eighteen was 21.9%, the highest recorded since 1983.
- 25% of children under six years old are poor.
- 33% of the children under six in families headed by a female are poor.
- There were 37.4 million Americans with no health insurance coverage.[59]

The working poor are suffering the most. The number of full-time workers who earn less than a living wage rose from 12% to 18% between 1979 and 1992. Primarily, those workers were young; many did not graduate from high school and did not attend college. They have nowhere to go since the reduction in the number of high-paying industrial job opportunities that used to offer routine production service jobs to those who were only high school graduates or, in some cases, dropouts. Among those 18 to 24 years old, 47% were earning low wages in 1992, whereas only 23% of that group received low wages in 1979. The 32% without a high school diploma earned the lowest wages of all.[60]

In the past two decades, the population of children living in working-poor families has jumped from 3.4 million to 5.6 million. Contrary to conventional wisdom, half of these children lived in two-parent homes; only 14% were born to teenage mothers. The Earned Income Tax Credit refunds lifted at least 1.7 million children of working-poor families out of poverty.[61]

About 7.6% of American families are classified as working poor. Because they work for companies that typically do not offer health plan benefits, almost 30% of them have no medical insurance. Indeed, the working poor often are worse off than those on welfare, who are eligible for medical care, food stamps, and other relief. Being a child of a poor working family means being less likely to be immunized against disease, less likely to enter school ready to learn and therefore less likely to graduate, and certainly less likely to attend college.[62] All these strikes against the child are guaranteed to continue the cycle of poverty.

To deal with this rising impoverishment, American families have held on by using some extraordinary coping mechanisms. The first of those, beginning in the late 1970s, was to have both spouses join the workforce. That is the primary reason women are in the workforce in such vast numbers.[63] They have to work to make ends meet for their families.[64] The second coping mechanism was to work longer hours. Today there are record levels of overtime; and many workers work a third shift, even a fourth shift, working 50 or even 80 hours a week trying to meet their bills.[65] The third coping mechanism was to have smaller families, because workers could not afford to have several children. Next came extraordinary use of credit and credit cards.[66] That practice has reached a saturation point, and defaults are soaring. Now families are beginning to dip into their precious savings or face even deeper debt.[67]

The impoverishment of the workers has a significant effect on their children. The General Accounting Office reports that poverty for American infants and toddlers increased 26% from 1983 to 1993, meaning that 20% of all preschool children were living in a poor family, defined in 1990 as an income less than $12,674 for a family of four and in 1994 as an income less than $14,335 for a family of four.[68] That was almost 7 million infants and toddlers in 1990 and 15 million in 1992. Today, according to analysts at Tufts University, the number of babies in poverty conditions is at an all time high.[69] In addition, 90% of the near-poor young children (an income of $23,446 for a family of four in 1990) lived in families with working parents.

School age children fare no better, with 17.5% of school-age youngsters (ages 5-17) living in poverty.[70] From 1973 to 1992 the number of white children living in poverty increased 56.6%, an increase of almost three million children. The number of Hispanic children in poverty increased 116%, an additional 1.6 million; and the number of black children in poverty increased 26.9%, another 1.03 million.[71] Overall, between 1972 and 1992 the number of children in poverty increased by 46.8% in spite of the sustained economic growth in the United States during the 1980s.[72] One organization, the Center on Hunger, Poverty, and Nutrition Policy, using 1990 Census Bureau figures, predicted that the number of children in poverty would rise to more than 20 million by the year 2010.[73]

The percentage of children living in poverty in the United States is more than double that of other major industrialized nations, according to a report by the United Nations Children's Fund (UNICEF). The UNICEF report corroborated U.S. figures that slightly more than 20% of U.S. children live in families with incomes below the poverty level, that is, incomes below 40% of median disposable income (currently $15,335). Child poverty has not gotten any better, even with a full recovery of the economy in 1996.[74]

Most other major industrialized nations have succeeded in reducing child poverty levels to well below 10%. The 20% rate in the United States is caused largely by the absence of a national health plan and the chaotic welfare, food stamp, and AFDC programs that might have mitigated some child poverty.[75] By contrast, other countries are successfully reducing poverty in the lives of children with their commitment to equitable taxes and income transfers. The United States does little in that regard, and the consequences for poor children are great, as Table 2.7 shows.

Table 2.7: Percentage of children living in poverty in industrialized nations, 1995.

Country	Before Tax/Transfers	After Tax/Transfers
Netherlands	14.1	3.8
Germany	8.4	2.8
Canada	15.7	9.3
Australia	16.4	9.0
United Kingdom	27.9	8.4
Sweden	7.9	1.6
United States	22.32	20.4

Adapted from "Dimensions, Children Living in Poverty," *Education Week*, 29 September 1993, p. 3.

Reviewing these data, one expert at the Center on Budget and Policy Priorities, a Washington research group, observed:

> When you have a child poverty rate that is four times the average of Western European countries that are our principal industrial competitors, and when those children are a significant part of our future work force, you have to worry about the competitive effects as well as the social-fabric effects.[76]

Children born in poverty are afflicted with all sorts of problems that affect their school experiences and that make them poor bets for a future world-class workforce. Poor children are much more likely to be born with low body weight, develop health problems, drop out of school, and suffer from neglect and abuse. A poor child is less likely to get the kind of good education a child growing up in a middle-class family receives.[77]

Good prenatal care helps to produce healthy children by school age. Poor care is indicated by the rate of baby deaths; and in that regard, America does not come off well. The infant death rate of 10 per 1,000 in the United States is much higher than the rate found in other advanced industrial nations (where the average is about 6.5 per 1,000). More black American babies die before their first birthday than do white babies. There are 17.6 baby deaths per 1,000 for blacks and 7.3 per 1,000 for whites. That rate of baby death is not only worse than in any other advanced country, but it also is worse than in some Third World countries, such as India. Low birth weight (3 pounds, 4 ounces or less) is a major cause of infant death, and low birth weight is caused by poor mothers getting too little nutritious food and too little prenatal care.

Another sign of caring about children is immunization. Immunization also is a cost-effective means of preventing sickness and big medical bills in the future and a way to make sure that children get an equal healthy start in school. Full immunization goals for measles, polio, and DPT (diphtheria, pertussis, and tetanus) have not been met in the United States. As a matter of fact, among the advanced industrial nations, the United States has the worst record of immunization against diseases that physicians everywhere know are totally preventable. The United States achieved 58% immunization for DPT, 74% for polio, and 77% for measles; other advanced countries in Europe were all at the 90% level. On average, our country managed to have only 67% of its children immunized by their first birthday. Even such emerging nations as India (83%) and China (95%) did better. When considering all the nations in the world, the average was 80% immunization before the first year.[78] Perhaps that is why UNICEF notes that the United States has a lower percentage of students (96%) reaching the fifth grade of school than do nine other industrialized nations.

Poverty also brings hunger to school children. One in eight American youngsters under the age of 12 goes hungry at some point each month; that is 6,000,000 children. The problem of hunger in the United States has been getting worse. Since 1985, for example, the increased need for food assistance has expanded by 89.5%. About 65% of American cities have to turn away people needing food assistance. And the problem is not just an urban one; poverty and hunger are found increasingly among rural families. The rural poor have been categorized as "Appalachian whites," because Appalachia is the historic rural poverty area in America. However, Appalachian white poor families now are found in rural areas all across the United States.[79]

For educators, the incidence of hunger in the United States is particularly worrisome. In comparison to non-hungry children, hungry children in school are almost four times as likely to suffer from fatigue, are almost three times as likely to suffer from concentration problems, are irritable, and are almost twice as likely to have infections, headaches, and frequent colds.[80] What kind of students are they? Will they be those students ready to take their place in the new workforce? Not likely.

Poverty also often leads to crime. America's crime rate was the focus of one of the Goals 2000 statements: a reduction in youth violence. But the rate of youth violence already has increased by 43% since the Goals were promulgated.[81] That is not exactly an ideal situation.

In addition to the effects of a growing two-tier economy on children and youths, the quality of life in the United States is changing for the worse for many others. Life expectancy is an indicator of a nation's overall health care. In the United States, life expectancy is 76 years; it is 79 years in Japan and 78 years in Sweden. Our country's death rates are 12% higher in poor rural areas and 19% higher in core metropolitan areas than in the affluent suburbs; and according to the National Center for Health Statistics, the disparity is getting wider.[82]

The level of education also has an effect on life expectancy. In 1989-90, death rates for men and women between ages 25 to 44 who did not have a high school education were three times those of college graduates. The difference, it appears, is that a college education not only makes a person more aware of health issues, it also affects the person's ability to get a good job in order to afford better living conditions and access to good health care.[83]

The quality of life in America is eroding as wages decline further and good jobs become harder and harder to find. The evidence is there for all to see: a lost middle class; class warfare; exclusivity; more police and police authority; more jails and prisoners, with billions spent for new prisons to house prisoners at $30,000 a year; more prostitution; more children sinking into mind-numbing poverty. Meanwhile, the fortunate ones get richer and control more of the institutional power. As the United States struggles to come to terms with its ailments, the ensuing debate often has gaping holes. Statistics are incomplete and interpreted differently. Such abstract concepts as "productivity" are tossed about with little clear link to people's daily lives. Rarely does the rhetoric get to the heart of people's *experience* of their economy, the trade-off they must make for a modicum of serenity, a chance to enjoy the things they have.

All of these statistics paint a dismal picture, but aren't most Americans happy and optimistic about their future? Not judging by recent polls.

Even the more-prosperous are worried. More than 70% of those Americans would sacrifice new cars, brand-name goods, and going out to restaurants to ensure a financially secure retirement. More than 60% of Americans between 29 and 47 say they will not have enough for retirement, no matter how much they save. The Municipal Board of Bond Investors Assurance Corporation says about 66% of the Baby Boomers believe their retirement savings are at risk.[84]

In contrast to the dismal social statistics, and in comparison with other nations, the United States has lots of goodies. Americans have more CD players, more answering machines, more automobiles, more microwaves, more computers, more food processors, and more of a host of other goodies than do most advanced industrial nations, including Germany, Japan, and France. But according to surveys, the United States typically is in the middle of the pack on its people's satisfaction with their lives.

Of course, the picture above is purposefully painted in dark colors to make a point. The surging productivity of America's New Economy is not bearing fruit for the ordinary American citizen. The consequence of that is reflected in the social statistics.

The United States has not succumbed completely to Third World status. And it does not need to do so if we put our minds to creative solutions to the problem of inequality. However, before we can solve the problem, we must first clearly identify the source of the problem. Then we can offer possible solutions. We will begin that process in the next few chapters.

Notes

1. Lawrence Mishel and Jared Bernstein, "The Joyless Recovery: Deteriorating Wages and Job Quality in the 1990s," *Economic Policy Institute Briefing Paper* (Washington, D.C.: September 1993), pp. 1-22.
2. Edward N. Wolff, *Top Heavy: A Study of Increasing Inequality of Wealth in America* (New York: Twentieth Century Fund Press, 1995), p. vi.
3. James Flanigan, "San Diego Offers Lesson on Economic Comeback," *Los Angeles Times*, 31 July 1996, pp. D1, D5.
4. Stephen R. Barley, "The New Crafts: The Rise of the Technical Labor Force and Its Implications for the Organization of Work," *EQW Working Papers* (Philadelphia: National Center on the Educational Quality of the Workforce, University of Pennsylvania, 1992).

5. James Risen, "Interview with Robert Reich," *Los Angeles Times*, 30 July 1995, p. M3.

6. Barley, op. cit., pp. 12-13.

7. Robert B. Reich, *The Work of Nations: Preparing Ourselves for the 21st Century* (New York: Vintage Books, 1991), p. 177.

8. Ibid., pp. 177-78. It is interesting to note that Reich did not include any government or highly qualified professional employees — such as physicians, teachers, government statisticians, researchers, and the like — in his classification of symbolic analysts; but he did include college professors and lawyers. But in function, if not remuneration, educators certainly would be considered symbolic analysts. Perhaps Reich's criterion that the talent has to be exportable excluded other types of symbolic analyst.

9. See, for example, "Bidding War Erupts for Young Programmers," *Los Angeles Times*, 30 July 1996, pp. A1, A14.

10. Reich, op. cit., pp. 227-28.

11. Ibid., p. 229. We will return to his four descriptors in more detail in subsequent chapters.

12. Christopher Lasch, "The Revolt of the Elites: Have They Canceled Their Allegiance to America?" *Harper's Magazine* (November 1994): 39-49.

13. Barley, op. cit., p. 11. Barley uses the term, *technicians*, for what are essentially craftworker occupations, but both terms mean the same thing.

14. Ibid., p. 14.

15. Risen, op. cit., p. M3.

16. George T. Silvestri, "Occupational Employment: Wide Variation in Growth," *Monthly Labor Review* (November 1993): 58-86.

17. Risen, op. cit., p. M3.

18. Silvestri, op. cit., pp. 58-86.

19. "Reich Says Jobs Fail to Offset Wage, Income Inequality," *Los Angeles Times*, 1 September 1995, p. A27.

20. National Retired Teachers Association, "Harsh Fate Awaits Many Caught Up in Downsizing," *NRTA Bulletin* (April 1995):1, 12; and "Where Do We Go From Here?" *NRTA Bulletin* (April 1995): 4-5.

21. Amy Harmon, "High-Tech Barn Raisin' Shows Disparity of Schools," *Los Angeles Times*, 6 March 1996, pp. A1, A15.

22. This description is loosely based on the observations of G. Alexander Moore, *Realtors of the Urban School* (New York: Doubleday,

1967); and Jonathan Kozol, *Savage Inequalities: Children in America's Schools* (New York: Crown, 1991).

23. See National Center for Education Statistics, *Youth Indicators, 1993* (Washington, D.C.: U.S. Department of Education, October 1993); National Center for Education Statistics, *The Condition of Education 1995* (Washington, D.C.: U.S. Department of Education, 1995); Bureau of the Census, *School Enrollment: Social and Economic Characteristics of Students* (Washington, D.C.: U.S. Department of Commerce, October 1993); Harold L. Hodgkinson and Janice Hamilton Outtz, *The Nation and the States: A Profile and Data Book of America's Diversity* (Washington, D.C.: Institute for Educational Leadership, 1992); and Harold L. Hodgkinson, *All One System: Demographics of Education, Kindergarten Through Graduate School* (Washington, D.C.: Institute for Educational Leadership, 1985).

24. "Is America Becoming More of a Class Society?" *Business Week,* 26 February 1996, pp. 86-91.

25. Ibid.

26. Keith Iradshie, "Gap in Wealth in U.S. Called Widest in West," Los Angeles Times, 17 April 1995, pp. A1, A4.

27. Note the key word here is *wealth*, not simply *income*, because wealth includes income as well as other tangible and liquid assets.

28. Iradshie, op. cit.

29. Organisation for Economic Cooperation and Development, *Economic Outlook, 1993* (Paris, 1993), pp. 53, 59.

30. Lynn A. Karoly, *The Trend in Inequality Among Families, Individuals, and Workers in the United States* (Santa Monica, Calif.: RAND, 1992).

31. Ibid., p. vi.

32. Ibid., p. vii.

33. Ibid., p. vi.

34. Ibid., p. vii.

35. "Income Disparity Between Poorest and Richest Rises," *New York Times*, 20 June 1996, p. A1.

36. Karoly, op. cit., p. 37.

37. Ibid., p. 42.

38. Ibid., p. 57.

39. Edward N. Wolff, op. cit., p. 1.

40. Ibid., p. 2.

41. Iradshie, op. cit., pp. A1, D4.
42. "Reich Cites Falling Wages as Administration Failure," *Los Angeles Times*, 6 June 1995, p. A26.
43. Robert B. Reich, "Meet the Frayed Collar Workers Getting the Boot," *Los Angeles Times*, 4 September 1995, p. B4; Tom Petruno, "Merger Frenzy Adds to Angst of Wage Earners," *Los Angeles Times*, 4 September 1995, pp. A1, A20; "For Many Uncertainty Laces the Labor Day Festivities," *Los Angeles Times*, 4 September 1995, p. B4.
44. "For a Pink Slip, Press 2," *Business Week*, 27 November 1995, p. 36.
45. Robert A. Rosenblatt and Stuart Silverstein, "State, US Jobless Rates Fall Sharply," *Los Angeles Times*, 6 June 1994, p. A1, A16.
46. "Is America Becoming More of a Class Society?" *Business Week*, 26 February 1996, pp. 86-91.
47. Ibid., p. 86.
48. "U.S. Confirms: Skimpy Raises Were the Rule," *Los Angeles Times*, 12 November 1995, p. D3.
49. Kevin P. Phillips, *Boiling Point: Democrats, Republicans and the Decline of the Middle Class* (New York: HarperCollins, 1993). In particular, see Chapters 6, 7, and 8 for a description of middle-class disintegration and the growth of an American rich/poor dichotomy.
50. Ibid., pp. 167-92.
51. Douglas P. Shiut, "Filling the Void," *Los Angeles Times*, 27 July 1995, p. B2.
52. Iradshie, op. cit., pp. A1, A4.
53. Edward N. Luttwak, *The Endangered American Dream* (New York: Simon and Schuster, 1993), pp. 125-26.
54. Ibid., pp. 117-27.
55. "Dimensions: Slipping Into Poverty: Family Income of Children After Marital Separation," *Education Week*, 13 May 1991, p. 3.
56. "Study Charts Dramatic Rise in Suburban Child Poverty," *Education Week*, 6 August 1994, p. 10.
57. James Risen, "Credit for Working Poor Exemplifies Tax Burden," *Los Angeles Times*, 4 April 1993, p. A5.
58. Luttwak, op. cit. pp. 125-26.
59. "Poverty in the United States, 1992," *Education Week*, 13 October 1993. The data were compiled from U.S. Census Bureau reports:

Poverty in the United States: 1992; *Money Income of Households, Families and Persons in the United States, 1992*; and *Measuring the Effects of Benefits and Taxes on Income and Poverty: 1992*.

60. Flanigan, op. cit.

61. "More Children in Working Families Found to Live in Poverty," *Education Week*, 12 June 1996, p. 10.

62. "Poverty on Rise for Children of Working Poor," *Los Angeles Times*, 3 June 1996, pp. B1, B6.

63. Karen Nussbaum, *Working Women Count: A Report to the Nation* (Washington, D.C.: U.S. Department of Labor, Woman's Bureau, 1994), pp. 5-10.

64. Families and Work Institute, *Women: The New Providers*, Whirlpool Foundation Study, Part 1 (New York: Whirlpool Foundation, May 1995), pp. 9-17. This study notes that women also value their participation in the workforce in addition to the income it brings to their families.

65. Juliet B. Schor, *The Overworked American: The Unexpected Decline of Leisure* (New York: Basic Books, 1992), pp. 51-65.

66. Robert D. Hershey Jr., "Americans Buying More Credit," *New York Times*, 30 July 1994, p. 33.

67. Risen, op. cit., p. M3.

68. "Number of Poor Children Increasing G.A.O. Says," *Education Week*, 27 April 1994, p. 12.

69. John T. Cook and J. Larry Brown, *Two Americas: Alternative Future for Child Poverty in the U.S.* (Medford, Mass.: Center on Hunger, Poverty and Nutrition, Tufts University, April, 1993), pp. 18-19.

70. U.S. General Accounting Office, *Infants and Toddlers: Dramatic Increase in Numbers Living in Poverty* (Washington, D.C.: April 1994), pp. 5-8.

71. Cook, op. cit., pp. 7-8.

72. David Briscoe, "It's Harder to Go to Work," *Los Angeles Times*, 2 October 1993, pp. E5, E9.

73. Cook, op. cit., pp. 18-19. Black children showed a smaller rate of growth because so many of them are already in poverty.

74. Robin Wright, "U.S. Child Poverty Worst Among Richest Nations," *Los Angeles Times*, 12 June 1996, p. A22.

75. "Dimensions: Children Living in Poverty," *Education Week*, 29 September 1993, p. 3.

76. Iradshie, op. cit., pp. A1, A4.
77. Janice Hamilton Outtz, *The Demographics of American Families* (Washington, D.C: Institute for Educational Leadership, March 1993), pp. 14-16.
78. Marlene Cimons, "Health Gap Widens Between Rich and Poor," *Los Angeles Times*, 16 September 1993, p. A18.
79. Ibid.
80. "Poverty's Hold on America," *Los Angeles Times*, 21 April 1993, p. A5.
81. Millicent Lawton, "Capital Backs Off Coordinated Effort to Curb Youth Violence," *Education Week*, 4 August 1993, p. 3.
82. Lawrence Mishel and Jared Bernstein, *The State of Working America, 1994-95* (Armonk, N.Y.: M.E. Sharpe, 1994), p. 318.
83. Ibid.
84. Marlene Cimons, "Health Gap Widens Between Rich and Poor," *Los Angeles Times*, 8 August 1993, p. A18; "Investing in Health, The World Bank's Report, 1993," *Los Angeles Times*, 10 August 1993, p. H6.

Chapter Three

Education and Supply-Side Dreams

Ordinary Americans — including today's high school and university students — are anxious and restive about the decline in good jobs, the drop in real wages, and the lack of opportunity. Certainly they have heard several explanations for the shortage of quality jobs. Some explanations blame technology and automation, some blame the influence of foreign competitors, and still others blame the population growth that is the Baby Boom. But no explanation has had such universal acceptance as the charge that our public schools and universities are not educating students in the knowledge and skills needed for success in today's workforce. And there is a corollary to that charge: Without a world-class workforce, the United States lost its competitive advantage, bringing on the misery described in Chapter 2. That message has been so powerfully ingrained in the minds of the public by pundits and the media that it has reached the status of "conventional wisdom" — everyone "knows" that schools are "failures" and that America does not have a quality workforce like the Japanese and Germans do.[1] Educators are advised to "reform and restructure" the schools or, as Gerstner and the conservative Hudson Institute group would have it, to adopt "solid" business practices and "re-engineer" the schools.[2]

The problem with the accusation that "it's education's fault" is that it is both logically and empirically false. Worse, the school remedies proposed by business would mutilate the essential mission of public education — educating children and young adults for social and personal competence — by having them focus merely on economic competencies.

Of course, just saying that does not dent the armor of "conventional wisdom." What is needed is a closer look at the issue. What is education's role in a nation's economy? What evidence and empirical work have economic scholars developed to clarify education's role in economic development? Are there alternative, more straightforward explanations for the economic downturn and sharp drop in standard of living experienced by the American people during the 1980s and 1990s?

Before addressing those questions, it will help to put current events into better perspective with a brief comment on America's economic circumstances up to the late 1970s, just before the economic downturn began. That was the period in which there was a tacit social compact between workers and their employers. With that compact, workers wages and corporate profits grew together, and jobs were secure. It is helpful to understand how and why there was shift from that social compact to a system in which companies considered workers to be sacrificial pawns.

The Social Compact

The cold-hearted shedding of American workers described in Chapter 1 was a radical departure from previous corporate practice. From 1947 to 1979, America's top corporations had an unspoken but real social compact with their workers regarding job security and decent wages. Then corporations insisted they had to have a "flexible workforce," that is, one in which companies can expand or contract whenever the "logic" of the marketplace dictates. In that world, the social compact between companies and employees became irrelevant; but its loss generated enormous anger among millions of Americans.

After World War II companies that had developed highly rationalized mass-production processes drove the American economy.

At the apex of those businesses were about five hundred key corporations that produced about half of America's industrial output, employed 80% of the country's workers, and made about 40% of the nation's corporate profit. These "core corporations," as Reich called them — U.S. Steel, General Motors, AT&T, General Electric, DuPont, IBM, Coca-Cola, General Mills, Johnson and Johnson, Proctor and Gamble, and others — were organized along the lines of "scientific management" as advocated by Frederick Taylor.[3] They were highly bureaucratic, with defined layers of authority from the top mangers down through middle managers, factory supervisors, and finally to frontline workers on the shop floor. These core corporations dominated their industries and set the standards for the nation in setting prices and wages and determining how goods were produced. Arrayed around the core corporations were large service and transportation firms — banks, railroads, shipping firms, insurance companies — and mass retailers such as Sears, Montgomery Ward, and J.C. Penney. Outside that circle were hundreds of thousands of independent smaller firms and small retailers who marketed and sold mass-produced goods.[4] With their size and wealth and influence, the core corporations became identified with the American economy itself. What was good for General Motors *was* good for the country.

The core corporations flooded the United States with their products and services. From 1947 until the middle of the 1970s, they also dominated world markets. No other industrial nation was in any condition to challenge the United States economically after the trauma and devastation wrought on their economies by World War II. But more important for our purposes, those core corporations also created millions of jobs, paying wages decent enough to single-handedly create a new, vital American middle class.[5]

In this period, the mission and role of education seemed quite straightforward. The top 15% of high school students were tracked in courses that enabled them to attend four-year colleges. As college students, they were tracked again to take, on graduation, executive, management, and professional positions within the core corporations or within business firms acting as satellites to the core corporations. Most of the remainder of the high school-age students — graduates and dropouts — gained decent-paying jobs as routine frontline workers and supervisors. Since mass production demanded little technical skill, no special training was needed beyond on-the-job training, except in a handful of specialized craftworker occupations.[6]

By all signs, those economic arrangements worked. Between 1947-1979, real gross domestic product (the measure nations use to assess their relative prosperity) grew steadily by 3.3%. Employment grew by 44 million during that same period; and at the average rate of 4.8%, unemployment remained marginal.[7] Productivity and wages also grew during this period; productivity increased by 2.6%, and wages kept pace by also growing by 2.6%. That pattern of equity between productivity and wages continued until near the end of the 1970s.[8] During this time, as productivity growth rates improved, core corporations were earning respectable profits and American workers decent wages. The War on Poverty's social programs, initiated in the 1960s, helped to mute the effects of poverty in the lives of most underprivileged Americans. Poverty rates declined by almost half, from 22.4% to 11.7% between 1960 and 1979, as more and more poor Americans were helped to move into the world of work.[9]

During much of the postwar period, American economic well-being was directly related to the tacit social compact that America's corporations had with their employees, a compact that assured workers decent wages and job security as productivity increased. Three primary factors supported that social compact: 1) the practice of workers and their firms sharing performance gains, 2) the continuous growth in consumption that resulted from rises in real wages, and 3) investment dynamics that emphasized expansion of capital stock, which in turn increased the growth rate of productivity and consumer demand.[10] The mass-production techniques used by the core corporations at that time made possible economies of scale and reduction of unit labor costs; and that, in turn, allowed prices to be kept reasonable. With those three factors in place, output increased and plants operated at nearly full capacity throughout the period. Prices fell in relationship to increased worker productivity. Good wages and reasonable prices made it possible for American consumers to purchase an inordinate amount of goods, and that strong demand favored increased growth in productivity. The corporations' profits came from price mark-ups of those consumer goods; thus when productivity increased, so did their profits. Unions in the core corporations negotiated for wage increases related to the average growth in productivity. Wage gains won by unions spread to non-union and satellite companies, thus assuring an additional strong consumer base for mass-produced products. As a result, the 1947 to 1979 period was characterized by rising real wages, falling prices, growing employment, a strong consumer base, and stable corporate profits.[11]

Economists call that phenomenon a "virtuous circle," summed up in this key economic principle: *Strong growth in demand favors growth in productivity and, conversely, productivity growth favors demand growth.*[12] It was a situation similar to the old saw about a "cat and rat" farm where the farmer has never-ending prosperity as he produces rats and cats. The cats he sells, the rats he raises for the new cat owners. In the real world, corporations produced goods and services, and they hired and paid workers well; in turn, the workers could afford to buy the goods and services that the corporations were producing.[13] The growth resulting from the "virtuous circle" interconnections ensured relatively decent jobs for most Americans regardless of their educational attainment. In addition, workers had reasonable job security; it was not unusual for many workers to have the same employer for 20 or 30 years. The combination of good wages and job security built a strong consumer base for Corporate America's products.[14]

It seemed that everyone benefited during the years of the social compact. The smooth "productivity = profit + wages" equation meant that investors reaped their rewards and consumers benefited from reasonable prices and plentiful products. The economy hummed along so well under those conditions that middle-class Americans, starting in the 1960s, felt confident enough to turn their goodwill toward helping less privileged Americans — the poor and the disenfranchised — and getting Americans on the moon by 1969.

But dark clouds were about to block out the sun. The self-satisfied confidence of being the world's economic power for such a long period of time deluded America's top business executives into complacency. And by the end of the 1970s, those executives were waking up to unanticipated foreign challenges. In panic, they began to try everything to fend off those challengers. In the process, educators became an unwitting tool.

Bearing False Witness: Blaming the Schools

The seemingly abrupt corporate abandonment of the social compact was not without rancor. From its earliest attempts to re-gain a so-called competitive advantage, Corporate America was faced with monumental worker and political outrage. Even before the 1990s, the early effects of the movement toward a New Econ-omy were felt by millions of Americans who lost their jobs and by new entrants into the job market who were unable to secure jobs for which they were qualified. Corporate America was accused of unilaterally breaking the social compact: firing long-term, loyal employees; reducing wages; going to war with unions; and mov-ing jobs and factories, first to low-wage areas of the United States and then to foreign countries. They were attacked as being unpa-triotic when they began to import technologically advanced but low-wage foreign workers — some highly skilled programmers, designers, and computer software experts — or merely buying their intellectual output.

Those business executives knew what they were doing. They felt they had to restore their corporations' competitive advantage against the foreign challenge. But the decisions they made seemed short-sighted and mean-spirited to many, leaving them vulnerable to a political backlash.[15]

America's businesses needed time to avoid that backlash. They needed time to retool, time to restructure, time to reinvest and modernize. Thus they needed a scapegoat, something that would deflect public anxiety away from them as they instituted their harsh changes. The government, which in the 1980s was under a conservative, pro-business leadership, was considered more of an ally than a scapegoat. But there was one major institution that was vulnerable to blame for its supposed major role for America's declining economic fortunes: America's public schools.

Since the end of World War II, it seemed that education was under constant attack from opinion makers for its purported weaknesses. A number of books and articles had been pouring out of academia and the popular press attacking education for one "evil" or the other. In 1949 the popular books by Bernard Bell, *Crisis in Education*, and Mortimer Smith, *And Madly Teach*, criticized education for contributing to the "unsatisfactory state of our life and culture." Albert Lynd's *Quackery in Public Schools* and Arthur Bestor's *Educational Wastelands* attacked the schools for their lack of "academic discipline" and frivolity in the 1950s.[16] A major contribution to America's loss of faith in its schools came with the publication of Admiral Hyman G. Rickover's *Education and Freedom* just as the United States was reeling from the Sputnik shock.

> [N]ow that the people have awakened to the need for reform, I doubt whether reams of propaganda, endless reiteration that all is well with our schools, or even pressure tactics will again fool the American people into believing that education can safely be left to the "professional" educators. . . . The mood of America has changed. Our technological supremacy has been called into question and we know we have to deal with a formidable competitor. Parents are no longer satisfied with [their] schools.[17]

To further buttress their arguments, America's corporations were not above using patriotism to add heat to their accusations about education's failures. In 1983 the National Commission on Excellence in Education issued its now familiar shock report, *A Nation at Risk*. It said:

> Our nation is at risk. Our once unchallenged pre-eminence in commerce, industry, science, and technological innovation

is being overtaken by competitors throughout the world. . . . The educational foundations of our society are presently being eroded by a rising tide of mediocrity that threatens our very future as a nation and a people. . . . If an unfriendly power had attempted to impose on America the mediocre educational performance that exists today, we might well have viewed it as an act of war. . . . We have, in effect, been committing an act of unthinking, unilateral educational disarmament.[18]

Such a dramatic charge had an immediate response from the public and the education establishment. As one analyst put it: "Within two years of the report, more than 300 national and state task forces had investigated the condition of public schooling in America. In 41 states, legislatures mandated that students take more courses in designated academic areas. Just 12 months after the report, the U.S. Education Department was declaring the arduous work of school reform was already bearing fruit."[19] The report's message maintained that America's schools, parents, the public, and government needed to rally around the flag to save American business from the threat of Japanese and German competitors or, more recently, from South Korea and Singapore.

Interestingly, as part of their drive to regain competitive advantage, America's core corporations ignored their own flag-waving messages. Indeed, they were busy rushing to build as many multinational links and economic footholds within foreign countries as was possible. In the process, American corporations ignored their own national boundaries, often at the expense of America's own economy. Adding insult to injury, many American corporations even formed alliances with foreign firms in the same countries which, they had warned, were threatening the destruction of the U.S. economy.[20]

Regardless of that hypocritical behavior, business had found the scapegoat it needed to deflect the political heat their actions were engendering. Soon American opinion formulators — corporate elites, policy makers, university experts, and media pundits — all began to assert that America was losing its ability to compete on a world-class level. They bemoaned the economic prowess of

Japan and Germany and warned of further competitive threats from rapidly industrializing, low-wage nations, particularly Asian nations. To demonstrate the decline in America's fortunes, they quoted gloomy statistics about trade deficits and stagnant productivity. In essence, America's corporate elite charged that their incompetence was not responsible for the loss of America's competitive advantage. The "real" reason was that the United States did not have a highly educated, world-class workforce. The schools were causing this economic decline, they claimed. And their media apologists perpetuated that charge.[21] Interestingly, none of those critics has ever defined clearly what was meant by "world-class," so educators may have been chasing a will-o-the-wisp when they contritely responded by tooling up to produce a "world-class workforce."[22]

Opinion formulators reported that American factories and jobs were going to foreigners because American students — high school and university graduates — were not educated well enough to provide American business with the kind of workers it needed They pointed to the educated workforce found in countries that were successfully eating into America's competitive advantage, such countries as Japan, Korea, Singapore, Germany, France, or whatever other country whose students appeared for the moment to have higher test scores than American students.

By placing the blame on the schools for America's economic doldrums, the decline in good jobs, and consequent rapid decrease in decent wages, business had found a potent vehicle for deflecting blame from itself. And the campaign worked. Their charges gave affluent Americans a rationale to understand business downturns, and they gave middle-class and working Americans a target on which to focus in hopes of preventing further wage slippage and unemployment. Suddenly, getting schools up to snuff became *the* American cause.

Academic credence was given to these anti-education arguments with the publication in 1987 of what proved to be a very popular research report, *Workforce 2000*. The authors of that study — both associated with the pro-business, conservative think-tank, the Hudson Institute — maintained that a labor shortage was developing in the United States because there was a growing mismatch between the skills needed by businesses and what was being taught in the schools. *Workforce 2000* argued — incorrectly, as it turned out — that by educating a huge new supply of workers for high-tech, high-skill jobs — what it called the supply-side push — productivity would be improved.[23] The authors argued, first, that "The rapid growth of high-skill professional and technical occupations is said to be rapidly upscaling the skill mix of jobs." Second, "the economy will face a 'labor shortage', due to a lack of workers with adequate levels of skill and education. The labor force will be increasingly dominated by workforce entrants with low skill levels (women and minorities) while, at the same time, the skill level of jobs to be filled will increase substantially. The results will be a *skills mismatch* between available jobs and available workers."[24]

Educators' collective ears began to perk up. The assumption was that employers would be demanding a workforce with high levels of skill and education, particularly professional and technical workers. Based on the *Workforce 2000* analysis, a labor shortage was inevitable because there was strong growth in high-skill occupations and too few trained workers. That argument brought demands that educators meet the coming need for a large workforce with better skills; that is, a supply-push for more workers with more education and training. That demand quickly became the mantra of America's businesses.

The problem with the *Workforce 2000* analysis was that it was wrong, as well as misleading. An independent analysis of the data showed the faults of the Hudson's Institute's analysis;[25] and the institute, in fact, tacitly admitted weakness in its analysis in a 1994 article.[26] But that did not prevent the supply-side argument from becoming the major rationale for business when assigning blame to the schools, nor does it prevent its continued use as a tool to drive education policy today.

Workforce 2000 gave little thought to how the actual *number* of quality jobs that would be available for the "new workforce" would affect the report's assumptions. Those numbers showed that, rather than increasing, job opportunities were actually being reduced as businesses used computer-based technology to deskill and eliminate decent jobs, causing huge layoffs. That reality dramatically off-set the effects of expansion of new high-skill occupations in various industries. In other words, *Workforce 2000* led policy makers to focus "only on the problems with education and training and not on the type jobs being created by the economy or on how employers structure work."[27]

Mischel and Teixeira, in a thorough critique of the *Workforce 2000* data and conclusions, conclude:

> The key policy implication of this scenario is that the *supply push approach will not produce the desired improvements in labor market performance or productivity*. This is because the obstacles to U.S. economic growth do not lie only, or even mainly, with the quality of the workforce. Just as important (perhaps even more so) are demand-side problems rooted in the sluggish response of U.S. employers to changing technological and market conditions. *Workers cannot fill high-skill jobs if such jobs are not widely available. . . .* thus, simply improving human capital levels . . . [through greater education and training of American workers] is not, and will not be, an adequate response to our labor market problems.[28] [Emphasis added]

By accepting the *Workforce 2000* argument at its face value, business leaders were able to mask the real problems with U.S. trade and competitiveness and let educators ignore their responsibility to demand that business reciprocate by finding ways to accommodate a growing supply of world-class graduates. Business executives and most policy makers were able to ignore any critical analysis of *Workforce 2000* and use the idea of an expanding "demand" for high-skilled jobs as a way to shift the blame from their own poor decisions to the so-called failure of America's education institutions. They managed to persuade the public that solutions to America's economic problems would be found when "educational deficiencies" were corrected. Corporate executives argued, and media pundits parroted, that America would regain its competitive advantage only when American schools restructured their curriculum to focus on business' needs.

"Reform the schools" became a rallying cry both for pundits and for those with their own pet projects to pander. *A Nation at Risk* rang a breathless alarm. *Workforce 2000* gave an intellectual patina to the danger. As a result, America's educators are making calculated efforts to educate American students for high-tech, high-performance jobs, regardless of whether those jobs will exist. Education entrepreneurs even adapted business language — "total quality management," for example — to convince harried educators that business techniques would solve their problems, as well as mollify corporate critics. For a while, TQM made a splash on the education market. It soon was replaced by more intriguing business adaptations, such as "re-inventing the schools," a spin-off of corporate re-engineering concepts.[29] Soon the country was caught up in the development of new standards, new reform measures, "restructuring," and new vocational curricula. A cottage industry, soon an army, of testers constantly measured results, often before new "reforms" had even a chance to work. Certain interest groups amplified the bad news in order to dismantle the public school system through voucher plans and privatization schemes. By the late 1980s even an American President got involved. He convinced some corporations that they should privately fund school restructuring efforts to better guide the schools in directions more conducive to business goals. Thus the New American Schools Development Corporation (NASDC) was born.

Educators do not escape some responsibility for creating this situation. They succumbed to accusations that America's schools were not producing a world-class workforce. Rising to what they thought was the task, America's school district and university leaders fell for corporate demands to restructure education's purposes and programs. Growing numbers of high schools instituted school-to-work programs, tech prep, apprentice training, and computer courses. Universities developed such majors as technology and software specialist, corporate planning, business investment management, entertainment specialists, design engineering, and system analyst. And in the late 1990s, as the nation is about to be inundated with new high-tech graduates, educators' contribution to the jobs dilemma will become even more pronounced. That will happen because educators assume that schooling alone can help most Americans get a good job. Educators pay lip service to the gloomy forecasts of economists and the Bureau of Labor, but they continue to perpetuate the myth that the current economic infrastructure will provide decent jobs — all they need do is "reform" and "restructure" America's schools to hold up their end.

Ironically, just as America's business firms are becoming "lean and mean," cutting back their workforce and in the process reducing opportunities for decent, high-quality jobs, schools and colleges are rapidly increasing the supply of high-skill workers and highly qualified college graduates. Educators assumed that these graduates would constitute America's new world-class workforce. Instead, huge numbers of superfluous workers are being produced, workers for whom education will certainly prove to be no advantage.

At any rate, by the late 1980s America's corporations had successfully deflected blame for the poor performance of the American economy away from themselves. Relatively free of political pressure, Corporate America was able to proceed with its own, more private, agenda: the economic restructuring of the U.S. economy, maintaining stagnant wages, becoming lean, improving its comparative advantage, and establishing the legitimacy of new multinational corporations that are beyond national controls.[30] That effort has succeeded. Corporate America has regained its competitive advantage and has generated super-profits for its stockholders and executives. Corporate America also has left millions of Americans unemployed or underemployed, witnessed the growing impoverishment of millions of Americans, and severely reduced the number of decent job opportunities for millions of qualified graduates.[31]

Education's Contribution to Productivity

Students graduating from schools and colleges who could have moved into high-quality jobs are discovering, instead, that fewer job opportunities are available. That has nothing to do with the inadequacies of the public schools. Even if the schools had not instituted reforms, there were still plenty of college graduates of high quality coming out of traditional programs, just as there had been in the past. But in today's New Economy, there is a surplus of college graduates, many of whom now take substandard jobs for which they are overqualified or earn so little that they move back in with their parents.

The so-called failure of America's schools to produce a world-class workforce was not the catalyst for America's economic ills. Business had done itself in. But the charges persist. Despite all that has been written to show that education has been doing its job and doing it well, conventional wisdom still assigns much responsibility for America's employment doldrums to education. However, the facts show that education has consistently and continuously been a major *support* for high productivity in the U.S. economy.

America's economic growth (any country's for that matter) has been an area of serious study by economists for several decades. The studies, called "growth accounting," attempt to identify and explain the *sources* of economic growth and measure the *effects* of various factors associated with that growth. Economists, including Edward Dennison, have identified three basic factors that are the keys to growth: 1) the amount that the country saves and invests in equipping its labor force with productive capital — tools, machinery, transportation equipment, and other human-made means of production; 2) improvements in the education and skills of its workforce; and 3) the pace at which new technology and improved techniques are introduced into the production, transportation, and distribution of goods and services.[32] Of course, all of those attributes change over time, making some a contributor to growth at one point and an inhibitor at other times. The problem for economists is the measurement and analysis of the potential growth-promoting or growth-retarding effects of these three factors.

Growth accounting has identified the chief factors that contributed to American productivity growth from 1948 through 1982. Table 3.1 shows the basic factors used by economists to determine the *weighted* contribution of individual factors to the overall economy, relative to *output per worker*. The output per worker declined after 1973 from its post-World War II heights (in this case, from 2.3 for 1948-73 to 0.2 for 1973-83). Note that the relative importance of almost every factor declined, meaning that technological advances, capital, and even hours of work decreased in importance as contributors to the output per worker. Only one factor remained consistently important to the effectiveness of the economy. That factor is education.

Table 3.1: Education's contribution to economic productivity.

Factor	1948-1973	1973-1983
Output Per Worker	2.3	0.2
Owing to Change in . . .		
Average Weekly Hours	-0.4	-0.5
Quantity of Education	0.4	0.4
Quantity of Capital	0.5	0.3
Economies of Production	0.3	0.2
Other Factors	0.4	-0.3*
Technological Advances	1.1	0.1

Adapted from Charles L. Schultze, *Memos to the President: A Guide Through Macroeconomics for the Busy Policymaker* (Washington, D.C.: Brookings Institution, 1992), pp. 228-35.

*This figure represents the massive switch of workers from rural farm jobs and self-employment into higher-productivity jobs.

The decline in three factors — reinvestments of capital, effective management processes ("economies of production"), and technological advances — suggest that corporate leaders failed to maintain their companies' productivity by neglecting the high levels of reinvestment needed to upgrade the quality of the tools, equipment, and technology and by failing to streamline management practices.

Researchers from the University of Oregon focused more specifically on education as a contributor to economic productivity. What they found was confirmation of Dennison's work: Education is not only an important component of economic productivity, it has been the most consistent contributor to maintaining economic growth.

But those researchers also found that, in the overall scheme of things, other factors, such as investment in technology, machine tools, and more effective operating processes, had more of a total weight than did education.[33] That finding confirms that management decisions, or rather the failure to decide, contributed more to economic decline than anything that education had done. A decade after the Oregon studies were reported, RAND Corporation did an in-depth review of contemporary growth-accounting studies. That report also confirmed that management's decisions about modernization and capital investments were the key factors.[34]

A common measure of worker productivity is Gross Domestic Product. However, a better measure is "Total Factor Productivity" (TFP). TFP measures the output produced for a given amount of labor and capital input. It measures an economy's efficiency. A high TFP growth rate indicates that productivity is growing substantially in relation to key input factors. By looking at the TFP growth rates during different periods, one can get a sense of how other industrial nations have been able to catch up with the United States.[35] Table 3.2 shows that during the 1950-73 period, as America's corporations remained self-satisfied, the growth rates of other nations soared. It was the lack of investment in capital stock — machine tools, computer-based technology, and so forth — that left the United States in a declining position after 1973.

Table 3.2: Total factor growth rates of advanced industrial nations.

Country	1913-1950	1950-1973	1973-1984
United States	1.19	1.05	-.27
Japan	0.04	4.69	0.43
France	0.61	3.11	0.93
Germany	0.19	3.61	1.13
Great Britain	0.38	1.53	.064

Adapted from Roland Storm, *How Do Education and Training Affect a Country's Economic Performance: A Literature Survey* (Santa Monica, Calif.: RAND, 1993), pp. 5-7.

When comparative purchasing power is added to the equation, the continued dominance of the U.S. economy is apparent, as

Table 3.3 shows. However, because they failed to keep up technologically, U.S. corporations have more company at the upper levels of productivity. That is because other foreign companies have *improved* their productive capacities, not because the American workforce declined.[36]

Table 3.3: Gross domestic product using purchasing power ratios, 1971-1991.

Country	1971	1991
United States	140	125
Germany	105	110
Japan	81	108
France	101	103
Great Britain	92	88
European Union Total	89	92
OECD Average	100	100

Adapted from Roland Sturm, *How Do Education and Training Affect a Country's Economic Performance: A Literature Survey* (Santa Monica, Calif.: RAND, 1993).

This table shows a comparison of how much could actually be purchased given the strength of an economy. The OECD used the average of all advanced industrial nations, 100, as the baseline. The higher the index number, the stronger the economy. Thus, even though Germany and Japan have gained in strength, the United States has been the clear economic leader from 1971 right up to today.

These data and analyses clearly indicate that indecision or inaction by top executives led to the decline of America's global competitiveness. But economists also raise another question about the entire issue of "global competitiveness." That is: Does global competitiveness exist, or is it another scapegoat issue?

There are many myths in the notion that the United States was losing the competitive battle against Japan, Germany, and other advanced industrial nations. First, entire countries do not compete; only companies do that. If a company does not compete well, it shuts down. But countries, even those that are not doing well economically, do not declare bankruptcy and shut down; too many other attributes make up a "country" — values, culture, language, mores, traditions — to give it unity and continuity.

A more descriptive term for comparing national economies is *comparative advantage*. All countries have something to sell or trade, but some countries have some things — goods or services

— in which they are superior. When they have superior stuff, they are said to have an *advantage* over other countries; and the more "superior things" a country has, the more advantages it has. When the world wants coffee, a country that can grow a lot of coffee has a comparative advantage over countries that cannot grow coffee.

Thus the dominant economic position of the United States results from its comparative advantage in a wide variety of "things." The greatest strengths of the United States are in technology-intensive information services and high-technology industries — quality products that people around the world want. However, the United States is not as advantaged in such areas of industry as chemicals and most equipment and machinery industries, including automobiles, which experienced the heaviest setbacks. Moreover, the data do not support the idea that United States' comparative advantages are shifting away from high-wage industrial products to low-wage sectors.[37]

Other countries learn the technology of advanced countries, especially by having their own citizens attend universities in those countries and through technology transfers. Those countries then use that information to "catch up"; and they even save R&D costs, thereby closing the comparative-advantage spread. The economies of all current advanced industrial nations are converging on that of the United States; and it is only a matter of time before they match ours, all things becoming equal. But "equaling" does not imply loss. It is not a zero-sum game, lowering to the least common denominator. Other countries have simply improved their capacity and therefore can produce certain goods that, comparatively speaking, are more desirable to people than those of other countries.[38]

Obviously, education is an essential strength of those countries that are able to join the ranks of advanced industrial nations, just as it is essential if the United States is to stay within those ranks. Maintaining a country's technological and innovative system is largely the task of a nation's intelligentsia and craftworkers. Maintaining a high level of manufacturing productivity is the role of high-tech workers joined with high-performance firms.[39]

When comparing the effect of education on various economies, it is important to look at the level of education attained in advanced industrial nations. In France the average number of years of education is 10.79. In Germany it is 9.48; Japan, 11.15; The Netherlands, 9.92; and Great Britain 10.92. In the United States the average number of years of education is 12.52. Even when that calculation is weighted to reflect the differences between elementary education and secondary/college education, the United States, with an index score of 16.18 years, is far ahead of other advanced industrial nations — France, 13.65; Germany, 11.86; Japan, 13.56; The Netherlands, 11.83; Great Britain, 13.14.[40] After an exhaustive review of studies directly related to education's input to economic growth in the United States, the RAND Corporation concluded:

> Regardless of the particular calculation, education and its effect through labor quality are generally found to be among the *most important* contributors to economic growth. [Studies] find that education contributed 15-20 percent of growth in per capita GDP. [Additional studies] estimate that education is responsible for 38 percent of the contributions of labor, accounting for over 90 percent in the change in labor quality.[41]

America's education system has been a critical element in the maintenance of the United States' worldwide economic prowess. Regardless of future considerations, America's schools traditionally have been doing something right and are continuing to make their contribution to the country's economic growth. Nay-sayers may continue to complain and scold educators, and they even may deny the facts. But there is one established fact that they cannot deny: Without completing any massive school "restructuring," "reform," "re-engineering," "re-invention," or whatever it will be called next time around, the American economy since 1992 has rebounded with a fury, as we shall see next.

The Comeback Trail

The U.S. economy is again hitting on all cylinders: strong growth, low inflation, and a steady stream of new jobs (albeit, mostly low-quality jobs). And U.S. companies, on the ropes in the 1980s, are again world-class players in 1997.[42]

The International Institute for Management Development, a Swiss firm, ranks countries each year on 230 different criteria. In both 1995 and 1996 it ranked the United States number one in competitiveness. That means that U.S. businesses were more competitive than those in Japan, which ranked second, and Germany, which fell to ninth. But the report's authors noted the social costs America paid to gain that position:

> The high rankings given the United States are likely to fuel passionate debate on the social costs of regaining competitiveness. The country's success is the result of bold economic reforms, deregulation and privatization, and renewed leadership in new technology. But at the same time, achieving this success implies that the revenue of certain employees were frozen while productivity was soaring.[43]

Corporations have been able to boost productivity through a combination of restructuring, downsizing, investment in new technology, outsourcing, and using the threat of international competition to hold down wages. Corporate America spent (and is still spending) billions of dollars for capital improvements, including rapid technological transformation and automation of work. It also is pouring hundreds of billions of dollars into new high-tech equipment and information systems. All told, corporations are spending well over 9% of the GDP on durable equipment, computers and computer systems, automated numerically operated machines, and other state-of-the-art technology.[44] As a result, American corporations today are way ahead of other countries in leading-edge, high-tech industries, such as software production, machine tools, biotech techniques, techno-informational services, and entertainment. That is shown by the tremendous increase in productivity since the 1980s, when productivity grew at a sluggish 0.06%.[45] Between 1990 and 1994, annual average growth in productivity was a healthy 2.2%. In the past decade, corporate productivity growth was strong at 3%, reaching levels not seen since the 1950s and 1960s. And it appears that productivity will continue to climb.

Corporate profits also soared, doubling between 1980 and 1994 — $240 billion to $480 billion, when adjusted for inflation. Profits increased another $65 billion in 1994 and more than $75 billion in 1995, an average of 11% for all corporations, and 13.8% for the top 500 companies. With profits high, prices rose slowly, since executives preferred profiting from low wages instead.[46] The idea was to keep costs low and returns high. The key to that was to keep worker wages stagnant or to reduce them by outsourcing, eliminating jobs, and hiring temporary help. In 1995, businesses added only a handful of workers to their payrolls, less than one-third the number added during the same period in 1994.[47]

Even the trade deficit has changed its basic characteristics. Instead of being heavily influenced by the importation of consumer goods, which add little to productive capacity, the deficit now comes from importing capital stock, which fuels economic growth. That should mean increased productive capacity. In turn, the new technological capability that capital goods provide the U.S economy should mean the trade deficit will be under control as the country enters the 21st century.[48]

So, everything is coming up roses for America's corporations. But the growth of the New Economy and the strength of the great increases in productivity were paid for by America's workers and the public. There also were long-term negative effects for most of America's educators, as we shall see. One interesting note is that the business people who had harped so much about the damage education had done to the country's economy gave no credit to education for the new "prosperity."

Where the Real Blame Lies

> The more he talked of his honor, the faster we counted our spoons.
>
> Ralph Waldo Emerson

How could the corporate comeback and expansion happen when education is, at best, just now tooling up to meet the business demand for high-skill, knowledge workers. The first kindergarten class since the *Nation At Risk* hullabaloo about education's failures has not yet graduated from college. Even so, the new highs in productivity and profits are a reality. One would think that if education was to blame for the bad times, it would be fair to give credit for producing these good times. Alas, that is not the case, because the real culprit for the downturn was not education at all; and top executives knew that.

However, business executives found that using the education system's supposed weakness to cover their own draconian re-engineering and downsizing worked so well that they began to believe their own propaganda. For one thing, it allowed them to refuse to recognize their own culpability for *losing* America's comparative advantage in the first place. It was the business executives' decisions that exacerbated the conditions that resulted in a downward turn in the economy *and* further loss of competitive advantage.

First, by not reinvesting in modernization and capital equipment improvement, business executives had let their corporations — especially industrial firms — become obsolete.[49] An in-depth investigation by MIT's Commission on Industrial Productivity placed the blame for falling profits squarely on CEOs who continued to use old-fashion production techniques and were satisfied with short-term returns. Those CEOs lacked the foresight that strategic planning would have provided. As a result, they failed to incorporate technological innovations, to adopt more efficient management processes, and to develop webs of suppliers to better rationalize production processes. Executive managers, the commission noted, also continued to use rigid bureaucratic management techniques, eschewed building cooperative relationships with employees, and generally turned off public support through arrogant environmental activities and pricing strategies.[50] With such obsolescence and archaic management, American business productivity went down the tubes.

Essentially, America's corporate leaders had two alternatives as they began to recognize the economic challenge posed by Japan, Germany, and other advanced industrial nations. One was to respond strategically to meet those competitive threats by rebuilding their companies' aging production infrastructures, developing sophisticated R&D programs, and adopting more effective management processes.[51] The other alternative was simply to tighten traditional management techniques and take only those measures that would give their firms momentary short-term relief from moribund productivity and falling profitability. Business executives chose the latter.[52]

The result was a sharp decline in America's economic prowess. CEOs — often for very personal reasons — developed short time horizons and adaptive strategies that allowed their shareholders to realize quick financial returns by squeezing out more profits from traditional processes.[53] Having that short-range strategic view, CEOs passed over modernization investments that required longer developmental periods before showing profits. But that approach was at the expense of the capital investment, innovation, and development of more effective management processes that were needed for corporate growth. It was a self-satisfied approach that took the rewards of the moment as an indication that all was well.

Investment in innovative processes and management techniques, on the other hand, would have expanded the ability of corporations to produce high-quality, low-cost goods and services at fair prices. Modernization investments would have let the corporation or business improve its technology, management processes, training programs, communications and transportation techniques, and shop-floor practices, which would have made the corporation competitive with state-of-the-art foreign firms.[54] The efficacy of those investment strategies was demonstrated by Japan, Germany, and other advanced industrial nations when they used them in the decades after World War II. Modernization investments led to innovations and management processes that slowly closed the wide gap between the U.S. economic productivity and their own.

For 30 years after World War II, corporations in general and the manufacturing sector in particular had generated enormous surpluses. Gross returns to investments greatly exceeded the cost of capital — those funds needed to maintain, expand, and improve a corporation and to pay off its debt. "Easy money" enabled most large companies to satisfy the demands of their investors and still have plenty of cash left over to pay rising wages and to invest in growth. In the 1970s, as the dual impact of growing infrastructure obsolescence and foreign competition began to hit home, America's corporations found themselves beginning to lose markets they once dominated, such as steel, electronics, and automobiles.[55]

Revamping America's economic infrastructure would cost billions. But as the United States entered the 1980s, the cost of capital got higher and higher and pushed the returns on investments lower and lower. Those "returns" are what investors counted on for their own economic security. The average profits rate in 1978-1979 was a healthy 16.5%, and the interest cost of capital was about 6.5% to 7%. But the interest rate surged in the early 1980s. From 1983 through 1986, when the average corporate operating profit rate had dropped to about 14%, the interest rate actually exceeded the profits rate by two or three percentage points.[56] With the double whammy of foreign competition and high interest rates, profits began to fall. Profits, of course, produced the money used to pay shareholders. Thus America's core corporations were not generating enough cash flow to reward shareholders with the returns on their investments they thought they deserved. Profit short-falls also meant that very little was available to finance innovative growth and reinvestment programs.[57]

With investors becoming angry, executives' immediate response was to engage in financial techniques to generate profits immediately. Between 1979 and 1989, for example, raiders and hostile take-over artists bought companies, artificially raising their value by taking them apart, selling subsidiary assets, slowing reinvestments, and controlling cash flow. Junk bonds were used to refinance companies' efforts to buy back their own equity. The fact that more than $640 billion in equity was removed from public trading indicates the fervor of these financial maneuvers. Many companies then reorganized themselves — sold assets, held back on investments, tightened operations, or reduced the amount paid in taxes — in an attempt to increase the returns to their investors.[58] But all that maneuvering produced only a momentary surcease in declining profits.

A second major factor driving the downturn in profits was the huge increase in imports from other advanced industrial nations and even from the more rapidly advancing, newly industrializing countries (NICs), such as South Korea, Taiwan, the Philippines, Thailand, Indonesia, and others.[59] Those new industrial nations had adopted Japanese models to build an industrial base that used the most sophisticated technological innovations in the manufacturing process. Some of them also adopted, again like Japan, worker-management relations that indicated not only a respectful relationship but also the interdependence management and workers needed to accomplish productivity goals.[60] The NICs, while arriving later on the scene, were soon in the thick of the competition. Productivity surged in those countries and, as they plowed profits back into further technological refinements, they began to cut rapidly into America's dominant economic position. Not only that, but those same countries — along with Japan and Germany — began exporting their quality products to the United States, building a loyal consumer base, thereby bloating America's trade deficit as Americans began to show preference for the quality and prices of imported goods.

By the time America's companies began turning around, a fundamental change had occurred in the strategy of the investors who controlled huge amounts of funds. Shareholders — especially the large institutional investors controlling pension and mutual funds — had become more insistent that the companies in which they invested continue to show growth in *profit rates*.

Think of the power those institutional investors held. In 1995, mutual funds totaled $2.78 trillion.[61] Pension funds held billions of dollars to invest and were, therefore, major shareholders. Institutional investors using traditional pension funds accounted for two-thirds of the trading on the New York stock exchange.[62] Institutional investors began to carry a lot of influence. For example, the nation's largest pension fund, the California Public Employees Retirement System (CalPERS), pushes companies with slow-moving stocks to improve their performance. The CalPERS attitude is that the corporations in which it invests should make money, not reinvest. That was made clear when the CalPERS investment chief recently moved the fund's investments more to stocks, rather than to more conventional bonds; she explained this was done to "earn more money."[63] And apparently the strategy works. CalPERS, with $93 billion in assets, has earned 10.3% on its investments over the last five years. Shareholders had become greedy.

With intense pressure on them to increase profits, corporate executives had to find ways to ensure continued increases in stock values. They realized that short-term financial machinations were no longer working, but their failure to reinvest during the 1970s and 1980s left America's corporations technologically unprepared for global economic competition. Most experts, and even some business leaders, saw that more fundamental corporate restructuring would be necessary.[64] They saw that the "slowdown in investment in the 1970s [had] led to slower growth in capital/labor ratio and in labor productivity in manufacturing and had given [other advanced industrial countries] an absolute advantage in several important industries."[65] To get the "real" savings needed to begin the restructuring process, business began cutting costs; and the most visible of those costs were wages and benefits.[66]

Corporate executives were under intense pressure from stockholders to get higher earnings, which they decided had to come from cutting costs even more aggressively. Many old-time corporate executives resisted the thankless changes demanded by corporate restructuring, and they were replaced by executives more willing to accommodate investors' demands.

> When a competitiveness problem (stagnant growth, declining margins, and falling market share, for example) can no longer be ignored most executives pick up a knife and begin . . . restructuring. The goal is to carve away layers of corporate fat and amputate under-performing businesses. Executives who don't have the stomach for emergency-room surgery, like John Akers at IBM or Robert Stempel at GM, soon find themselves out of a job.[67]

To ensure the executive's commitment to increase value for shareholders, more creative ways to compensate the corporate executives were devised. The traditional way of setting executive compensation prior to the 1980s was a relatively straightforward process. Salaries and bonuses were the major components of executive compensation, with salaries largely determined by the size of the company and bonuses based on how fast the company was growing. But in the 1980s the pay of CEOs began to be tied directly to the return they achieved for shareholders. The method used to do that was to tie executives' pay to increases in the value of the corporation's stock. Thus, *stock options* rapidly became a central component of executives' compensation packages.[68]

Stock options ensure that executives' salaries are directly related to the corporation's stock performance and the shareholders' returns. A stock option gives executives the right to buy their company's stock at a given price (called a "strike price") at some point in the future. Imagine that a company's stock is selling for $50 and it grants its CEO an option on 100,000 shares of the company stock with a purchase price of $50. If the stocks increase to $75, the corporate CEO can exercise his option and realize a gain of $2.5 million. If the company's stock price falls to $45, the executive receives no gain. But he also *loses nothing* since he has not used any of his money to actually purchase the stock at $50; it is only a paper pledge. Thus the stock option gives the executive virtually unlimited potential for gain and no penalty if prices fall. As one observer puts it:

> The holder [executives] of the option does not risk nor commit any capital to the corporation during the years that the corporation could certainly use the capital, but the holder nonetheless shares in the gains from the corporation's capital at the same rate as shareholders who did shoulder the risk. A holder of an option gets to buy stock after the results are in.[69]

Stock options soon came to be a basic part of an executive's earnings, rather than simply a reward for superior performance. That means an executive's pay does not necessarily suffer even when a corporation performs poorly. In many instances when it appeared that a corporation's stock might decline in price because of lack of performance, the company's directors often "repriced" company stock to ensure that their executives received excellent compensation anyway. For instance, AT&T Chairman Allen's cash compensation actually was cut in 1995 by 15%; but an enormous option grant of 858,000 shares — up from 72,854 the previous year — more than made up the difference. Allen's overall compensation in 1995 rose 139% to $16 million. That came in a year in which Allen ordered layoffs of as many as 40,000 AT&T employees to help the company recover from failed strategies for which he was responsible. Stock options also can be a bonanza for executives in bad times. For example, in 1993 Walt Disney Company's chairman, Michael Eisner, did not receive a bonus because of the poor returns from the EuroDisney project. Still, Eisner took home $203.2 million in 1993 by exercising his stock options.[70]

Is it any wonder that top executives have learned to focus on short-term stock market performance so they can exercise their options when conditions are most advantageous? When executives take their options early, they often are able to establish a higher level of base pay *and* get more options in their new compensation packages. Other executives who are not CEOs still get stock options and receive handsome compensation, sometimes better than their CEOs get.

The overall performance of a corporation and its capacity to serve as a foundation for long-term wealth and prosperity for both shareholders and employees is not a major consideration.[71] For example, recent stock option packages in the computer industry took neither company size nor performance into consideration. The five top-performing technology companies in 1995 paid their executives $1,556,000 on average (the range was $383,000 to $5,236,000). In contrast, the bottom five companies received a very low performance rating but gave their CEOs stock options worth $2,172,000 on average.[72] Go figure!

Even so, shareholders, including institutional shareholders, apparently knew what they were doing when they tied compensation to stock prices. Indeed, in today's world, stock options have become the most important component of corporate executives' compensation packages, as Table 3.4 shows:

Table 3.4: Source of executive income by percent, 1985 and 1993.

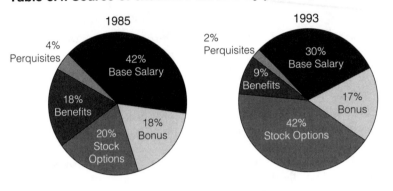

Adapted from "Execs' Biggest Fears: Stock Option Accounting Rule," *Chicago Tribune*, 21 March 1994, Section 4, p. 3.

The use of stock options has been so effective in increasing returns to shareholders that it is little wonder that many corporations insist their executives own company stock. Indeed, executive stock ownership has increased yearly. For example, in 1970 America's 200 core corporations set aside about 3% of their shares for stock options for their executives. In 1995, they reserved 10%. These stock options have given executives a vested interest in increasing shareholder stock prices by whatever means necessary, because as they do so, they also increase the value of their own personal wealth.

If not growth and expansion and productivity, how are stock option compensations increasing share values? Stock options were the driving force behind the massive layoffs and elimination of quality job opportunities in the United States over the past decade.[73] Among the list of the 15 highest paid executives are those whose companies — IBM, General Motors, Sears, Martin Marietta, General Dynamics, General Electric, RJR Nabisco, Time Warner, ITT, and Unisys — downsized and laid off workers to enable executives and shareholders to realize higher share values. So while the rest of the country's workers experienced stagnant or falling wages, top executive pay continued to increase, sometimes by a lot. For example, in 1995 executive compensation jumped 23% for an *average* executive pay of $4.37 million. That was the same year in which the stock market reached record highs, corporate chiefs got annual bonuses of $1.22 million and stock options grants worth at least 77% of their annual pay, and *3.26 million American workers were fired*. The growth rate at the top handily beat the growth of corporate profits themselves. Indeed, executive raises seem to parallel brutal downsizing — with some of the biggest raises going to the CEOs with the sharpest hatchets. Is that coincidence? Stock market analysts know better:

> Rising corporate profits, driven by lower costs associated with a smaller work force, are one reason the stock market has been rising so fast. That's why there's a relationship between fired Americans and $4.4 million-a-year corporate executives.[74]

The pressure to downsize to push up stock prices has spread in the 1990s. Firing workers and even middle managers has proven personally profitable for top executives ever since stock options came into vogue. CEO pay continues to shoot up, showing a 34% increase between 1993 and 1995, while ordinary workers were getting a paltry 2.9% increase. In fact, the pay of top U.S. corporate managers continues to grow so fast while frontline workers wages are stagnating that it has become an economic and political cause célèbre. But it hasn't slowed them down.

Even profitable companies that could easily pay decent wages and benefits, such as Proctor and Gamble, AT&T, Eli Lilly, and Mattel Toys, have downsized to cut blue-collar workers and restructured to eliminate middle managers and white-collar employees.[75] When AT&T cut 40,000 high-tech and professional employees in 1996, its stock value rose immediately by almost 3%, bringing a huge increase in compensation for AT&T executives with little more effort than firing thousands of employees.[76]

Thus the "common interest" of shareholders, institutional investors, directors, and executives is a search for easy, fast money.

Nonetheless, the downsizing, restructuring, and intimidation of employees to hold down wages worked. Corporate productivity shot up, labor costs dropped, and stock prices rose through the roof.[77]

It is pretty clear that the downturn in the American economy was closely linked with executive mismanagement, short-sightedness, and avarice, to put it mildly. Here is how two leading experts summarize what happened to America's leading corporations that caused the weakening of the country's competitive advantage:

> With no or slow growth [in the late 1980s, early 1990s], these companies soon found it impossible to support their burgeoning employment rosters, traditional R&D budgets, and significant investment programs. The problems of low growth were often compounded by inattentiveness to ballooning overhead (IBM's problem) diversification into unrelated businesses . . . and paralysis imposed by unfailingly conservative corporate staff. It is not surprising that shareholders are giving moribund companies new marching orders: Make this company "lean and mean"; "make the assets sweat"; "get back to basics." Return on capital employed, shareholder value, and revenue per employee became the primary arbiters of top management performance. Although perhaps inescapable and in many cases commendable, the resulting restructuring has destroyed lives, homes and communities — to what end? For efficiency and productivity. Although arguing with these objectives is impossible, their single-minded — and sometimes simple-minded — pursuit has done as much harm as good.[78]

And what was education's role in this? Educators were involved in the rush to judgment. They kowtowed to business demands and held out their hands for federal dollars tied to school-to-work strings. They asked for help from business advocates in order to define the expectations for our graduates almost solely from business interests, often to the exclusion of our real clients: the schools' students and parents.

However, most educators knew something was amiss as businesses, impatient with the slow processes of "reform" and "restructuring," turned their moral and fiscal support to truly undemocratic and threatening notions — vouchers and privatization schemes — that would have, if successful, destroyed the covenant public educators have had with their communities for more than a hundred years. Those two shifts by the business community and their media and think-tank cronies were the wake-up calls for thoughtful educators. Most educators are aware that schools are not as efficacious as they should be in preparing students for the 21st century, but they want to find ways to improve schooling without destroying its historic mission to serve all students.

A Look Ahead

Many businesses took the short-term route. They vitiated production standards in order to produce cheaper goods, rather than better goods. They aggressively reduced worker wage and benefit levels, and they used the federal government to make the workforce docile and to cut back safety-net social programs.[79] Clearly, if blame needs to be assigned for American businesses losing their comparative economic advantage to foreign competitors and for causing the horrendous economic downturn in the 1980s and early 1990s, it needs to be leveled directly at the poor decisions made in that period by chief executive officers of America's corporations and the short-sighted greed of major stockholders.[80]

As we shall see in later chapters, not all business executives were frozen into passivity by the challenge of foreign competition and productivity, nor were all executives so wrapped up in satisfying their own and their stockholders' avarice that they were willing to ignore their companies' need for modernization. On the contrary, a number of business firms began to change themselves aggressively by introducing new technology, adapting Japanese productivity and management processes, and adding a factor unique in American culture — the willingness to take risks and capitalize on an entrepreneurial spirit. Those firms, as we shall see, became success stories in an otherwise relatively dismal economic climate. While other businesses were downsizing and re-engineering to benefit CEOs and shareholders at the expense of their companies, the top executives of high-performance firms were preparing their companies for growth.

Fortunately for the United States, those companies and executives did not succumb to the manipulation of financial assets and to the brutalities of downsizing and re-engineering in order to gain short-term profits. These companies are exemplary models of modernization, worker relationships, and innovation for all of America's corporations. And that development and those high-performance companies are the harbinger of future corporate operations, as we shall see in the next chapter.

Notes

1. Laurence Ogle and Patricia Dobbs, "Good News, Bad News," *Education Week*, 13 March 1996, p. 46.
2. Louis V. Gerstner Jr., Roger D. Semerad, Denis Philip Doyle, and William B. Johnston, *Reinventing Education: Entrepreneurship in America's Public Schools* (New York: Dutton, 1994).
3. Robert B. Reich, *The Work of Nations: Preparing Ourselves for 21st Century Capitalism* (New York: Vintage, 1991), p. 46.
4. Ibid., pp. 46-47.
5. Kevin Phillips, *Boiling Point: Democrats, Republicans and the Decline of Middle-Class Prosperity* (New York: Harper Perennial, 1993), pp. 3-31; and Reich, op. cit., p. 48.
6. Lawrence A. Cremin, *The Transformation of the School: Progressivism in American Education, 1876-1957* (New York: Alfred A. Knopf, 1961), pp. 188-93.
7. Ronald E. Kutscher, "Historical Trends, 1950-92, and Current Uncertainties," *Monthly Labor Review* (November 1993), p. 3; also, Lawrence Mishel and Jared Bernstein, *The State of Working America, 1992-1993* (Washington, D.C.: Economic Policy Institute, 1993), p. 216, gives data over a longer period.
8. Mishel and Bernstein, op. cit., p. 132.
9. Ibid., p. 274.
10. Eileen Applebaum and Rosemary Batt, *The New American Workplace: Transforming Work Systems in the United States* (Ithaca, N.Y.: ILR Press, 1994), pp. 14-15.

11. David M. Godon, "Chickens Home to Roost: From Prosperity to Stagnation in the Postwar U.S. Economy," in *Understanding American Economic Decline*, edited by Michael A. Bernstein and David E. Adler (New York: Cambridge University Press, 1994), pp. 55-68.
12. Applebaum and Batt, op. cit., pp. 14-15.
13. Godon, op. cit., pp. 55-68; see also, Reich, op. cit., pp. 48-51.
14. Robert Boyer and Pascal Petit, *Kaldor's Growth Theories: Past, Present, and Prospects* (Paris: CEPREMAP, 1989).
15. Gary Hamel and C.K. Prahalad, "Competing for the Future," *Harvard Business Review* (July-August 1994): 124.
16. Cremin, op. cit., pp. 339, 344-45.
17. H.G. Rickover, *Education and Freedom* (New York, 1959), as quoted in Cremin, op. cit., p. 347.
18. National Commission on Education, *A Nation At Risk: The Imperative for Educational Reform* (Washington, D.C.: U.S. Government Printing Office, 1983), p. 5. Interestingly, the "risk" document was written by university-level writers and people from think tanks. The one exception was the lone member of the task force with classroom experience, and he wrote a scathing rebuttal to the other task force members.
19. Richard DuFour and Robert Eaker, *Creating the New American School* (Bloomington, Ind.: National Educational Service, 1992), p. 1.
20. Richard C.J. Barnet and Jon Cavanaugh, *Global Dreams: The Imperial Corporations and the New World Order* (New York: Simon and Schuster, 1994), p. 422.
21. Laurence Ogle and Patricia Dobbs, op. cit., p. 46.
22. "Matter of Definition: What Are 'World Class' Standards?" *Education Week*, 15 June 1994, p. 11.
23. W.B. Johnston and A.E. Packer, *Workforce 2000: Work and Workers for the 21st Century* (Indianapolis: Hudson Institute, 1987).
24. Ibid., pp. 95-96.
25. Mishel Mischel and Ruy A. Teixeira, *The Myth of the Coming Labor Shortage: Jobs, Skills, and Income of America's Workforce 2000* (Washington, D.C.: Economic Policy Institute, 1991), p. 4.
26. Alan Reynolds, "Workforce 2000: The Future of Jobs in the United States and Europe," in *Societies in Transition, the Future of Work and Leisure* (Paris: Organisation for Economic Cooperation and Development, 1994), p. 48-53.

27. Mischel and Teixeira, op. cit., p. 40.

28. Ibid., p. 41.

29. Gerstner et al., op. cit., passim.

30. Reich, op. cit., p. 46.

31. Barnet and Cavanaugh, op. cit.

32. Growth accounting was devised by Robert Solow, then at the Massachusetts Institute of Technology, for which he received the 1957 Nobel Prize. The method later was expanded by Edward Dennison, and it is his results that are reported in this section. See Charles L. Schultze, *Memos to the President: A Guide Through Macroeconomics for the Busy Policymaker* (Washington, D.C.: Brookings Institution, 1992), pp. 228-35.

33. Wynn DeBevoise, *The Contribution of Education to Economic Productivity* (Eugene, Ore.: ERIC Clearinghouse on Education Management, 1983), pp. 2-15.

34. Roland Sturm, *How Do Education and Training Affect a Country's Economic Performance: A Literature Survey* (Santa Monica, Calif.: RAND, 1993).

35. Ibid., pp. 5-7.

36. Ibid., p. 8.

37. Ibid., p. 9.

38. Ibid., pp. 8-13.

39. Ibid., p. 9.

40. The education growth factor is slightly skewed in Germany and The Netherlands because both countries have a full, sophisticated apprentice system that trains skilled workers on the job. That education and training is not included in the education growth factor numbers because it is not "formal" education. Germany has very high productivity. When its index for education growth is adjusted to reflect its investment in education and training, the contribution of quality labor to that productivity is higher than in any other advanced industrial nation, including the United States.

41. Sturm, op. cit., p. 9.

42. Michael Mandel, "Plumping Profits, Slumping Paychecks," *Business Week*, 20 January 1995, pp. 86-87.

43. "Competitiveness Yearbook Puts U.S. at No. 1," *Los Angeles Times*, 27 May 1996, p. D2. Other high ranked countries include Switzerland (10), Denmark (6), Norway (6), The Netherlands (7), Sweden (14), and Taiwan (18). Low rank was for countries that were depen-

dent on their natural resources: Indonesia (41), Mexico (42), and South Africa (44).

44. Christopher Farrell, Michael Mandel, and Joseph Weber, "Ridin' High: Corporate America Now Has an Edge over Its Global Rivals," *Business Week*, 9 October 1995, p. 137.
45. "The Big Picture: Productivity's Powerful Pace," *Business Week*, 25 September 1995, p. 8.
46. Sumita Wadekar Bhargava, "Profits: Reality Pays a Call," *Business Week*, 13 November 1995, p. 130.
47. Robert B. Reich, "Meet the Frayed Collar Workers Getting the Boot," *Los Angeles Times*, 4 September 1995, p. B4.
48. Farrell, Mandel, and Weber, op. cit., pp. 134-46.
49. Bennett Harrison and Barry Bluestone, *The Great U-Turn: Corporate Restructuring and the Polarizing of America* (New York: Basic Books, 1988), p. xiii.
50. Ibid., Ch 1.
51. Gary Hamel and C.K. Prahalad, *Competing for the Future* (Boston: Harvard Business School Press, 1994), pp. 27-48.
52. Harrison and Bluestone, op. cit., pp. 11-14.
53. Ibid., pp. 22-52.
54. William Lazonick, "Creating and Extracting Value: Corporate Investment and American Economic Performance," in *Understanding American Economic Decline*, edited by Michael A. Bernstein and David E. Adler (New York: Cambridge University Press, 1994), pp. 79-113.
55. John P. Kotter, "Leading Change: Why Transformation Efforts Fail," *Harvard Business Review* (March-April 1995): 59-67.
56. Margaret M. Blair, "CEO Pay: Why Such a Contentious Issue?" *Brookings Review* (Winter 1994): 23-27.
57. Ibid.
58. Ibid.
59. Pete Emgardo Barnathan and John Wingenberg, "Asia's New Giants," *Business Week*, 27 November 1995, p. 65.
60. Harrison and Bluestone, op. cit., pp. 11-12.
61. "Demand for Stock Funds Still Zooming," *Los Angeles Times*, 29 December 1995, p. D3.
62. James Flanigan, "A Contradictory Economy Driven by Steady Investors," *Los Angeles Times*, 14 January 1996, pp. D1-D2.
63. *Los Angeles Times*, 11 December 1995, pp. D1, D3. As the devastating effects of such a stance have become obvious, CalPERS may

be changing its approach. Recently it announced that it would be pushing companies in which it held significant stock to look for alternatives to layoffs, such as "retraining" and "redeployment." See "The Layoffs Love Affair Is Cooling," *Washington Post Weekend Edition*, 4-10 March 1996, p. 21.

64. Michael J. Mandel, "Can U.S. Companies Afford to Take the Long View?" *Business Week*, 1 May 1995, p. 36.

65. Eileen Applebaum, "High Tech and the Structural Employment Problems of the 1980s," in *American Jobs and the Changing Industrial Base*, edited by Eileen L. Collins and Lucretia Dewey Tanner (Cambridge, Mass.: Ballinger, 1984), p. 24.

66. Harrison and Bluestone, op. cit., pp. 22-52.

67. Hamel and Prahalad, op. cit., p. 124.

68. Blair, op. cit.

69. Calvin H. Johnson, "Stock Options Aren't Free Compensation," *Los Angeles Times*, 8 April 1994, p. B7.

70. *Los Angeles Times*, 4 January 1994, p. D1. The Walt Disney Co. also added another executive, President David S. Ovitz, for a compensation package worth $101 million, including $71 million in stock options and a clause for escalating his stock options by 20% every year after 1998. "Ovitz's Disney Pay Includes Stock Options that Could Total $110 Million," *Los Angeles Times*, 15 November 1995, p. D1.

71. Mandel, op. cit., p. 36.

72. *Los Angeles Times*, 24 September 1995, pp. D2, D10. The average performances and stock option figures were derived by dividing the performance and stock option data of the ten major computer companies to get an average amount for top and bottom performers.

73. *Los Angeles Times*, 15 June 1996, pp. A1, A22-A23. This article goes on to say that guilt is motivating more companies to grant shares to regular workers, but only 3% of the top 1,000 companies are doing that.

74. "CEO Bask in Stocks' Banner Year; Average Pay Rises to $4.37 Million," *Los Angeles Times*, 5 March 1996, p. D2.

75. Margaret M. Blair, "CEO Pay: Why Such a Contentious Issue?" *Brookings Review* (Winter 1994): 27; Lester C. Thurow, "America Reverts to the 19th Century," *Los Angeles Times*, 29 January 1996, p. B9.

76. "Market Starts '96 with Bang as Dow Soars 60," *Los Angeles Times*, 3 January 1996, pp. D1, D3. Many critics of AT&T's down-

sizing alleged that CEOs were toying with Wall Street by manipulating their stock prices; see "AT&T Split into 3 Firms to Cost 40,000 Jobs," *Los Angeles Times*, 3 January 1996, pp. A1, A9.

77. "4% of AT&T Employees Accept Buyout Offer," *Los Angeles Times*, 29 December 1995, p. D3; "Demand for Stock Funds Still Zooming," *Los Angeles Times*, 29 December 1995, p. D3.

78. Hamel and Prahalad, op. cit., p. 8.

79. Harrison and Bluestone, op. cit., pp. 14-15.

80. John P. Kotter, "Leading Change: Why Transformation Efforts Fail," *Harvard Business Review* (March-April 1995): 59-67.

Chapter Four

The New
Social Compact

The forces driving the New Economy are decisions made by the powerful owners and executives of America's corporations. They are the people who decided to use technological innovation to shed workers and make a quick buck, rather than to search for more creative solutions to technology's challenges and opportunities. Thus America's standard of living dropped.

Nor does the standard of living seem to be improving for most Americans. The economic expansion of the mid-1990s did little to create high-quality jobs or to increase wages. In 1995 wages averaged a paltry gain of 2.9%, the smallest gain since government statistics have been kept.[1] Millions still remain unemployed or underemployed in temporary and part-time jobs with lousy wages and no benefits. And businesses have not stopped downsizing. More than one million workers were laid off just in 1995 and 1996.[2] And in all likelihood, corporate executives will use the next recession as a rationale to shed even more workers.

There are, of course, beneficiaries of the New Economy other than the major stockholders and the managerial elite. Those who find work as symbolic analysts are winners in the New Economy. However, these professionals, technical specialists, and knowledge workers constitute only 20% to 25% of the working-age population.[3]

Unfortunately, it is the success of these symbolic analysts and other knowledge workers that vectored business-people and concerned educators away from more realistic solutions to the jobs dilemma. Business people, appealing to educators, were saying: "Look what's happening. Computer-based manufacturing and electronic information processing are radically changing how we produce goods and deliver services. Give us workers with more education and more training, so they will be able to *use* that technology effectively." Educators took that appeal at face value. Indeed, they took up that challenge and have been enthusiastically pushing the system's resources to graduate better-equipped students, both in quality of education and in training.

Educators had fallen prey to the incessant pitch of conventional wisdom concerning the need for a high-tech workforce. Thus educators have kept right on producing graduates educated for high-quality jobs that may never exist. High schools continue to tool up to produce graduates with the skills and attitudes America's business firms say are needed. Universities and colleges are graduating an ever-growing number of students with the sophisticated skills and conceptual understandings they need to be valuable to America's corporations. But most American businesses continue to use short-term measures to increase their immediate stock values, which, in turn, reduces the job opportunities for both skilled high school graduates and knowledgeable university graduates.

Educators assumed, as did many government officials, that the solution to the technological changes occurring in the workplace is simply better preparation of students for the world of work through more education and more training. They did so without any analysis of how many of those nifty jobs would be available. They did not ask: Will the demand for knowledge workers match or exceed the supply being graduated? Because they did not ask that tough question, educators were nonplused when Corporate America realized that companies could gain greater profits by shedding their workers and investing in more machines. Thus opportunities for decent, challenging jobs were rapidly diminishing even for symbolic analysts and high-tech, skilled craftworkers.

In the United States, where unemployment benefits are relatively skimpy and of relatively short duration (normally 26 weeks), the unemployed find themselves without health insurance and workers have little choice but to accept jobs no matter how low the pay. Thus U.S labor markets have been, in the fine euphemism of official documents, "flexible."[4]

Other advanced nations face the same dilemma. Europe — especially Germany, the leading economy in Europe — also has a severe unemployment problem brought on by technological innovations that reduce the availability of high-quality jobs.[5] Japan, for the first time since the end of World War II, is faced with the prospects of ending its guarantee of lifelong employment for its high-skilled workers.[6] However, the difference between these countries and the United States is that Europe and Japan are searching for humane, long-term solutions to the jobs dilemma, whereas U.S. corporations seem content to let "market forces" determine who works and who does not, who prospers and who is poverty stricken. This "let the chips fall where they may" attitude is fraught with political ramifications.

In the "joyless recovery" of the early 1990s, the angry response from ordinary Americans to the lack of decent jobs, underemployment, and rising unemployment was an attack on what Americans perceived as the causes of their misery. Thus there was strong antagonism expressed against immigrants, political steps to eliminate "affirmative action," angry anti-feminist media, and attempts to abrogate thirty years of environmental protections, all in the name of "saving jobs." There also has been growing a deep mistrust of government solutions to *any* problem.

All of that loss of work has come at a great cost — costs that go beyond economic. The loss of a decent job is more than just the loss of pay; it is loss of identity. "What do you do for a living?" is a common question when people first meet. Work also makes people feel that they are using their time productively. So in addition to the loss of security, independence, health insurance, vacation pay, pensions, and other benefits that came with having a job, there is the onerous emotional toll of not having a decent job.

As the growth of the jobs dilemma moves to crisis levels, both here and in other advanced industrial nations, thoughtful business, labor union, and political leaders have begun to question the wisdom of the decisions that led up to the crisis. They have begun the search for alternative solutions, those that not only will militate the distressful effects of economic restructuring but also will result in a long-range, institutional solution to the jobs dilemma.

Some American companies already have seen the problems created by mindless downsizing and are attempting to manage their workforces creatively in order to avert layoffs. For example:

- The executives at Pinnacle Brands, a Dallas trading-card company, urged staffers to save their jobs by devising money-saving or money-making ideas. The first suggestion came from a custodian, who urged elimination of a $50,000-a-year expense — sodas and bottled water in conference rooms and executive offices. A public relations manager arranged for Pinnacle to distribute pins for the 1996 Olympics — bringing in nearly $20 million in sales.
- Chevron Corp., the San Francisco-based oil giant, encourages job-hopping among its units to balance staffing. It trains workers to bring them up to speed in new skills.
- Harman International Industries Inc. in Northridge, California, a maker of audio and video products, pushes employees to grow through education and job training. Harman also operates an in-house job bank for shifting workers to new projects should their current jobs become "surplus."
- Other companies have developed a worker swap program that helps them even out seasonal production vagaries. Some companies even temporarily cut every worker's pay and trim work schedules to save jobs.[7]

Such innovations are the exception. But they indicate that with a modicum of creative thinking, alternatives to layoffs can be found when employees are valued. But the United States needs more than patchwork efforts.

However, even the fact that some corporations are thinking about alternatives is a good sign. Up through the mid-1990s, not many people in the United States had spent much time looking for alternatives to the jobs dilemma. As a people, we had accepted the argument that, because of some mysterious and inexorable "market forces," Americans would have to suffer stoically, enduring the pain and distress of economic restructuring. It is as if one had no choice — an economic hocus-pocus had caused the layoffs, lower wages, poverty, class divisions, and other effects of economic restructuring. In fact, those effects were the results of decisions made by people — corporate executives, institutional investors, Wall Street, or even, sometimes, business consultants — to restructure the economy. Many analysts now argue that it is time to re-evaluate the assumption that so-called invisible market forces — those that apparently value machines over humans — have actually caused this dilemma; perhaps, with the appropriate *structural* interventions, it might be possible to resolve the jobs dilemma by viewing it through a different model: putting people first.[8]

Putting People First

In the past, when a major change in the economy increased productivity, it resulted in people working shorter hours. For example, when the economy shifted from an agricultural to an industrial base, work hours gradually lowered from 80 hours a week to 60 hours a week. Other changes brought the average work week to 40 hours, until the 1970s.[9] However, in today's techno-information economy with its unheard of productivity levels, work hours actually have *increased* for American workers, that is, those who still are left after downsizing and re-engineering. Today, with fewer workers in the economy, workers can produce what Americans enjoyed in 1948 in less than half the time it took then.[10]

Technology severely reduces the *number* of high-tech workers that are needed. Even now, Japan has a fully automated model factory that needs only minimal human intervention to operate and maintain itself while turning out excellent products. As the

121

trend continues, especially within the advanced industrial nations, the job opportunities for knowledge workers will continue to decrease.

Corporate America has taken advantage of that trend to shed workers to save wages. But eventually even American corporations are going to realize that shedding workers from good-paying jobs will prove self-defeating. Downsized workers make lousy customers; and customers are the backbone of the new techno-information society — accounting for 75% of the nation's GNP — just has they were in the old economy.[11] In addition, the American people eventually are going to realize that they have been left out of the "economic miracle" of the New Economy and will begin making political demands for a more equitable and just distribution of the benefits of technologically driven high productivity. When that happens, there will be an active search for ways to accomplish that redistribution — one that takes human needs as its first consideration. And work still will be a central element of any new system.

There are two attitudes toward technology and work in the techno-information age. From one view, the *technocrat* view, computer-based technology must inevitably eliminate workers in order to gain lower unit labor costs and higher profits. In this view, it is a zero-sum game. By 2005, more than 90 million of the projected 124 million jobs in America could be eliminated or marginalized by applications of computer technology.[12] Even now it is common to find automated machinery, robots, and increasingly sophisticated computers doing the repetitive work associated with routine production, tasks that typically employ three-quarters of the workforce in advanced industrial nations. As we move further into the computer age, advances in artificial intelligence will challenge much of the traditional "brain-power" work done by craftsmen and such professionals as physicians, lawyers, nurses, and teachers.[13]

The other point of view, the *instrumental* view, puts people first and involves structural modification of the economy. It does not assume that technological advances will automatically eliminate all but a core of highly skilled, technically competent workers, leaving the rest of us wretched. Rather, it sees technology as the means for reducing the work of *all* workers, with people *sharing* what physical work remains to be done. That will include the creative work of symbolic analysts, as well as the high-skill, high-tech humans needed to tend to the machines. It also will mean the development of essential service tasks that will employ many millions more Americans in exciting and challenging work.

The instrumental view sees computer-based technology as a *tool* that humans *decide* how to use, including how it is used to affect employment. In that context, technology can be used as a means for reducing everyone's work and spreading the available work around to an expanded workforce base, rather than a means to eliminate or marginalize jobs. Technology would be used to increase the amount of freedom humans have. Work then becomes something in which *everyone* engages only "part-time." Machines would do most of the work while human activity is directed elsewhere — family, friends, social activities, avocations, invention, creativity, voluntary civic activities, charity, and just plain leisure. In the instrumentalist view, technological innovations in the workplace should be accelerated, rather than suppressed, in order to achieve that end.

Viewing technology instrumentally, as a means for producing more jobs and creating greater "free-time" for everyone, is not at all science fantasy. Indeed, in two ways, analytical research and real-world experience, the instrumental option is given substantial support. The first tests of the instrumental view were feasibility studies that calculated how many hours the work week would need to be reduced in order to produce a significant number of "freed-up" hours so that others also could work at those jobs.[14] Without, for the moment, considering what that would cost either workers or the businesses, what would it take to reduce hours sufficiently to gain a large number of job opportunities for craft-workers and symbolic analysts? The feasibility studies have shown that it is possible, at least theoretically, to increase the number of good job opportunities for millions of additional workers.[15]

But will it work in reality? The real-world test of the idea comes from studying the effects of what is happening in Germany and other Western European countries that are reducing work hours to accommodate more jobs. Those policies will be discussed in more detail below. The point here is that the concept of using technology to expand job opportunities is not a fantasy but an idea that has both empirical and pragmatic validity.

There are three ways that hold promise for job expansion: *work-sharing*, *profit-sharing*, and *public jobs*. Putting more people to work at decent jobs also will help resolve the concomitant issues of stagnant wages and poverty, as well as reduce the huge discrepancies that have grown between the wealthy elite and the rest of us. Basically, job expansion means expanding the number of decent high-tech, knowledge worker, and symbolic analyst job opportunities for qualified school and university graduates.

Job-Expansion Policies

We can anticipate at least some of the socioeconomic effects that will accompany technological change and plan accordingly. Indeed, rather than fatalistically accepting whatever distress that future portends, it is more useful to deal with those effects proactively by determining and implementing policies to mitigate some of technology's predicted negative consequences. Sufficient information already exists to do that.

Consider this: It is now well known that the decline in manufacturing jobs among advanced industrial nations is just continuing a long-term trend. That trend allows us to anticipate at least the immediate future. We know that manufacturing always will be a significant part of the GNP; but as we introduce more sophisticated technology, it will produce goods with many fewer workers. Even now a high-skill worker, with computer-based technology, can do the work of three or more unskilled workers. Being *aware* of that trend permits us to consider a number of alternatives. One choice is simply to continue to shed workers until only a handful of craftworkers are needed to do work — a problem that Germany is facing right now. A second choice is to keep everyone working and to push the costs of production so high that we price our products out

124

of the global competitive market. A third choice is to try to isolate ourselves from the rest of the world.

All of those choices are self-defeating. Yet we cannot continue to do nothing. As the pressure of underemployment, unemployment, and wage inequality mounts, it is becoming increasingly urgent for government officials, business planners, and educators to institute policies to make the transition to a full techno-information society as smooth and beneficial to Americans as possible.

A fourth choice — job expansion — is the most effective response to the growing phenomena of technologically driven joblessness, low-wage service jobs, and income inequality. However, that choice depends on government officials, business people, educators, and opinion makers not only accepting the basis of the New Economy — the combination of computer-based manufacturing and information technology — but also to go even further by actively supporting the *expansion* of the economy's technological capacity. Expanding the opportunities for decent jobs demands the mutual development of government, corporate, and education policies.

There are three major interconnected programs for job expansion: *work-sharing* for the industrial sector, *profit-sharing* for the service sector, and *public works* for the chronically unemployed. Here is how they work.

Work-Sharing

One of the most effective ways to expand jobs is through *work-sharing*. Economists recognize that work schedules need to be modified if there is to be any hope of accommodating new workers.[16] As Juliet Schor explains:

> It is now very unlikely that the U.S. economy can generate large numbers of jobs without reducing the hours associated with each job. The measures advocated [here] (especially job-sharing, trading income for time, guaranteed vacations, and the abolition of mandatory overtime) should have a major impact on job creation.[17]

Work-sharing is a program in which currently employed workers reduce the number of hours they work in order to "free up" time that can be used to hire new employees. In an obviously oversimplified but accurate example, let's say that a company has 10 full-time workers working eight hours a day. That is a total of 80 hours per day or 400 hours per week. If work-sharing were in operation and the 10 full-time workers cut back to four hours per day, 200 hours per week would be available for hiring 10 new employees who also would work four hours a day.[18] There is a variety of ways in which the new employees could be used. They could work at the same tasks as the first employees but on different shifts. They could fill in on a rotating basis to give other employees extended vacations. They could take over a job for an extended period of time so that other workers could be retrained in preparation for an expected technological upgrading. They could be used to cover for sabbaticals in which employees could pursue further education or personal and family activities. Or they could simply work beside the original employees in order to eliminate overtime, which has become a very common practice used to keep production rates high.

While it may be a new notion for some business people, work-sharing should sound familiar to educators. Many educators are familiar with the practice of "job-sharing," which has some of the features of work-sharing. Job-sharing typically involves two valued teachers who wish to teach for only part of a school year. A district usually permits that when both teachers are excellent and valuable members of the staff. The school districts that have such a policy budget one full-time equivalent (FTE) salary, which the cooperating teachers must share in proportion to the part of the school year they teach. Health benefits for the cooperating teachers are handled in a variety ways. Those range from the fully paid participation of both teachers to having the teachers make payments to the district to make up the deficit for participation in the district's plan. However it is managed, everyone gains. The students gets the benefit of the excellent teachers' services; the teachers get the time to attend to the personal matters that moti-

126

vated them to seek the job-sharing arrangement; and the district experiences little increased cost. Work-sharing is a bit more complicated, but the same basic principle applies: one set of tasks with more than one person acting on it.

Some forward-thinking companies in America — Hewlett-Packard, Texas Instruments, and Aetna Life and Casualty, for example — have tried job-sharing as a way to give their employees more personal flexibility. In a 1994 nationwide survey of 505 corporations, 37% offered job-sharing — two workers splitting one full-time job — compared to 28% in a 1990 poll.[19] Partners split the wages and share one benefit package. Companies like it because they can retain prized, highly skilled employees, especially women with young children, and avoid training costs and new-hire catch-up time. Even some "long-suffering" CEOs are job-sharing, with two executives sharing the CEO tasks.[20] But job-sharing, which usually is a temporary arrangement, does not have the full systemic advantage that work-sharing has for creating new job opportunities.

In a market economy, work-sharing is a bit more complex than in the above examples. There are several issues that must be resolved to make the practice work effectively. In the industrial sector, work-sharing could have a cost for both workers and businesses, at least at first. Many economists propose that these costs could be distributed equitably among the involved parties. 1) Workers would accept reduced work time with some reduction in wages. 2) The business would pick up a portion of the wage reduction and invest in labor-saving technology, automation, and information systems. 3) Government would establish national health programs to relieve business of that cost, establish policies to encourage portable pension programs to accommodate flexibility in the workforce, and establish tax policies that reward work-sharing and technological capital investments.[21]

Each participating group would realize a cost-benefit from work-sharing. Workers will find that work-sharing allows for decent wages and benefits while also increasing leisure time. Business will find that a high-quality workforce joined with appropriate technology and management processes will increase productivity and reduce unit labor costs, and that tax benefits and elimination of medical plan costs will *offset* slight increases in wages. And government will find that an increased number of workers in the workforce will increase tax receipts. In addition, the implementation of a national health program will reduce everyone's medical costs and will provide care not only to workers, but to all Americans, including the elderly and indigent.[22] Finally, government will be able to avoid the predictable social and economic unrest that surely will arise as more and more Americans experience their standard of living plummeting, joblessness increases, and more people are impoverished. Thus every major vested group has a stake in resolving the jobs dilemma.

As it is, American workers are being worked to death and suffer from increased levels of stress. Work-sharing would be a healthful solution to the worker situations described here:

> In the twenty-five years that work time has been rising, so too has unemployment and underemployment. At each business cycle peak, unemployment and underemployment rose — from 7% in 1969 to 14.5% in 1989, before the last recession began. This is no coincidence. Employers are hiring fewer workers in part because they are using their existing workforce for more hours. Factory overtime has now reached its highest recorded level, in the midst of a recovery which has long been dubbed "jobless." In the automobile industry, where tens of thousands of workers have been laid off, daily overtime has become standard. In the Detroit area the average workweek is 47.5 hours, Saturn workers have a regular 50-hour week, and in some plants, workers are doing 60 hours a week. The United Auto Workers (UAW) estimates that *59,000 automobile jobs would be created* if the plants were on a 40 hour week. High per person costs of fringe benefits, especially medical costs, are a big part of the problem. Those will only be solved with publicly-funded health care.[23] [Emphasis added]

Work-sharing is *not* the practice of simply rearranging the hours per week or hours per day as a way to get more work out of employees. While employers complain that overtime laws restrict them from optimizing the flexibility of hours (the law says that anything over 40 hours a week is overtime), that is a disingenuous argument, because in reality they do not want to hire additional people to do the work that needs to be done. Business is trying to squeeze every moment out of workers but is not willing to pay for extra help or the benefits for new employees.

Instead, business has been dealing with worker exhaustion and stress by fiddling with a number of schemes. A popular one — a shortened work week — seems to benefit the company more than workers. One typical "shortened" week is just four days of 10 hours each. Nationwide, 25% of companies offer four-day work weeks with longer daily hours.[24] Another typical schedule is working four 9-hour days for a total of 36 hours in one week, then working 44 hours the next week (nine hour days with an additional eight hours on Friday). None of those schemes are true work-sharing, since the intent is not to hire new workers but to work the current workforce as much as possible without killing the workers.

There is growing empirical evidence that work-sharing practices can produce new jobs. The most recent study of work-time, for example, states it is possible "to create jobs at lower costs by providing incentives or mandating cuts in daily hours rather than by cutting days of work."[25] Cutting the number of hours in the work week is even more effective. If the work week were reduced, even if nothing else was done, almost ten million *new* jobs could be made available in the United States. Economists have calculated that if work time were reduced to an average of 35 hours a week, from the current forty hours, 9.2 million new full-time jobs would be created for every 100 million persons employed.[26] With 124 million people projected to be in the work-force by 2005, that could mean at least 10 million *new* jobs. Most of the 12 million unemployed and underemployed would be able to get better jobs. Given such a large number of new jobs created by simply reducing the work week by five hours, imagine the number of jobs that could be generated by reducing the work week to 30 hours. Think also of the changes that increased leisure time would mean for families in the United States.

Consider this scenario regarding how work-sharing and increased leisure time could be phased into the economy: Assume that wages are at reasonable level and that workers defer further wage increases in exchange for more leisure time, a time-for-income exchange (as the surveys reported below suggested they might). If spread over 12 years beginning in 1997, the total number of hours worked each year could decline from about the current average of 1,765 hours to about 1,500 hours by 2008. American workers could have a 33-hour work week and an 11-week paid vacation each year by the year 2009. For a labor force of 100 million, that would be an aggregate reduction of about 12.6 billion hours, or 6.2 million full-time work years. Since aggregate economic productivity would be maintained through technological innovation, much of the foregone work time could be used for hiring additional high-skill craftworkers.[27] And when we consider that 15 million college students and 16 million high school seniors will graduate in 2004, all potentially looking for jobs, the 10 million new jobs that will be generated, plus the replacement of retirees, will go a long way toward resolving the jobs dilemma.[28]

The demand for high-quality workers in the United States will increase only if there is a well-developed work-share program. However, such programs would not be possible in low-technology business organizations, such as those providing hands-on assembly or other routine production services; but those jobs are the ones most susceptible to elimination through technology. Effective work-share programs require a greater use of technology. The increased use of technology is necessary to increase productivity, which in turn is necessary to increase income and leisure time.

The reduction of wages and maintaining productivity are central issues in work-sharing programs. Today, with the millions of workers who have been laid off — at least 3.2 million manufacturing jobs lost since 1979 — productivity and profits are at an all time high.[29] Thus a work-sharing program would result in little noticeable diminution in productivity, especially if phased in over a decade. In addition, the empirical evidence suggests that if companies cut standard work time to increase "employment demand, cutting daily hours would generate fewer costs [to productivity] than would cutting the number of work days."[30] But the hourly reductions needed to make work-sharing feasible would devastate worker incomes unless economic productivity soared.

Productivity is the key to job expansion. The more productive a company is, the more able it is to expand job opportunities. The aircraft manufacturer, Boeing, is a prime example of that. In 1995-96 it aggressively sought and won contracts with several countries — including China and Saudi Arabia — for billions of dollars worth of airplanes. Because of that, production shot up. Boeing not only stopped downsizing, it actually added 5,000 new employees in 1996 and gave its craftworkers a substantial raise.[31]

Under present conditions, America's corporations would be able to continue their productivity momentum even with reduced work time. And continued investment in computer-based manufacturing, automation, information systems, and re-engineered management processes will make it possible to achieve even higher production rates.

However, the issue of worker incomes is more complex. What would motivate workers to take a cut in pay, especially since wages in America have been stagnant for more than a decade? Several reasons have been suggested. The first is that American workers are overworked. The most dramatic evidence of that condition occurred in 1995 when auto workers in General Motors went on strike specifically to get GM management to relieve the pressure of overwork. GM had downsized from 350,000 in 1990 to 250,000 in 1994, and the remaining workers were physically and mentally exhausted.[32]

The strike was dramatic, but there is other evidence that suggests workers would prefer having more time for personal pursuits. For example, in a survey that gave respondents a chance to decide between the typical 40-hour work week versus other options, only 23% of the workers who responded indicated that they would choose to work full-time. Another 29% preferred part-time work, 19% preferred voluntary work, and 25% preferred working at home caring for their family.[33] Another survey asked if workers would exchange all or part of a 10% pay *increase* for free time: 26.8% of the workers were willing to trade for shorter workdays, 43.5% were willing to trade for longer weekends, and 65.6% were willing to trade for extended vacations. However, most workers were a bit more reluctant to give up much of their *current* pay for more free time. Still, 23% were willing to forego 2% of their current pay for shorter days; 26.2% were willing to do the same for longer weekends; and 42.2% were willing to give up 2% of the current income for longer vacations.[34] It would appear that if the family had an adequate income, workers may be willing to exchange a wage hike for free time.

However, under current conditions, it would be foolish for workers to take less pay in trade for more free time. While American workers have pushed corporate productivity to record high levels, their wages and benefits have declined since 1979. While wages and benefits decreased for most workers, they increased for executive managers (including CEOs) and high-level professionals. In addition, workers put in an average of 76 more hours per year than they did in 1979![35]

Harvard University economist Juliet B. Schor estimates that, in an attempt to maintain their standard of living in the face of declining compensation, workers spent the equivalent of four weeks *more* a year on the job in 1989 than they had two decades earlier. A large part of that increase came from the flood of women into the labor force. Their participation rate shot from 42.7% to 57.4%. In many families, that helped stem the decline in hourly earnings, but only temporarily. But the addition of more family members into the workforce clearly has brought its own pressures.[36]

Most experts now agree that to expect workers to carry the full cost of work-sharing is neither necessary nor ethical. With U.S. corporations earning record high profits, there should be a commitment from them to absorb some of the costs of work-sharing. Obviously, the way to do that is to share the results of high productivity with their workers by giving them wage increases. Corporations also could offer workers shares in the company so that profits can be shared more equitably, though that would be a less satisfactory option.[37] The point is to increase the paltry incomes of most goods-producing and service workers, as well as the salaries of those professionals whose practice is within organizations, such as teachers, nurses, social workers, and similar professionals who do not have a private practice.

One critical element for the success of work-sharing is that the freed-up time is actually used by business for new hires, and not merely as another way to downsize. Federal and state regulatory policies must clearly spell out corporate responsibility for work-sharing. In addition, there are three other major areas in which government policies would support work-sharing efforts: 1) tax incentives when businesses actually implement work-time reductions, 2) a national health plan to help reduce or eliminate corporate responsibility for health benefits, and 3) a progressive tax that penalizes overtime work and a legal mandate that overtime pay starts after 30 hours of work, rather than the current forty hours.[38] Such a realignment of tax policy would give tremendous incentives to business and workers to reduce work time. It also would level the playing field by severely penalizing a company that attempts to gain a short-term labor savings by requiring overtime instead of hiring additional workers.

The real motivation for businesses to support work-sharing programs and decent wages is self-interest. Workers are also customers. Work-sharing produces more workers earning decent incomes. As customers, those workers can now afford to buy the products that the corporations produce and the services they provide. Such spending benefits the entire economy. When a decently paid worker buys a car, for example, a number of peripheral workers also are supported — salespeople, mechanics, gasoline station owners, insurance agents, and others. With such a consumer base, the entire economy could expand, perhaps even re-establishing a virtuous circle.

If there was a reduction from the 40-hour week to a 32-hour week, work-sharing would create 8% to 10% more goods-producing jobs.

That is about 15 million *new* job opportunities by 2005. Yet even with that many new jobs, there is a limit to how many goods-producing jobs will be needed. There still will be a need for a commensurate effort to increase the number of decent jobs in the service sector. That, too, is manageable.

Profit-Sharing

The second major program for expanding job opportunities, especially in the service sector, is profit-sharing. Profit-sharing is the practice of dividing the economic gains made by businesses with employees who *add value* to services or products. In one of the most detailed studies of the effects of profit-sharing, productivity, and job growth, the conclusion was clear:

> Profit sharing can improve company performance by encouraging worker effort, cooperation, and sharing of information. [But even more important] it leads to greater employment and output stability for firms and the economy as a whole, by changing employer incentives to *hire* and retain employees.[39] [Emphasis added]

Someday, of course, the transformation to the New Economy will be complete and service sector workers will have come into their own:

> The time may come when most tax lawyers are replaced by expert systems software, but human being are still needed — and well paid — for such difficult occupations as gardening, house cleaning, and the thousands of other services that will receive an ever-growing share of our expenditure as more consumer goods become steadily cheaper. The high-skill professions whose members have done so well during the last 20 years may turn out to be the modern counterpart of early-19th-century weavers, whose incomes soared after mechanization of spinning, only to crash when the technological revolution reached their own craft.[40]

Until that time, the service sector will continue to have huge income extremes between well-paid professionals and the in-person service workers at the lower rungs of the income scale. However, profit-sharing can benefit *both* ends of the service sector and their business firms through expanded productivity, jobs, and increased wages.[41]

So far, the IPS workers, commonly called "Low Service" employees, have not benefited from the transformation to the New Economy. Technology has had a broadly negative effect on job opportunities in the Low Service sector. Computer-based machines need fewer workers to program and tend them, and they have eliminated the need for certain categories of jobs — for example, bank tellers, telephone operators, and architectural drafters. While technology is a boon for symbolic analysts, the "High Service" jobs, it has been a bane in the Low Service sector by deskilling jobs and driving wages down.

The service sector also is facing substantial restructuring, which may reduce jobs and wages even further. The deregulation of such industries as telecommunications, airlines, trucking, and financial services, combined with changes in technology, has accelerated domestic competition among service providers.[42]

The problem is different in the service sector than in manufacturing. "In-person service" is labor-intensive, whereas "goods" are capital-intensive. Add more machines in a factory, and productivity will increase and workers can work-share to expand jobs. But in the Low Service area, which already is crowded with low-wage workers, it is not that easy. Thus a way must be found to let all service employees experience wage increases in direct relation to their labor output.

Job expansion is not the only issue in the Low Service area; wages need to be increased to provide service employees with a decent standard of living. Profit-sharing can accomplish those twin goals for the service sector.

Profit-sharing is based on the concept of *value added*. For example, imagine a group of computer programmers who devise standardized applications but also give their programs special touches to make them more user-friendly. Customers begin snatching up those programs, increasing the wealth of the company.

Rather than sharing those profit gains with only company executives and shareholders, which is the traditional practice, profit-sharing would give a goodly portion of the profit gain to the programmers themselves. In that way, three parties have a vested interest in the welfare and growth of the company: executives, shareholders, and the employees who receive a direct benefit from their productivity.

This value-added criterion can be used in the retail trades, financial services, transportation services, communication services, medical services, and a host of other service areas. The value-added concept also applies to service jobs that add value only indirectly. For example, there are specialized service workers who repair and maintain computer-driven machines and other technology. They may not be producing a "product," but their service needs to be recognized and rewarded.

When it comes time for rewards, employees may receive bonuses, salary increases, and other shares commensurate with the company's profit gain.

The key to job expansion in the service sector is productivity. In that sector, however, productivity relates directly to customer satisfaction, something that good retailers have always known. The *more* service a company can provide its customers, the more all of the employees, executives, and shareholders will prosper. Adding additional service providers will enable them to increase their level of service even more.

We all have had the annoying experience of having to wait to get questions answered or to check-out or to get other help because no person was available because a consumer-oriented business had radically downsized its sale force. Contrast that feeling with how appreciative we are of a store or business that took the opposite tack and increased the number of persons available to make us feel special while in that store or seeking that service. We often are more willing to make a purchase in the service-oriented store, even if it costs a few more pennies than in the other place. That is the way in which profit-sharing *expands* jobs in the service areas.

There are several mechanisms to both increase wages and expand jobs through profit-sharing programs. The same basic concept applies for all of them: Give the employees a stake in helping the company increase its productivity and its profits, and then give those employees a fair cut of the gains. Here is a brief description of two such programs.

Employee Share Ownership Program: ESOPs are designed to give employees a stake in businesses by providing them owner-ship shares in the company through pension plans and stock bonus plans, usually in lieu of cash payment for benefits. The typical plan works this way: Workers are given a set number of shares in the company with an option, or "strike" price, deter-mined when they are issued, just as the executives are given such an option. Thus if a worker were given a two-year, 10-share option in 1996 when the stock price was $25 and, by 1998, the stock had increased in value to $75, then workers would get to keep the difference ($500). There are more complex plans, but that is the basic way in which ESOPs work.[43]

ESOPs also are an effective vehicle for job expansion. Once employees have sufficient shares to gain or buy control of a com-pany, they tend to explore all avenues to expand and protect jobs. Of course, those actions always are contingent on the company's productivity; but worker ownership has proven to be a major way of ensuring productivity. It appears that more companies are beginning to see the wisdom of ESOPs. About 3% of the top 1,000 publicly held companies make some grant of stock options or other forms of stock sharing to *all* employees, while another 9% to 13% have ESOP plans for at least 60% of their employees. And they are successful.

ESOPs appear to be most popular as a means of augmenting compensation in two kinds of companies: service/retail and high-tech.[44] There are hundreds of employee ownership programs across the United States, ranging from Hallmark Cards to Avis Car Rental to Parson's Engineering.[45] Many of the plans are very gen-erous. For example, full-time workers in PepsiCo's fast-food operations, which earn 37% of Pepsi's profits, get 10% of their prior-year salaries as a stock bonus. High technology companies have had ESOPs in place for a long time, with the first, Hewlett Packard, starting in 1957. Over half the high-tech companies now offer stock options to their employees.

There has been a steady increase in the number of workers involved in stock ownership — from 5 million in 1983 to well over 10 million in 1996, even though some traditional "command and control" managers have resisted the trend.[46] The results are very positive for both workers and management.

ESOPs even have enabled employees to purchase their companies, including everything from supermarket chains to steel mills.[47] For example, workers in Pennsylvania were able to buy a steel plant that was going to go out of business. The workers' union joined with an investment firm and turned the steel factory around. The workers' jobs were saved; the union got involved in decision making with two director's seats on the board; and production-floor decision making was implemented.[48] Even when employees do not have full ownership, their shares in a company can give them a higher degree of influence over jobs and hiring.

Perhaps the most celebrated case is the employee buy-out of United Airlines in 1993. United was failing at the time and was wracked with labor strife. Once the buy-out was complete, United's employees, including pilots and machinists, voluntarily took a cut in wages. The company increased flights and introduced a new short-line shuttle service. The employees at United gained three seats on the board of directors and hired a new president, who promptly democratized the company. Just as important, United employees were able to show management how to significantly increase profits. For example, workers recommended using electricity, rather than jet fuel, to keep jet engines idling while at loading gates, an idea that saved United $20 million a year. With that and other creative worker ideas, United's profits soon began to grow. As customer demand soared, the airline added more than 1,700 *new* employees into service jobs — pilots, reservations, flight attendants, and mechanics — and the company has continued to expand its employment.[49] United's stocks have more than doubled since the ESOP program was instituted. Every traditional indicator — rising productivity, stock prices, profit margins, market share, and expansion of its workforce — show that United's ESOP is a success.[50] But for our purposes, the real success of United's ESOP was that the company hired 7,000 new employees, a real indicator that job expansion in the service sector through ESOPs really works.

Because of their success as a way to provide more decent jobs, ESOPs have become widely accepted as a method of job expansion in the service sector, as well as a way to deal with wage stagnation. One leading business magazine grudgingly put it this way:

> ESOPs are no panacea, but in the debate over solutions to wage stagnation, it is the one concept that can raise both corporate competitiveness and employee wealth without gumming up the free market. . . . ESOPs are worth a look.[51]

Gain-sharing: Gain-sharing is similar to an ESOP, but the returns to employees are faster. Gain-sharing is the practice of dividing the profits a company earns with its employees on the basis of some criterion. One national company, Ben and Jerry's Ice Cream, is well-known for its gain-sharing program. Gain-sharing is designed to motivate employees to expend greater effort and teamwork and thereby to increase productivity.[52] The *gain* from that increased productivity is then shared on a more equitable basis between workers, management, and stockholders. In Ben and Jerry's case, gain-sharing proved instrumental to its growth from a local small business to a national powerhouse competing with giant companies.

Most effective gain-sharing plans, such as the one found in Saturn automobile plants, mix a basic wage into the compensation package. Saturn workers get a bonus for increasing productivity and maintaining quality control. The evidence is fairly straightforward that gain-sharing does increase productivity. But the gain-sharing plans that have been the most effective in increasing worker productivity involve both union membership and worker participation in decisions about goals and techniques.[53]

Public Jobs

The third method for expanding job opportunities is one that divides some Americans — the creation of public jobs. Whereas work-sharing and profit-sharing are dependent on increases in economic productivity to be affordable, public jobs use government funds. Even so, public jobs are needed, especially by those groups of Americans who have been left behind in the surge of technology and those who, for no fault of their own, have been relegated to the ranks of the chronic poor. There also are those workers who find themselves between jobs as they shift from one career or occupational area to another. And there are managers who have been re-engineered out of their positions. All these are people in situations with which neither businesses nor individuals alone can deal effectively.

All government interventions are not necessarily bad or ineffective. There are a number of laws and government regulations that have helped solve certain problems — for example, the environment is improving, the threat of war is greatly lessened, public health is improving, and race and gender barriers are eroding. One major government intervention was a program of which many living American educators were even recipients — The Serviceman's Rehabilitation Act 1944 (GI Bill) — which funded their college tuition and books and provided a modest stipend ($500 a year for college money, $50 a month to live on). The GI Bill was as great for the country as it was for individuals. Nearly 8 million veterans were educated — they became the managers and entrepreneurs who helped build the prosperity of the postwar decades.

Whenever a nation as large and diverse as the United States has a common purpose — whether it is war, depression, poverty, or encouraging industrial growth or agricultural policy — it has turned to the federal government. Then why shouldn't the government have an important role as we wrestle with the transformation to the New Economy? It is time for the federal government to take action again.

Job Corps: Many Americans have difficulty developing the skills needed for finding a new job or for applying old skills in new situations. Education by itself cannot do it all. For Americans in those circumstances, federal and state governments need to organize a Job Corps charged with rebuilding the nation's infrastructure and preparing it for future demands. For the individual participant, the corps would have three primary goals: 1) provide meaningful, useful, paying jobs for the chronically unemployed; 2) provide training in new employability skills, perhaps in newly redesigned high school learning-center facilities; and 3) eliminate welfare and unemployment payments.

Those government-sponsored workers-in-training will have their work cut out for them. The American infrastructure — roads, railroads, airports, harbors, ships, inland waterways, water resources, bridges, tunnels, dams, and the like — plus damaged environmental resources and dilapidated government facilities all need to be restored. Forty percent of the nations' bridges are deficient. Twenty-eight million Americans have inadequate sewage plants. By 2005 traffic delay because of inadequate roads may cost $50 billion annually in wasted fuel and lost wages. Fifty-eight major international airports — including those in such major cities as Los Angeles, Newark, and Chicago — will be so seriously congested by 2005 that the nation's passengers will be severely delayed.[54] The 1993 estimate just to fix bridges and roads was $40 billion. Estimates for fixing the entire infrastructure exceed $500 billion!

The United States now spends a great deal on maintaining and rebuilding its infrastructure; but it is not enough, nor does it match levels spent by other advanced industrial nations. Those countries, especially Germany and Japan, are obsessed with maintaining their infrastructures. Japan, Germany, France, Italy, Britain, and Canada all spend more public funds per gross domestic product than does the United States — Japan spends the most at 3.0%

141

of GDP, Germany 2.5%, while in the United States it is a paltry 0.6%. And it shows in dilapidated cities, crumbling interstate highways, decaying buildings, polluted waters, and other problems in essential areas.

However it is financed, rebuilding the infrastructure will create millions of jobs for the chronically unemployed, discouraged workers, and those workers who have been deskilled by technology. Rebuilding also will allow managers who have been re-engineered out of jobs to re-apply their skills and experience in new situations. The workers-in-training will learn valuable craft-worker skills and develop strong work ethics that will carry over to private workforce behaviors. And their work will benefit the country as well. Even more important, those jobs will help reduce the pressure on other job opportunities: Each dollar spent on the infrastructure translates into an estimated 50,000 additional public and private jobs.[55]

When first entering the Job Corps, most workers, especially the chronically unemployed, will have limited skills. Education would play a major role in providing generic vocational and career training, as well as teaching any fundamental skills that might be lacking. In addition, the program could include a master craftworker who would act as mentor to the new apprentices, so that Job Corps participants could learn from the best while earning a living and doing something worthwhile for the country. In the end, millions would have improved their salable skills, and the country would have a magnificent infrastructure, one capable of supporting America's increased productivity and global competitiveness.

The public job process also can be used to expand job opportunities. As the nation moves from an industrial-based to an information-based economy, the physical infrastructure needs will be entirely different. Instead of locomotives, the engines of modern business are fiber-optic cables, satellites, computerized switches, cellular phones, and the millions of lines of software codes that knit them all together. Nations that cannot put these ingredients together into advanced communications grids will not be able to take full advantage of the increasing flow of global commerce.[56]

Expanding the new information-age infrastructure will be expensive. Putting in fiber-optics cable, for example, will cost $325 billion by 2005. Analysts project that another $60 billion will be needed for public works and facilities just for new information and communication services. Since the info-highway benefits the states as well as individuals, the states could reasonably be expected to pay a small but reasonable portion of the costs, while private business, the main beneficiary, pays the rest. It is estimated that U.S. businesses could save $23 billion a year by using advanced communications (including telecommuting) to replace only 20% of the business activity that requires transportation.

One factor that holds potential for weakening the effects of a job-expansion programs is the re-entry of retirees into the job market. People are living longer, and healthy citizens often prefer to work than to spend a life of inactivity. With their polished skills and abilities, they would be very attractive to businesses. To keep retirees retired, we need to have alternate useful activities for them to perform, if they choose. Local governments would help to keep retirees productively engaged in their communities, and therefore less tempted to take a job that some working-age person might need. Therefore, public work should include voluntary work, too. Local governments should establish agencies to train volunteers for a variety of temporary jobs: school volunteers, hospice workers, clean city campaigns, park managers, etc. Retirees also should be encouraged to use their skills and talents as teachers, mentors, master craftwork instructors, nurses aides, and many others.

The Catch

Job-expansion policies rest on sound economic principles. However, like everything in life, there are complexities involved when trying to implement job-expansion practices. That implementation is not solely the responsibility of businesses. Rather, Corporate America must join in a partnership with government, labor unions, and educators. Each of those partners has a distinct role and set of responsibilities.

Government scaffolds are needed to protect those businesses that attempt to expand job opportunities. Such scaffolds include tax relief and, perhaps, paying part of any reduction in wages that may be needed to make job expansion work. The federal government also needs to devise a manageable national health plan to relieve employers of the exorbitant contributions to medical plans. And it must devise a portable pension program to help workers move from company to company without loss of pension funds and thus retirement security.

Labor unions have the dual role of supporting alternative means of compensation — such as more vacation time, personal time, and sabbaticals in lieu of wages — rather than the usual wage demands. Labor also needs to be willing to participate in democratic activities on the job, such as setting goals and making decisions at frontline production.

Assuming that Corporate America's commitment to job expansion is real and government regulations support job-expansion policies, the role of educators becomes more significant and ethical. Their primary role will be to get ready for the increased demand for symbolic analysts and highly skilled craftworkers. They must redesign schools and university programs to make them more congruent with 21st century social and economic realities.

There are a number of systemic actions that this partnership needs to take if we are to accomplish the goal of job expansion. Here is a summary of nine necessary conditions that most analysts agree should be met by a business, organized labor, government, and university/high school collaborative:[57]

1. Invest heavily in research and development to design and produce new products, to establish businesses that address new problems (for example, the environment or the infrastructure), and to stay on the cutting edge of product development.
2. Use technology wherever possible to reduce unit labor costs, increase productivity, lower prices, and expand market share.
3. Reduce work hours for workers, increase vacations, increase compulsory education age limits, and establish a compulso-

ry retirement policy, all of which will increase the number of jobs that can be shared through work-sharing policies.

4. Prohibit executive salaries being tied to stock options or ownership and establish confiscatory tax policies for any salary that exceeds 20 times that of the highest paid frontline worker.

5. Develop more cooperative business-labor union negotiations and participatory relationships to ensure that main players are involved in setting goals and making shop-floor decisions. The necessary corollary to that is more effective government labor policies and easing business regulations.

6. Expand leisure service industries to provide educational and voluntary leisure experiences for employees.

7. Use grants, foundations, and other means to reinforce the quality of university education, including teacher preparation, college-public school partnerships, and inservice professional development.

8. Make heavy investments in school plant rehabilitation and telecommunications readiness, and establish a new tax base for education.

9. Establish a universal National Health Program and expand the purpose and function of the Social Security pension operation to allow workers portable pensions between jobs and career moves.

Some of those recommended measures (for example, numbers 1, 6, and 8) involve long-range, developmental strategies that should be implemented now but that probably will not come to fruition for two decades. Others involve changes in policy and values (numbers 4 and 5, for example). Still others (such as numbers 2 and 3) can not be implemented fully until other measures in the list have been in place for a time. Two, numbers 7 and 9, already have begun; but they will require continuous support to maintain momentum. In spite of those various timelines, America could move forward with job expansion processes now if it had the political will to do so. Poll after poll shows that Americans are highly anxious about the economy and their own jobs or lack of jobs.[58] Indeed, in the absence of some action to resolve the jobs dilemma, many analysts predict the country will experience increasing social turbulence.

The Government's Role in Job Expansion

Regardless of the voluminous talk about how "global economics" and "multinational corporations" are superseding national polices, government still plays a critical role in how an economy functions.[59] It is especially in the area of job expansion that government policies can inhibit or abet progress. According to Harvard economist Juliet Schor, the government must take three basic sets of actions to translate job-expansion proposals into reality.[60] First, the government must establish a scaffold of social and taxation policies to provide a solid framework for both business and labor participation in job-expansion programs. Second, discussed above, is the public jobs program to rebuild the nation's infrastructure. And third, government must restructure federal and state allocation policy to focus funding more clearly on transforming the education system.

The federal and state governments need to change labor policies that affect hours, wages, and benefits. The governments also must reward businesses for implementing high-performance work organizations and must liberate businesses from restrictive and inhibiting regulations. Both workers and businesses need a government legal scaffold to make job-expansion practices work.

Worker Policies: Government policies must deal with certain related issues: work hours, minimum wages, early retirement, delayed entrance into the workforce, and profit-sharing regulations. But there also is a need to consider policies that would provide the scaffold for job expansion: national health care, portable pension programs, and an expanded earned income tax credit.

An effective work-sharing system depends on employees sharing the workload that remains after computer-based technology has reduced the need for physical labor. For such programs to succeed, changes must be made in current government regula-

146

tions that define a standard individual work week as 40 hours. By law, any time over 40 hours is considered overtime for which businesses are required to pay a penalty wage — time and a half up to triple-time, depending on the hours worked.

Analysts have suggested the standard hours in the United States could go as low as 30 hours a week with little adverse effect on productivity.[61] But to even approach that level, businesses need the assurance that the "standard" will be enforced equally. Their rightful concern is that "cheaters," those who work their workers overtime but do not pay them, would gain an unfair competitive advantage. That assurance would come from an enforceable government 30-hour standard and by disallowing all overtime, except under extraordinary and monitored circumstances. Even when overtime is necessary, businesses and workers would be required to give compensatory time off that is equal to the time worked. Those businesses that fail to conform to the requirement could be severely penalized, just as they are now. The result would be millions more job opportunities for craftworkers.

There are additional policies that would support those work-hour reductions, two of which appear to be relatively easy: early retirement and extended compulsory schooling. If the official retirement age of 65 were dropped to 55, it would free up additional jobs. The law enabling that early retirement would necessarily have to restrict retirees from rejoining the workforce; but it also should encourage voluntary work, since most retirees will be healthy and active at 55. On the other end of the age-span, young adults of high school age should be encouraged or even required to continue their formal education through community college, school-to-work programs, career academies, or apprentice programs. That additional education would reserve the job opportunities for those adults between the ages of 20 to 55, approximately 120 million men and women out of a total potential workforce (age 16 to 65) of 150 million.[62] Obviously, fewer people clamoring to enter the workforce would reduce the pressure on the economy.

Government policies also can help American workers to share in the fantastic productivity increases that have taken place in the economy since the beginning of the 1990s. Some of these policies involve the minimum wage, a "GI Bill" for displaced workers, union organizing, and work councils.

Minimum Wage: When America's wage structure is compared with those of other advanced industrial countries, America's corporations look really cheap. The data for the United States actually is skewed even further away from those in the other countries because it contains benefit costs, such as Medicare, that most other nations handle through a national health and pension plan.[63] Thus while German workers get $30.32 an hour to spend, their American counterparts actually get only an average of $11.85 per hour. The United States has a long way to go before reaching the pay levels of other advanced industrial nations. Table 4.1 shows the average hourly wage and hours per week and per year in industrial nations.

Table 4.1: Wages, hours, and hours per year of AIN countries, 1996.

Country	Wage	Hour/Week	Hours/Year
Germany	30.32	36.6	1620
Switzerland	28.60	40.5	1838
Belgium	25.76	37.8	1729
Norway	25.06	37.7	1740
Japan	24.83	40.0	1880
Austria	24.27	38.6	1722
Netherlands	24.05	38.8	1714
Denmark	23.73	37.0	1687
AIN Average	**22.31**	**38.9**	**1768**
Sweden	21.38	40.0	1824
France	19.84	39.0	1755
United States	19.29	40.0	1896
Italy	18.76	40.0	1744
Canada	18.22	40.0	1824
Ireland	15.28	39.0	1794
Britain	15.21	38.6	1752

Adapted from Mary Walsh, "Germany's Reckoning," *Los Angeles Times,* 25 February 1996, pp. D1, D3.

After much jockeying, Congress passed an upward revision of the minimum wage from $4.25 to $5.15 an hour. When that is compared with the $11.85 per hour average worker wage — and especially with the power elite's wage of $425 per hour in Washington, D.C. — it tends to put "minimum" in a better perspective. And make no mistake, the current minimum is a poverty wage as defined by the U.S. Department of Health and Human Services. A family of three requires $12,980 a year to rise above the poverty level. A 40-hour week at the current minimum of $4.25 generates $8,840 a year.

The new minimum raises the wages of 12 million people; and contrary to the conventional wisdom that most of those earning the minimum are kids, 75% of those 12 million are adults. More than 39% of them are the sole wage-earner in their family; 58% are women; 47% work in full-time jobs; and another 32% work at least 20 to 34 hours a week. Only 11.7% are teenagers in families with above-average incomes. All together, those earning a minimum wage make up 12% of the workforce. In addition, another 8.9 million workers earn just slightly more than the minimum.[64]

The major reason minimum wages are important is that they eventually affect the entire wage scale; the minimum pushes on the next layer, and so on up the line as employers work to keep their employees ahead of minimum by raising wages. And as the minimum goes up, the entire country's standard of living goes up, stimulating more consumer activity and more productivity.

A "GI Bill" for Displaced Workers: If the post-World War II GI Bill helped millions of Americans get educated and prepared for decent jobs, workers whose wages helped make the virtuous cycle of prosperity a success, why not do the same for workers who have been passed over or for those who have been deskilled by technological innovations. In addition, the tax code could be changed to allow displaced or "redundant" workers to take courses to train for *new* jobs; the current code allows deductions for improving skills only in one's current job. Some call that a *human resource investment* tax break, since it would be similar to the tax breaks that businesses already get for *capital resources investments* for new machinery and technology, called the Capital Investment Tax Credit.[65]

Union Organizing: In Europe, where unions are strong and have been able to make sure that increased profits are distributed equitably, it was not difficult to get them to reduce hours so that others could get decent jobs. In other advanced industrial nations, union membership increased and their economies still showed rapid economic growth — for example, 2.7% in Germany and 3.3% in Canada — while economic growth remained marginal at only 1.9% in the United States as union membership decreased.[66]

Historically, union strength has been a major determinant of American prosperity. Economists explain that unionization increases productivity because unionized establishments have greater labor discipline and lower turnover, which result in more experienced and loyal workers. Employee involvement programs also increase productivity, but even those programs work better under union conditions. In union shops, the argument goes, workers feel more free to make suggestions that may challenge established ways of doing things, because they know a union contract protects them from retaliation.

Current U.S. laws weaken workers' rights. One in particular undercuts union activity: the right of businesses to hire permanent replacements for those who are legitimately on strike. Instead, we need national policies to increase unionization.

Work Councils: In 1996 there was an abortive attempt to get better management-worker relations started by establishing collaborative groups. However, certain members of Congress placed too many anti-union amendments in the bill; and it was defeated. But the germ of an idea was there.

In Europe, it is traditional to have worker councils in which management and workers, and sometimes a government representative, meet regularly to plan, set goals, evaluate progress, solve problems, and so forth, as *equal* participants. The idea of councils is to empower workers as participants in the welfare of the company and to open a straight channel of communication to employers. The government role essentially is one of arbiter. Work councils bring democracy to the workplace.

Business and Labor Policies: There also are government policies that would benefit all citizens, including both businesses and their employees. These include such policies as profit-sharing rules, portable pensions, health programs, childcare programs, and earned income credit.

Profit-Sharing Rules: Policies in this area would establish uniform regulations for any profit-sharing program in the same manner that the Security and Exchange Commission makes rules for the marketplace. The intent of any law on profit-sharing would not to be to dictate to businesses but to establish the ground rules to be enforced by an independent regulatory body. In that way, both employers and employees will know that fairness is practiced.

Portable Pensions: More than half of U.S. workers have no pension plan. The statistics are worse for employees of small businesses, only 14% of whom have pensions. Those that do have pensions are fearful that they may lose them if they have to take a new job because they are laid off or want to make a career move. Thus one of the major stumbling blocks for establishing a more flexible workforce has been the fear that workers would lose their pensions when they were laid off by one firm, even if they were hired again by another. The recent legislative agreement to legalize portable pensions is very important because it makes movement from job to job more humane and will increase the flexibility of the workforce.

"Portable pensions" means just what the title implies. Laws in this area guarantee that workers who have established pension funds in one firm would be able to carry them into a new job, thereby not losing what had been earned. The law allows workers to save a certain amount each year as a tax-exempt payroll deduction. The program provides expanded tax-exempt options and protection of pensions if a company — or even a government, such as Orange County, California — goes bankrupt.

To make pensions more widely available and portable, analysts say the program should:

- Make it easier for employees to move money in the 401(k) salary set-aside plans from job to job.
- Enable employees to move into such plans as soon as they begin work with an employer, instead of having to wait six months to a year.
- Increase federal protection for "multi-employer plans," used in the construction industry and other businesses where workers shift frequently between jobs. If the fund goes broke, the federal pension guarantee would be increased to about $13,000 from $6,000 each year.
- Protect public employee pension funds from being at risk in the event of a government bankruptcy.[67]

Health Programs: In 1996, 42 million Americans had no medical insurance. That figure has been growing steadily; it was 39 million in 1993 and 33.7 million in 1988. Experts say the increase in the numbers of people with no medical insurance is the result of the continuing decline in employer-provided coverage and funding cuts for Medicaid. About 62% of Americans under age 65 currently receive medical insurance through the workplace, but more than 66% did so in 1988. About 12.5 million people lost employer-sponsored coverage just between 1988 and 1993, the most recent years for which comparable data are available. In addition to the 42 million uninsured Americans, another 29 million (or 18.5% of those under 65) are underinsured, meaning that they cannot afford out-of-pocket medical costs that exceed 10% of family income.[68]

The lack of medical coverage is not confined to the poor. A third of the uninsured live in households with annual incomes of more than $30,300 — almost twice the official poverty level for a family of four. The consequences for them are as bad as for every other uninsured family: Lack of insurance is associated with a 25% higher risk of death. Even worse, for uninsured children who are injured, only 73% were as likely as insured children to receive treatment. A national health plan similar to those found in Europe and Canada would relieve that problem. Those plans consider health care to be a *right*, not a privilege.

If such a plan were adopted in the United States, it would relieve businesses of the partial payment they have to make for private plans, which also takes money out of the pocket of their workers in the form of benefits costs that did not go to wages. In addition, workers and the rest of the citizenry would benefit from lower health premiums and, even more important, from the better health care that comes from universal health care systems.[69]

Childcare Programs: The Census Bureau reports that the number of working mothers is rising. Fifty-three percent of the women who had babies within a 12-month polling period were back in the workforce. And with millions of women now in the workforce, that makes childcare a top priority for today's families. While some companies provide in-house childcare, most parents are forced to use the private businesses, which can be expensive.[70] While college-educated workers usually can afford private childcare, the other 60% also need reasonably priced childcare. That is where local government, especially school districts, can help. School districts can offer low-cost childcare services, perhaps operated by an independent contractor hired and overseen by the district. Such childcare programs can be supported by local companies, thus earning money for the schools while providing a reasonably priced service for working parents.[71]

Earned Income Credit: Regardless of the vitriolic commentary and media hype, the facts show that Americans generally do not want to be on welfare. The charge that many people use welfare to avoid working is contradicted by the fact more than 71% of adult AFDC recipients have a work history; and more than half of them go back to work, when it can be found, after they leave welfare. In addition, 66% of all AFDC recipients, 9.4 million people, are children, whose average age in 1993 was 7.4 years.

Most Americans want to work, and not just for the income; the pride and self-identity associated with work also are important. However, some American workers are pushed into poverty and welfare through inequitable taxes. A family of four is classified as poor when its income drops below $15,335 a year, which is

$1,278 a month for four people. Workers making just over the minimum wage ($6.00 per hour) earn $11,520 a year, or $960 a month. If both parents work, they still would earn only $1,920 a month, $642 more than a family on welfare. But then there are childcare fees, transportation costs, and other work-related expenses that pull that $1,920 a month below the amount of welfare payments. And one of the biggest deductions, of course, is that the working poor pay taxes, while welfare recipients do not. Paying only the minimum tax rate would take another $800 or so off the top of their lousy wages, pulling them down below poverty levels.

The Earned Income Tax Credit (EITC) is a government guarantee of income, a subsidization of wages to guarantee that no *working* American will live below the poverty line. The need for the program is shown by the fact that the working poor are making less than they did in 1972. With two children, the working poor's average disposable income in 1972 was about $16,000 a year. That dropped to $14,000 in 1980 and $11,900 in 1990, and it rose slightly to $14,500 in 1995.[72]

EITC works much like a tax refund. Workers with incomes near or below the poverty level file a special income tax report and receive a check from the IRS, which in most cases is higher than what was deducted for taxes from their paychecks. That has lifted more than 4 million Americans out of poverty. Even conservatives have praised it, because no new federal bureaucracy is needed to run the program.

In 1980 only 6 million families with annual incomes of less than $10,000 qualified for EITC, and the maximum credit was $500 for a household with two children. By 1996 the program covered 20 million families, the poorest fifth of the American workforce, who receive $1,341 in cash benefits. The maximum benefit of $3,560 goes to families with incomes below the poverty line, which now stands at about $15,335 for a family of four. But since it is a graduated program, half the funds go to families earning more than the poverty level, with incomes as high as $28,524 for working families with two children.

Business Policies: There are a number of things the government can do to make it easier for business to be a willing partner in job-expansion actions. Business itself has identified several essential government policies.

Job Tax Credit: Among the top candidates for relieving some of the costs of job expansion for businesses is a job tax credit, which is much like the investment tax credit for modernizing plants and equipment When the unemployment rate in an area exceeds a predetermined level — for example, 7% — a federal tax credit of 10% would be given to local businesses for all the salaries and wages they paid in the area. This would encourage employers not to lay off workers and would act as a magnet for jobs from areas where the tax credit is not available. Those other areas, where unemployment is low, could profit by shipping some business to the low-wage, underemployment area to save from the tax credit.[73]

The tax credit would be applied to each eligible company's tax liability. A company with a monthly payroll of $1 million would get a $100,000 tax credit. Companies operating in the red could sell their credits to profitable companies in order to stay in business while they worked to become healthy again.

Advocates of this business-relief program agree that the tax credit needs to be in effect for at least two years, long enough to encourage the desired behaviors by business executives. The tax would not worsen the deficit, because more workers would continue to work, pay taxes, and stay off welfare. Also, the credit would be targeted to restricted areas and not spread evenly to all low unemployment areas.

Faster Depreciation: To encourage business to reinvest in computer-based technologies, which will allow them to increase productivity and support job-expansion programs, the U.S. and state governments should allow businesses to immediately write off the cost of new machines and worker training, rather than waiting for long-term depreciation.

Relief from Monopoly Rules: Chapter 5 recommends that core corporations form alliances with networks of suppliers to save money and increase productivity. These alliances would function in much the same way as Japan's *keiritsu*. However, such alliances currently are restricted by anti-monopoly laws. The government should carefully rewrite those laws, giving the public proper safeguards against high prices and unsafe products while encouraging business to form alliances.

No Health Contribution: This is the same benefit mentioned above for workers. Business would no longer have to make a contribution, because payment for medical service under a national health plan would be spread equitably among all citizens.

Limit CEO Compensation: One regulation top executives will not like will be to disallow stock options as compensation and to establish a ratio limit on executive salaries, like similar limits in Europe and Japan. If the ratio is set at 30 to 1 and the best frontline worker income is $60,000, that would allow a CEO to earn almost $2 million in salary. If stock options were removed from CEO compensation, executives would be able to concentrate on the professional leadership of their corporations. Executives still would receive bonuses for a job well done, but in the same proportion as frontline workers. In that way, executives would be motivated to become proactive to maintain their companies' competitive advantage. But in this plan, the rising ship would carry everyone.

Change SEC Rules: The United States needs long-term investments, but current regulations favor short-term gains. Congress and the Security and Exchange Commission need to change the regulations, and shareholders need to be motivated to accept the slower, but consistent, growth and security associated with long-term returns.

Regulatory Relief: Contrary to conventional wisdom, many employers and union representatives support the need for workplace regulations, according to an in-depth study by the General Accounting Office. That study concluded:

> In terms of compliance burdens, workplace regulation is not as significant as other issues: taxes, trade, and environmental issues loom far larger.[74]

However, there were many complaints about the arbitrary enforcement of regulations. Many of the employers interviewed in the study said that the approach used by many regulatory agencies is adversarial, characterized by poor communication, unfair and inconsistent enforcement, and vague regulatory language that increases the potential for lawsuits. Most union leaders in the study agreed with this assessment, though they also believed that many agencies were not vigorous enough in enforcing existing regulations. In addition, employers in both large and small companies remarked that they rarely were confident that they knew all the laws and regulations for compliance and often could not get accurate information on applicable statutes or on how to comply. And union representatives suggested that their role be expanded during agencies' enforcement procedures, such as having greater participation in back-wage settlements under the Fair Labor Standards Act.[75]

Most employers and union representatives urged agencies to adopt a more service-oriented approach to regulation. They viewed such an approach as fostering a more collaborative relationship between employers, unions, and workers that ultimately could ease compliance and help to achieve legislative goals. Proposed elements include making information more accessible to employers, workers, and unions; providing more technical and education assistance to employers, workers, and unions; and permitting more input from employers and unions into agencies' standard-setting and enforcement procedures. If the government follows up on these legitimate concerns, regulations would be more manageable and meaningful.

There already are responses to the regulatory issue. For example, the Occupational Safety and Health Administration is drafting an ergonomic protection standard to reduce the incidence of muscle and bone disorders. But unlike most OSHA standards, this one would not contain myriad requirements for such things as table heights and chair designs. Instead, it would require that companies respond constructively to worker injuries and complaints. Businesses would have the responsibility to solve the problem, not simply to follow dozens of arbitrary rules.[76]

Government-Supported Research and Development: Research conducted by various government agencies could prove very beneficial to both large and small businesses. Large businesses often benefit from government R&D and often work on projects with various government R&D agencies. The problem, however, is the lack of an overall R&D focus and the lack of diffusion of good ideas. There are, for example, some 700 to 800 federal laboratories, all with their own narrow mission; but these laboratories often do not correlate their efforts with other labs.

A major assumption of job expansion is that job opportunities will grow only as innovative, technology-driven productivity increases. Thus America needs to build a national strategy for maintaining its preeminence in science and technology.

Education's Infrastructure Needs

Part of the government's responsibility is to ensure that the public schools prepare students to use technology. But before students can receive the full benefit of modern technology in the schools, that technology has to be acquired, and school buildings need to be retrofitted to accommodate it. Needless to say, achieving that goal will be costly. Almost a third of the nation's schools were built before 1950, and 43% were built in the 1950s and 1960s.[77] Practically all are due for replacement or refurbishment, according to the American Association of School Administrators.

Reports from around the country cite crumbling brickwork, rotting window frames, and rusted steel frames with the tensile strength of a chocolate bar. Some schools leak so badly that classes cannot be held. In Alabama a school ceiling collapsed just 40 minutes after the kids had left. Chicago does not have enough electric power and outlets for the new computers it bought, so they remain in their shipping boxes. Some suburban schools in Philadelphia are so crowded that students cannot carry backpacks because there is no place the store them. In Los Angeles, it takes 30 to 40 years for a school to get repainted, and that is just the outside! Things were so bad in Washington, D.C., that schools could not even be opened in September 1994 because the fire marshals had ordered the district to correct 4,000 citations for fire code violations, including defective boilers, wiring, clogged sprinklers, unworkable windows, and many other life-threatening situations.[78]

A business or government agency would not accept such structures; instead, they would raze or totally refurbish them. Interestingly, while a recent Congress was rejecting a request for $100 million to help refurbish schools, it approved $20 million for the Department of Education to renovate its building. Apparently, dilapidated school buildings are okay for kids but not for federal functionaries.

Thus the last major role of state and federal governments in helping to reduce the jobs dilemma and to produce a world-class workforce is financing the massive infrastructure development that is needed by schools, including bringing them up to date with technology.[79] Right now, school districts cannot afford to do all the things they need to do. Many schools are so dilapidated that those repairs need to be done before technological upgrades can be started. And many school districts already have a huge expense from complying with the disability act. A GAO report estimates that schools have spent $1.5 billion to improve accessibility for the handicapped in the past three years, or an average of about $40,000 per school.[80] The GAO estimates that schools nationwide will spend $5.2 billion between 1994 and 1998 to comply with the Americans With Disabilities Act.

The states are doing little to build schools and repair the nation's education infrastructure, according to the U.S. General Accounting Office. According to the GAO study, only 13 states have comprehensive school-facilities programs. State legislatures appropriated $3.5 billion for school construction in 1994, a fraction of the $112 billion that federal officials and experts say is needed to build and fix schools nationwide. Other than Alaska and Hawaii, no state spent more than $300 per pupil on facilities in 1994, and 17 states spent less than $100 per pupil.[81] Nor has Congress been serious about the need. The $100 million allocated in the federal budget to repair 80,000 schools was eliminated in 1995.

States and the federal government also have not prepared for the anticipated increase in enrollment of children. There will be lots of kids and too few classrooms. Nationwide the number of elementary and secondary students is expected to reach 56 million by 2004, up dramatically from the 47 million in 1991 and even exceeding the previous high point of 51 million reached in 1971.[82]

Add to those problems the new demands for more flexible, more technologically up-to-date school buildings, and the dimensions of the problem grow huge. But no concerted efforts are being made even to bring schools up to safe standards, much less make them capable of handling the demands of modern technology. Modern technology means more than just installation of computers. It also means installing wiring, computer connections, modems, telephone lines, software, systems maintenance, and a host of other things. A GAO report in 1995 stated that schools are not equipped to use modern technology and that it would cost $112 billion to prepare them.

The technology needs and problems of schools have been spelled out very clearly in a report by the U.S. Office of Technology Assessment, *Teachers & Technology: Making the Connection*. In addition to limited hardware and software, other factors that affect access include:

- Costs are high for purchasing and connecting technologies and for training people to use them.
- Technologies may not be located in or near the classroom.

- Hardware in schools today is old (50% of the computers in schools are 8-bit machines) and cannot handle many newer applications.
- New or additional wiring or phone lines are necessary for telecommunications networks.[83]

If education is to play a central role in preparing a world-class workforce, it is critical that schools be brought up to date with technology. That is a responsibility that cannot be turned over to private interests. Schools and society cannot wait; there is an urgent need for government intervention and support now.

Our Competitors Already Have Started

In the United States, the idea of job expansion has been considered utopian, which means that many hard-nosed decision makers will refuse to consider it seriously. Work-sharing and profit-sharing are relatively new ideas in the United States. But other nations already are implementing many of these practices.

The advanced industrial nations of Europe are facing a jobs dilemma much like that in the United States. The same forces that led to less pay and an overqualified workforce in the United States also led to unemployment for millions in Europe. Unemployment in the European Union now stands at 10.8%, with the rate for people under 25 nearly 20%. Older workers are not retiring fast enough to accommodate the young, who get discouraged and stop seeking meaningful work. About two-thirds of the unemployed have been out of work for more than six months, at a cost of about $200 billion for all EU countries. In addition, experts predict that only three million of the European Union's 16 million unemployed can be absorbed into the workforce, even with the cyclical upturn that started in 1993.[84]

Unlike those in the United States, unemployment payments in the EU exceed the wages the unemployed would earn in an entry-level factory job. That produces huge deficits for EU governments. Thus, if work-sharing practices expand in Europe, two positive results will occur: unemployment expenditures will be reduced, and people will have dignified work.

The United States, with just two-thirds the population of Europe, has added 24 million new jobs since 1980; but most of those jobs are lousy. Europeans in that same time period added only 9 million new jobs, also mostly lousy, according to the *New York Times*.[85] One difference is the slow growth of the service sector in Europe, unlike in the United States, so that low-income service jobs have been unable to absorb those who do not get manufacturing jobs.

Another difference is that Europeans have been searching for creative solutions to their jobs dilemma. The Europeans have been able to escape much of the hardship associated with downsizing by granting unemployed and underemployed workers generous social benefits. European companies have downsized, but they usually have done so by means of attrition and early retirement. Early retirement also is encouraged so that new job opportunities are created.[86] Thus many of Europe's unemployed are over 50 or young people in their early 20s. But the unemployed and retired do not generate taxes, so most European countries have had to devise alternative means for humanely resolving their jobs dilemma.

European countries have worked to gain the consensus of the three parties that must agree on a course of action — business, labor unions, and government — which, in Europe, have a long tradition of working together. Those solutions tend to focus on getting more people to work in decent jobs with decent wages — not merely to provide substandard, "hamburger slinger" types of jobs. As a result, European labor unions, businesses, and governments have been experimenting with work-sharing and other programs.

Labor unions have been particularly willing to reduce the weekly work hours to accommodate work-sharing. But the discussion of relief from high unemployment has also generated several other creative ideas, some of which could be adopted in the United States. Here are some of the ideas Western Europeans are experimenting with as a way to resolve their jobs dilemma:[87]

- In Belgium the government has implemented a "Plan for Redistribution of Work in the Public Sector." Under the terms of that plan, all government employees have the right to a four-day, 32-hour work week. More than a quarter of a million federal, regional, and local government civil servants and employees of state-owned companies eventually will qualify for the plan. Those who opt for the plan will receive between 86% and 90% of their original pay. Government economists predict that the plan will create thousands of new jobs.
- In Denmark the government is sponsoring a sabbatical program for employees in industry and the public sector. The one-year sabbaticals are designed to allow workers to devote more time to their families and private affairs or to take advanced training and education. About 60% of those on leave (86,000 employees in 1996) have been replaced by permanent new hires, but the government plans to make room for workers returning from sabbatical.
- In the Netherlands trade unions and employer organizations have a national agreement that requires employers to meet worker *requests* for modified working hours. A quarter of the Dutch work force today works less than full time. Labor statistics indicate that the shift to four-day weeks has opened more than 30,000 new jobs in the Netherlands over the past three years and will produce up to 100,000 new positions in Dutch industrial and service sectors. That many new jobs in the Netherlands equals 20% of its current unemployment rate.

Things are happening all over Europe to deal humanely with the jobs dilemma issue. Another work-sharing variation in Europe calls for operating factories six days a week. Workers work only four days a week but are rotated around a flexible six-day schedule. That means some weekend work for some workers — something many European workers have long resisted. Some European business analysts have suggested that with weekend

163

schedules, businesses may be able to hire up to 500,000 new workers.[88]

Wages are important. When European workers volunteer to work-share, even if it means earning less, it is because of their affluence. Their governments encourage work-share efforts with permissive regulations and financial support; and all EU countries have national health plans, which relieve businesses of the high costs of medical benefits. The governments pay part of the fringe costs of those hired into new jobs; and some of the governments also reimburse employees for about half their income lost by shifting to a four-day week.[89] Europeans, of course, pay higher taxes than Americans do in order to support their social programs and national health plans. The major reason for Europeans' willingness to assume such a tax cost is the high wages made by European workers, much higher on average than those of American workers. The value expressed in Western Europe is that social programs and health care are the natural right of people and thus the costs for those rights also should be shared through taxes. Thus support for work-sharing efforts involves a three way partnership among labor, business, and government.

Work-sharing programs in Germany are the most likely model for what might work in the United States. German jobs pay the highest wages in the world, and the government provides full health coverage and pensions, making the German workers the best compensated in the world, too. There are few low-wage jobs, though there is a gray market of freelance workers and foreign workers who take many of the less desirable jobs. When there is a need for low-wage jobs, German assembly plants move to foreign countries. Ironically, the United States is one of those low-wage countries.

The entire German labor system is set up to train high-quality craftworkers through education and apprentice programs. The problem is that few high-quality jobs open up, and few new job opportunities are created because computer-based technology is used to reduce unit labor costs. With few low-wage jobs available and a lack of decent job opportunities, Germany has a much higher unemployment rate — about 10.9% in 1996 — than does the United States — about 5.6%.[90] However, as was noted earlier, if the United States counted its part-time workers as unemployed, as the Europeans do, our unemployment rate would approximate that of Germany. The fact is, both countries face a huge jobs dilemma.

However, the German approach to their jobs dilemma demonstrates their concern for social justice. The major component of that approach is work-sharing. It was not easy. At first, the German Federation of Trade Unions resisted any reduction in hours if it meant a reduction in pay. Business people felt that any reduction in hours would hurt productivity. But as unemployment reached crisis proportions, the trade unions realized that their resistance was hurting other workers.[91] They began reviewing alternatives that would broaden job opportunities for new graduates, apprentices, women, and the unemployed.[92] And when government devised a financial scaffold to absorb certain business costs, business executives' reluctance began to dissipate.[93]

As a result, powerful German unions, in alliance with major corporations, have implemented work-sharing programs. The program at Volkswagen, the country's largest automaker, is one example. VW's 100,000 employees voted overwhelmingly to work and earn less, so the automaker successfully implemented a work-share program by reducing the work week from 36 to 28 hours. The union's immediate motivation was to save the jobs of nearly one-third of its workers, who were about to be laid off as VW downsized during the auto industry's deep recession. The company's motivation came from knowing it will save $1 billion as a result of not having to pay for those hours and that they will preserve their core of highly skilled workers.[94]

More recently, IG Metall, Germany's most powerful union representing more than 3 million automotive, steel, electronics, and engineering workers, announced that the union would not seek any additional wage or benefit increases over the next three years. Its workers will voluntarily reduce the number of hours worked; and any overtime in the future is to be compensated with extra time off, not wages. If they can get agreement from the German corporate executives, anywhere from 150,000 to 300,000 *new* job openings will become available to qualified workers. That represents up to 1% of the 30 million people in Germany's total workforce.[95]

Germany offers an example of dealing with the jobs dilemma in two ways: First, it is demonstrating that work-sharing is a viable concept in practice, not just theory, by actually increasing new job opportunities by almost half a million. And second, it is demonstrating that paying decent wages results in more cooperative labor actions, again demonstrated by the voluntary steps German workers are taking to help their fellow citizens gain decent jobs.

American workers are the most productive in the world, even more so than Germany's or Japan's, yet their wages have been stagnant. If America's job dilemma is to be addressed effectively, Corporate America must realize that it is in its interest to find fairer ways to distribute the wealth it earns from labor's productivity. Germany offers it a good example.

A New Social Compact

The government interventions discussed above, even if implemented soon, obviously will take time and be phased in slowly over the next decade. But whatever the time and cost demands, the United States will never resolve its jobs dilemma without such an investment in people and the infrastructure, the two things that underpin the effectiveness of America's economic system. If all those changes come to pass, a new social compact with the American people will be formed. And America's workers, many economic experts argue, need a new social compact that reflects the economic exigencies of the New Economy and recognizes the human needs during the transition to that economy.[96]

It is naive to expect Corporate America, by itself, to become more socially responsible. Today's business community clings to its faith in the restorative powers of the marketplace. Instead, the new social compact will be a collaboration between business and government. It will be based on a "stakeholder economy," where a company's employees, customers, and communities enjoy legislated rights. Only government initiative can ensure more social responsibility, and most Americans understand this.

Some companies are trying to humanize the transition to the New Economy on their own, using such methods as stretching out layoffs and providing funding for retraining. But only the government can contribute the legal and social scaffolding to ensure a national movement toward a more humane economy, as well as the necessary legal underpinning to make those programs work.

The new social compact most likely will be a social safety net provided by local, state, and federal governments and the provision of "employability skills" by education and businesses. Education is rapidly tooling up for that task.

Educators can no longer afford to neglect the preparation of students for a *future* society — including a future world of work. The National Center on the Educational Quality of the Workforce (EQW) points out the obvious:

> The productivity of American businesses is intrinsically linked to the success of the nation's schools and the educational attainment of its students and workers. As firms transform themselves — shedding outdated production systems, recasting older forms of work organization, adopting new technologies, and instituting high-performance systems — they will have to depend increasingly on schools to supply a workforce capable of adapting to these new modes of working. This reliance will require that firms articulate their skill needs to schools. Similarly, to dismiss schools from their share of the responsibility — to let them "off the hook" — is to lessen the capacity of American enterprises and American workers to compete successfully in an increasingly challenging global economy.[97]

And yet, as we are preparing students for the future world of work, we are helping to further exacerbate the jobs dilemma. To avoid that, government, education, and business leaders must all recognize that the jobs dilemma is a multifaceted problem. If education continues to crank out high school and college graduates qualified for participation in a world-class workforce, and if business does not concomitantly find ways to provide job opportunities for them, then the jobs dilemma will remain a problem. Only a partnership among business, government, and education will ensure success.

Notes

1. Michael A. Hiltzik, "More Firms Giving a Stake to Employees," *Los Angeles Times*, 15 June 1996, pp. Al, A22-A23. This article goes on to say that guilt is motivating more companies to grant shares to regular workers, but only 3% of the top 1,000 companies are doing that.
2. See "This Year's Pace of Layoffs Is Fastest of Decade," *Los Angeles Times*, 11 June 1996, p. D2; and "January Job Layoffs Highest in Two Years," *Los Angeles Times*, 7 February 1996, pp. D1, D3.
3. Christopher Lasch, "The Revolt of the Elites," *Harper's Magazine* (November 1994): 39-49.
4. Paul Krugman, "Technology's Revenge," *Wilson Quarterly* (Autumn 1994): 57. Krugman is an economist at Stanford University.
5. Meinhard Miegel, "Full Employment: A Socioromantic Utopia?," in *Work in the Future, The Future of Work*, the Second Annual Colloquium of the Alfred Herrhausen Society for International Dialog (Stuttgart, Germany: Schaffer-Poeschel Verlag, 1994), pp. 23-34.
6. James Flanigan, "In Japan No More Life Long Job Guarantee," *Los Angeles Times*, 14 July 1996, pp. D1, D5. From 1990 to 1996, Japan went through its own hard times. But the Japanese are not planning to change their schools, or even to blame them for the economic downturn. Instead, they are taking the same business steps that all capitalist countries take when the economy turns bad: They lay off people.
7. Maria Cone, "Compatible Partners Make Job Sharing a Win-Win Option," *Los Angeles Times Careers Supplement*, 6 February 1995, pp. 5-6.

8. Eileen Applebaum and Rosemary Batt, *The New American Workplace: Transforming Work Systems in the United States* (Ithaca, N.Y.: ILR Press, 1994); Richard B. Freeman, ed. *Working Under Different Rules* (New York: Russell Sage Foundation, 1994); Jeremy Rifkin, *The End of Work* (New York: G.P. Putnam's Sons, 1995); Stanley Aronowitz and William Difazio, *The Jobless Future* (Minneapolis: University of Minnesota Press, 1994).

9. Juliet Schor, *The Overworked American: The Unexpected Decline of Leisure* (New York: Basic Books, 1991), pp. 29-31; Jeremy Rifkin, *The End of Work: The Decline of the Global Labor Force and the Dawn of the Post-Market Era* (New York: G.P. Putnam's Sons, 1995), p. 222.

10. Schor, op. cit., pp. 29-31.

11. Juliet Schor, *A Sustainable Economy*, Open Magazine Pamphlet Series No. 131 (Westfield, N.J., April 1995), p. 10.

12. Lewis J. Perelman, *School's Out* (New York: Avon, 1992).

13. Ibid. In Perelman's view, computer-based technology and electronic information processes will obviate the need for teachers at some point in the near future.

14. Fred Best, *Reducing Workweeks to Prevent Layoffs* (Philadelphia: Temple University Press, 1988).

15. Ibid.

16. "Worker" in this context means "craftworker," those who are able to add value to products and who earn high wages.

17. Schor, *A Sustainable Economy*, p. 10.

18. Best, op. cit., pp. 1-2.

19. Maria Cone, op. cit.

20. Nanette Fondas, "Job Sharing in Executive Suite: An Idea Whose Time Has Come," *Los Angeles Times*, 16 April 1995, p. D2.

21. Best, op. cit.

22. Herbert J. Gans, *People, Plans, and Policies* (New York: Columbia University Press, 1993), pp. 256-61.

23. Schor, *A Sustainable Economy*, p. 10.

24. "Finding the Week that Works," *Los Angeles Times*, 13 November 1994, p. D3.

25. Daniel S. Hamermesh, *Workdays, Workhours, and Work Schedules* (Kalamazoo, Mich.: W.E. Upjohn Institute, 1996), p. 141.

26. U.S. Department of Commerce, *Statistical Abstract of the United States, 1993* (Washington, D.C.: Bureau of the Census, 1993), p.

401; Fred Best, *Reducing Workweeks to Prevent Layoffs* (Philadelphia: Temple University Press, 1988), p. 133. I have taken the liberty here to extrapolate the number of new jobs based on the total employment in 1978 as discussed by Best. His description of shortened hours is negative, because its focus was on preserving jobs to avoid layoffs, while the focus here is on creation of new jobs to accommodate qualified graduates.

27. Best, op. cit., pp. 139-45.
28. National Center for Education Statistics, *Projections of Education Statistics to 2004* (Washington, D.C.: U.S. Department of Education, October 1993), pp. 49-52, 53-64.
29. "Labor Markets Hit a Slow Boil but Inflation Keeps Its Cool," *Business Week*, 22 August 1994, p. 21; "Downsizing Slows but Sheepskin Set Is Still Scrambling," *Business Week*, 22 August 1994, pp. 6, 20. That study indicated that a tiny, 1.1% increase in hiring new college graduates was the lowest in 14 months and came nowhere near making up for the huge loss of job opportunities reported by the Census Bureau.
30. Hamermesh, op. cit., p. 141.
31. See "Boeing to Increase Production Next Year to Make Up for Strike," *Los Angeles Times*, 20 December 1995, p. D2; "Boeing Will Reportedly Add 5,000 Jobs in '96," *Los Angeles Times*, 29 January 1996, p. D4.
32. Donald W. Nauss, "GM Faces Strike by 12,000 Workers," *Los Angeles Times*, 27 September 1994; pp. D1, D6. Another strike was called in March 1996 over the same issue at a different plant; see "3000 Workers Strike GM Plants," *Los Angeles Times*, 5 March 1996, p. D2.
33. The Harris Poll, 10 May 1992, reported in Schor, *A Sustainable Economy*, p. 9.
34. Best, op. cit., pp. 36-37.
35. Lawrence Mishel and Jared Bernstein, *The State of Working America, 1994-95* (Washington, D.C.: Economic Policy Institute, 1994), p. 112.
36. Schor was quoted in "The New World of Work," *Business Week*, 17 October 1994, pp. 76-93.
37. "Options for Everyone," *Business Week*, 22 July 1996, pp. 80-84. There are many problems with this program, but the primary one is that it is a payoff for working long hours when others have been fired, exactly the reverse of work sharing.

170

38. It would still be possible for a worker to work overtime on occasion, especially among professional workers. But instead of receiving monetary compensation, the worker would take compensatory time off.

39. Douglas L. Kruse, *Profit Sharing: Does It Make A Difference?* (Kalamazoo, Mich.: W.E. Upjohn Institute, 1993), p. 101.

40. Krugman, op. cit., p. 64.

41. Kruse, op. cit., pp. 45-68.

42. Applebaum and Batt, op. cit., p. 4.

43. Michael A. Conte and Jam Svejnar, "The Performance of Employee Ownership Plans," in *Paying for Productivity: A Look at the Evidence*, edited by Alan S. Binder (Washington, D.C.: Bookings Institution, 1990), pp. 143-82.

44. "More Firms Giving a Stake to Employees," *Los Angeles Times*, 15 June 1996, pp. A1, A22-A23.

45. Len Krimerman and Frank Lindenfeld, eds., *When Workers Decide: Workplace Democracy Takes Root in North America* (Philadelphia: New Society Press, 1992). This collection describes the successful business experiences of worker-owned companies and cooperatives throughout the United States and Canada.

46. When traditional management has actively resisted worker ESOP influences, companies have gotten into trouble, rather than succeeded. See "Why ESOP Deals Have Slowed to a Crawl," *Business Week*, 18 March 1996, pp. 101-02.

47. James Flanigan, "Employee Ownership: One More Way of Coping," *Los Angeles Times*, 12 June 1994, pp. D1, D6.

48. Keith Alexander and Stephen Baker, "If You Can't Beat 'Em, Buy 'Em," *Business Week*, 24 October 1994, p. 80.

49. *Los Angeles Times*, 16 December 1993, p. A39; *Los Angeles Times*, 15 July 1994; *Los Angeles Times*, 17 August 1994, p. D2.

50. "Gross Compensation?" *Business Week*, 18 March 1996, pp. 32-33, 96-100; Graef Crystal, "Growing the Pay Gap," *Los Angeles Times*, 23 July 1995, p. D2.

51. "A New Look at Employee Ownership," *Business Week*, 18 March 1996, p. 124.

52. Alan S. Binder, ed., *Paying for Productivity: A Look at the Evidence* (Washington, D.C.: Bookings Institution, 1990), pp. 5-7.

53. Martin L. Weitzman and Douglas L. Kruse, "Profit Sharing and Productivity," in *Paying for Productivity: A Look at the Evidence*,

171

edited by Alan S. Binder (Washington, D.C.: Bookings Institution, 1990), pp. 95-142.

54. "Rebuilding America: The Mind-Numbing Cost," *Business Week Special Edition* (December 1992): 186-98.

55. Most analysts now agree that redeveloping the nation's infrastructure will benefit business and government in the long run. See "Record Cost Cited to Fix or Rebuild Nation's Schools," *New York Times*, 26 December 1995, p. A19.

56. Christopher Farrell, "The New Economic Era," *Business Week Special Edition* (December 1992): 24-25; "The Highway to Tomorrow," *Business Week Special Edition* (December 1992): 200; "Rebuilding America: The Mind-Numbing Cost," *Business Week Special Edition* (December 1992): 186-98; "Mutating into a Second Era," *Business Week Special Edition* (December 1992): 175-77.

57. Martin Neil Bailey, Gary Burtless, and Robert E. Litan, *Growth with Equity: Economic Policymaking for the Next Century* (Washington, D.C.: Brookings Institution, 1993), passim; Charles L. Schultze, *Memos to the President: A Guide Through Macroeconomics for the Busy Policymaker* (Washington, D.C.: Brookings Institution, 1992), Part 3; Herrhausen Society, *Work in the Future* (Stuttgart, Germany: Schaffer-Poeschel Verlag, 1994), p. 4. See also the Organisation for Economic Cooperation and Development's *Employment Outlook* (Paris, July 1994), Chapter 2.

58. Robert Kuttner, "Needed: A Two-Way Social Contract in the Workplace," *Business Week*, 10 July 1995, p. 22; "Writing a New Social Contract," *Business Week*, 11 March 1996, pp. 60-61.

59. Robert B. Reich, *The Work of Nations: Preparing Ourselves for 21st Century Capitalism* (New York: Vintage, 1991).

60. Schor, *A Sustainable Economy*, pp. 12-28.

61. Best, op. cit., pp. 36-37.

62. Bureau of the Census, *Statistical Abstract of the United States, 1993*, 13th ed. (Washington, D.C.: U.S. Department of Commerce, 1993), Table 622.

63. Mary Walsh, "Germany's Reckoning," *Los Angeles Times*, 25 February 1996, pp. D1, D3.

64. Mishel and Bernstein, op. cit., Chapter 3; and "A Higher Minimum Wage Will Benefit Majority of Americans," *Democrats' 2000 Progress Report* (Summer 1995), pp. 1, 6.

65. Robert A. Rosenblatt, "Beyond Mere Slogans, U.S. Needs a GI Bill for Displaced Workers," *Los Angeles Times*, 25 February 1996, p. D2.

66. Richard Rothstein, "Productivity Forever: New Bargain or No Bargain?" *The American Prospect* (Summer 1993): 32-47.

67. Paul Richter and Robert Rosenblatt, "Clinton Proposes Simpler Pension Plan," *Los Angeles Times*, 12 April 1966, pp. A1, A11.

68. Apparently, as these conditions worsen, more politicians are beginning to worry. See "Numbers Without Health Insurance Rises," *Los Angeles Times*, 27 April 1996, pp. A5, A16.

69. James C. Franklin, "Industry Output and Employment," *Monthly Labor Review* (November 1993): 41-57.

70. *Los Angeles Times Careers Supplement*, 12 August 1996, p. 4.

71. When I was a superintendent, I developed just such a childcare contractual relationship with a number of large corporations within my school district's boundaries. The program not only earned a large cash infusion for district coffers, it also engendered enormous good will from the employers and employees of the companies involved. Other superintendents should investigate this ongoing income source.

72. Mishel and Bernstein, op. cit., pp. 115-17.

73. Bruce W. Ballenger, "Federal Jobs-Creation Tax Credit Could Lift California's Economy," *Los Angeles Times*, 30 July 1995, p. D2. The ideas expressed here are not those of a radical left-winger. Ballenger is a partner in Ballenger, Budgetti, and Associates, a management consulting firm that specializes in corporate reorganizations and profit improvements.

74. General Accounting Office, *Workplace Regulation: Information on Selected Employer and Union Experiences*, GAO/HEHS-94-138, Vol. I2-8 (Washington, D.C., June 1994).

75. Ibid.

76. Samuel C. Florman, "Regulating the Regulators," *Technology Review* (April 1995): 73.

77. "Record Cost Cited to Fix or Rebuild Nation's Schools," *New York Times*, 26 December 1995, p. A19.

78. Lynn Smith, "Reading, Writing, and Ruin," *Los Angeles Times*, 9 November 1994, pp. E1, E7

79. "States to Not Spend Enough to Fix, Build Schools, Report Says," *Education Week*, 10 January 1996, p. 22.

80. "Accessing the Disabled Costly, Report Says," *Education Week*, 8 February 1995, p. 9.

81. "States to Not Spend Enough to Fix, Build Schools, Report Says," *Education Week*, 10 January 1996, p. 22.

82. "Record Cost to Fix or Rebuild Nation's Schools," *New York Times*, 26 December 1995, p. A19.

83. Office of Technology Assessment, *Teachers & Technology: Making the Connection* (Washington, D.C.: Congress of the United States, April 1995), pp. 18-24.

84. Tyler Marshall, "Europe Rethinks Job Sharing," *Los Angeles Times*, 14 February 1995, pp. H1, H4.

85. *New York Times*, 20 June 1996, pp. A1, C17.

86. Ibid.

87. Marshall, op. cit.

88. Miegel, op. cit., pp. 23-34.

89. Marshall, op. cit.

90. "German Union Forges Plan for Creating Jobs," *Los Angeles Times*, 13 January 1996, p. A2.

91. Ibid.

92. Marshall, op. cit.

93. There is still a core of business holdouts, those who wanted to use the recent German recession as an excuse to rescind 50 years of labor laws and who would have emulated American hiring and firing practices. Labor resisted. Now that the German economy is in a growth period, less is heard about radical departures from the traditional partnership of labor, business, and government.

94. "VW, Unions OK 20% Reduction in Work Week," *Los Angeles Times*, 25 October 1993, p. M1.

95. Organization for Economic Cooperation and Development, *Employment Outlook* (July 1994), p. 201.

96. Lester C. Thurow, "America Reverts to the 19th Century," *Los Angeles Times*, 29 January 1996, p. B9.

97. Advisory Board, National Center on the Educational Quality of the Workforce (EQW), *EQW Policy Statement* (Philadelphia: University of Pennsylvania, 1995), p. 1.

Chapter Five

Fighting Fire with Fire

Regardless of what business executives and government officials tell us, education and training by themselves will *not* resolve the jobs dilemma. No matter how exquisite or sophisticated or intense the training and education programs are, if there are no jobs available for graduates, getting educated will not be an advantage for millions of young people. If no changes are made in the way corporations and other businesses conduct business, there will be a growing mass of highly educated but unemployed or underemployed university and high school graduates demanding change.

The American economy must become more effective for all its citizens, rather than just for a lucky elite. An effective economy meets three criteria: 1) it raises the standard of living of all citizens, 2) it ensures that all groups share in prosperity, and 3) it has sustainable growth.[1] A nation must meet all three of those criteria or be exposed to weaknesses that ultimately may lead to economic or political turmoil.

In that sense, the New Economy's jobs dilemma and its potential political ramifications may prove to be the Achilles heel for America and other advanced industrial nations. While generally effective in a purely economic sense, the New Economy is not raising the standard of living and personal well-being of many Americans. The New Economy is not leading to social and economic benefits for all Americans, especially children and young adults. Failure to change direction means exacerbation of the dismal economic conditions described in the previous chapters — a declining middle class, low wages, poverty, no medical coverage, disease, squalor, short life-spans, and citizens with a good education and no place to go.[2]

Educators have felt the pinch of the New Economy's stinginess. Declining economic support, attempts to disassociate the well-off from public schools through voucher programs, rejected tax increases, defeated facility bonds, and declining professional incomes are the most obvious signs of the New Economy's mean-spirited side for educators. Much worse than those blatant signs are the less obvious consequences of the New Economy's rampant disregard for the lives of ordinary Americans and their children. It is harder for the public to see the effects of crowded classrooms, dilapidated buildings, and the intellectual loss of impoverished children. It is harder to see the loss of purpose among university graduates who had anticipated professional and business careers, but who find themselves having to grasp at any job, however menial, to make a living.

Older Americans also are threatened by the New Economy as its political ramifications get translated into deficit cutting that challenges precious entitlements, including Medicare and Medicaid. But older Americans cannot begin to imagine the plight of high school and university graduates, because they did not have to face the same occupational traumas. There were jobs for them. Working hard to get ahead paid off. But what will happen to their children and grandchildren?

Job-expansion techniques — work-sharing, profit-sharing, employee stock ownership plans, and others — have shown potential for relieving the jobs dilemma. However, there has been little interest in achieving that potential in the United States. Downsizing and re-engineering are an easy way to increase returns to institutional investors and top executives, so little concern has been shown for the long-range implications of those retrogressive tactics. That may be changing. As the adverse consequences of those tactics begin to negatively affect America's middle and working classes, politicians and analysts have begun to revisit such ideas as work-sharing and profit-sharing not just as a means to save jobs but, more important, as a way to expand job opportunities. The United States already has the economic capability to implement such practices. All that is missing is the political consensus among major decision makers and top business executives to move forward.

There is no technical reason that the American economy cannot support significant job expansion. That expansion would provide more Americans a chance to secure high-wage, challenging symbolic analyst and craftworker jobs. Why haven't we chosen that path?

Some would have us believe that "mysterious, invisible market forces" drive the economy. That is not so. The economy is not like the weather. The weather has to be taken the way it comes; the direction the economy takes is based on human decisions. The reason we seem unable to expand job opportunities lies much more with the lack of creativity and strategic foresight among business executives and politicians.[3] It is no surprise that when top managers look at technological innovation, all they see is the opportunity to increase profits by shedding workers, which they did with a vengeance.[4] Top executives wanted only the fastest way to gain a large return on investment for their shareholders (including themselves). Machines cost less than workers, so they started downsizing. That needs to change.

The growing income inequality that resulted from those actions has led many people of good will to question an economy that can produce such riches for a small elite and yet not meet the needs of the vast number of Americans. They are beginning to ask if it is right to allow "invisible market forces" to run roughshod over lives, exempting only the chosen few. They are questioning why the New Economy, with its prowess and technological inventiveness, cannot fulfill Americans' need for security, education for their children, and a renewed sense of community. Millions of Americans are joining those thoughtful analysts to ask what the economy is for.

The search for answers is leading many authorities to compare how Western Europe and Japan are addressing the jobs dilemma. They are finding some very fundamental differences in attitudes regarding the purpose of an economy. Those attitudes guide how other countries approach economic decisions and how each assesses the effects of those decisions on the well-being of its citizens in this techno-information age. Americans may have something to learn about the function of an economy by studying the experiences of other advanced industrial countries.

What Is the Economy For?

James Fallows, a noted analyst and author, poses the central policy question the United States will face as it approaches the 21st century: What is an economy for?[5] In the course of comparing American economic thought about the function of the economy versus the views of other advanced industrial nations — especially Japan and Germany — Fallows' incisive analysis describes four essential differences between economic models of other advanced industrial nations and that of the United States.

1. *The purpose of economic life.* The basic drive of the American economy is to raise the consumer's standard of living. The American goal is materialistic. Corporate America believes:

> Economic development means "more." If people have more choice, more leisure, more wealth, more opportunity to pursue happiness, society as a whole will be a success. In theory, any deal that the market permits will in the long run be good for society as a whole.[6]

Other advanced industrial nations believe the purpose of an economy is to increase the collective national strength and to make the nation independent and self-reliant, so that it does not rely on outsiders for survival.

2. *The view of power.* The American view is that concentrated power is evil, and elaborate means have been developed to reduce the concentration of power. For the other advanced industrial

nations, power is a fact of life, something that needs to be used for the long-term national good. Therefore the advanced industrial nations permit their governments a much more active role in directing their economies than does the United States.

3. *The view of unpredictability.* In the American corporate model, surprise is viewed as the "key to economic life." It is because markets are fluid and unpredictable that they work. The other advanced industrial nations distrust the market. They see competition as a way to keep businesses alert, but not as the way their countries should be run nor as the way to determine where their economies should move. They work to avoid surprise. Planning is a rational policy among the other advanced industrial nations. In the United States, planning is anathema.

4. *The view of national borders.* Corporate America's model accepts a division of the world's people into the "have and have-not" economic classes, regardless of national status. Therefore, they are unwilling to put the needs of the American nation first, preferring to let market forces take their course. Other advanced industrial nations assume that there are "us" and "them" and that they have to look out for their own people first.

Those differing economic views have led the United States in a different direction from other advanced industrial nations. With its acceptance of the idea of "market forces" acting as if they were the hand of God, Americans have, for the most part, let events unfold with little attempt at planning or coordination of economic matters. With the exception of the Federal Reserve Board's role of vicar, manipulating the flow of money and the interest rate, little direct intervention in the economy is found in America. Thus Corporate America, left to itself, has preferred a quick, short-term solution to the jobs dilemma: Get jobs for everyone, regardless of the job's quality or wages, and attack the unlucky and impoverished as wastrels. Lack of a job is seen as an *individual's* problem — get more education or training and everything will be okay. Perhaps it is time to change that view.

The result of Western Europe's different approach to decisions about their economies has been more humane policies for both the employed and the unemployed. The attitude in Europe is "people come first," and the economy is the tool for providing for their well-being. All European countries have capitalist economies, just as the United States does. But their capitalism is moderated by their people-come-first values.

That difference between the United States and other industrial countries is seen most clearly in the approaches those other nations are taking to their own jobs dilemma. Europeans have a core of highly skilled, high-wage craftworkers. They also have their own unemployed millions, which will grow even larger when the millions about to graduate from their universities and apprentice programs cannot find jobs. Instead of considering that a problem of individual decision making, European advanced industrial nations address the jobs issue as a *social* problem. They continue to search for viable *social* solutions for their jobs dilemma. They are experimenting with work-sharing, profit-sharing, and various support systems while trying to perfect a long-term systemic solution.[7] In the meanwhile, those countries let their social welfare policies provide a modest but livable income for the unemployed.

The other industrial nations have not yet found a systemic long-term solution for the jobs dilemma. So far, their efforts have focused on relieving current unemployment and continuing the search for solutions. However, decision makers and opinion formulators in the United States are even less sure of a path to follow. Until quite recently, our country's best minds have been slow to formulate strategies that could show us a way out of the dilemma. Some pundits have even thrown up their hands. Their thinking is constrained by what they see as inescapable joblessness. That pessimism has been:

> premised on [the] rhetoric of global marketplace and information-based society. This vision of the future is not questioned and is assumed to be inevitable. The global corporate culture and the economy that goes with it is, indeed, a juggernaut with incredible power and momentum. But that does not preclude

the ability of our democratic institutions to play a role in shaping the future of the world of work.[8]

Just what options are available? And can we afford them?

Getting There: Output Enhancement Technology

The jobs problem in America is growing worse, but some authorities are generating ideas that could profoundly affect the future world of work. They have begun to investigate a solution to the jobs dilemma that blends the best practices of the industrial world. These solutions combine the best of capitalist initiative with a renewed concern for social welfare.

Any solution necessarily must rest on sustainable high productivity, and that means computer-based technology. Instead of limiting business R&D and government support in order to constrain further computer-based manufacturing and electronic information processing, we must do just the opposite. We must push those developments to the limit in order to create a true techno-informational economy. The resultant productivity would make it possible to expand the number of decent employment opportunities through work-sharing and profit-sharing and to implement a social welfare scaffold to support individuals who are in transition from the old economy to the New Economy.

That solution, of course, depends on just how the technology is used in the workplace. Technophiles wax optimistically about how technology will change the world and education, but they show little understanding or concern for the effects of technology on jobs.[9] Others see technology replacing humans and pessimistically predict the "end of work" and a "jobless future" that no amount of creative planning can overcome.[10] And using technology in the workplace merely as a way to increase productivity without addressing the central issue of jobs could bring about a jobless future. Indeed, that is what has caused the current jobs dilemma. Technology should be seen as a way to enhance human labor, not replace it.

Companies install new technology to remain competitive, not to make more jobs. If technology is to expand job opportunities, it simultaneously must satisfy business needs. Computer-based technologies allow companies to increase productivity, to get a better return on shareholders' investments, and perhaps even to lower prices by reducing production costs. They also reduce the human work time that is needed. But these technologies also are critically important in the drive to expand job opportunities. They can do so only if companies devise effective human-computer interconnections.

That "interface," economists and business academics tell us, is called *enhanced-output technology*, or EOT. Enhanced-output technology is the use of computer-based technology by talented symbolic analysts and skilled craftworkers to enhance, or add value to, products and services. For example, a computer-assisted design program can produce a prototype airplane. But if the airline wants all its airplanes, regardless of size, to give all passengers ample leg room, they need a person who can imagine creative ways to do that, who can manipulate data and program the computer to test different prototypes, and who can make an expert recommendation to designers. Symbolic analysts are needed to do that. And craftworkers must translate the design into actual working airplanes.

Continuing the analogy: After the final computer/symbolic analyst design is used to guide production, unanticipated problems often emerge as skilled craftworkers do the delicate work of assembling the airplane. They need to decide how to correct those problems on the shop floor. They may need to make small correction in the math formulas driving the computer programs, or they may need to discuss their interpretation of diagrams and written instructions with their work team. In such situations, merely counting on computer-based technology to direct the operation of low-skill workers would never work.

Thus technological advances affect job opportunities in two ways, one negative, one positive. Negatively, technology may be used directly to eliminate jobs by automating and using robots. By re-engineering job structures and modifying managerial processes, corporations can eliminate as many employees as possible and then replace them with computer-based technology. This direct

182

application of technology has been the choice of many of America's corporate executives. It represents a short-term, profit-driven, and short-sighted choice; and it results in the massive loss of decent jobs. Companies that adopt direct-application strategies fail to recognize the potential effect on their consumer base. Impoverished and unemployed workers make lousy customers. The strategy also ignores the political ramifications posed by creating a large body of underemployed, angry workers.[11]

On the positive side, when technology is used to enhance output, it emphasizes the critical role of craftworkers and symbolic analysts in the production equation. With enhanced output technology, high-tech craftworkers perform value-added functions in the manufacturing processes. The skills, knowledges, and experiences of workers allow them to use technology more efficiently and effectively. Because of this interaction of man and machine, the enhanced technology approach allows work-sharing and profit-sharing programs to be implemented easily.

It is important to note that the choice of approach — enhanced or direct technology — is a human decision; it is not caused by a technological imperative or economic law.[12] Both approaches save money through increased productivity. Executives who choose the direct approach decide to maximize shareholder returns in the short term by using technology to shed workers. Executives who choose the enhanced technology approach, in contrast, seek long-term growth for their business by investing in computer-based technology, redesigning management-employee interactions to tap the expertise of their frontline workers, employing larger cadres of core craftworkers, and establishing an alliance of suppliers and distributors to form an integrated network. They plan to maximize productivity by using technology to keep unit labor costs low, but they rely on the skills and knowledge of their craftworkers and symbolic analysts to add value to products and to maintain innovation. With the enhanced approach, a strong core of highly skilled, high-tech craftworkers is essential.

Enhanced technology firms are prototypes for work-sharing. The reduction in unit labor costs is gained primarily by giving computer-based machines responsibility to do routine functions. That, in turn, can allow a reduced schedule for all of the firm's craftworkers. And that frees up time that could be used for work-sharing. In a large empirical study of the effects of both direct application and enhanced technology on employment, economists Robert Levy, Matianne Bowes, and James Jondrow concluded:

> The degree of direct labor displacement is . . . lessened by the indirect output-enhancement effect of technology — that is, technological advance leads to lower output prices, increases the quantity of output sold, and increases employment.[13]

The high quality and lower cost of products produced through a combination of technological innovation and worker sophistication also will strengthen the competitive advantage of American corporations, giving them a larger market share — more customers. Increased market share means higher profits and even greater productivity, which should mean better income for employees, managers, and stockholders. In addition, computer-based manufacturing techniques make it possible to customize products, and customization and quality are the marketing secrets the rest of the world learned from Japan's corporate leaders.[14] The technology to accomplish these goals already exists.

The trick to all this, of course, is to get top corporate executives and their satellite companies to understand that, in the long run, switching to an enhanced-technology and job-expansion mode of operation is in their very best interest. The larger the core of well-paid craftworkers and the better the bonuses that service workers earn from gain-sharing, the larger the customer base for American products and services.

The Productivity Base for Job Expansion

"All well and good," one might agree, and then question: "But even if such technological expansion took place, could we *afford* job-expansion policies and still stay competitive?" The answer is yes. The capacity of America's economy to support job expansion is real, especially if certain business decisions and government policies are in place. For the economy, business must set in motion five things to start moving in a high-performance direction:

- Top management develops the foresight to better project long-range trends and how those trends will affect their companies.
- Research and development explores new areas on the frontiers of knowledge, as well as how best to rebuild the national infrastructure.
- Business firms expand productivity and establish a strong market share through increased global trade.
- Business organizations transform into high-performance work organizations.
- Investment rules are revised to reward long-term investments, thereby empowering management to take a longer view.[15]

Government, too, will need to develop a solid scaffold to aid business and labor as the transformation to high performance takes place. Among those actions are:

- Establish tax rewards for job-expansion practices and investments in technological innovation.
- Reward reductions in the work week and daily hours and penalize overtime.
- Modify investment rules to reward long-term investment in stocks and safeguard profit-sharing programs.
- Establish national health and retirement programs and a livable minimum wage.
- Create laws encouraging equitable and collaborative labor-management relationships and worker councils.
- Provide a scaffold for workers in transition from old to new skills, as well as training programs for the unemployed and underprivileged.

Transforming American corporations into high-performance, highly competitive work organizations will result from the combined efforts of those business and government actions. The cumulative results of those actions will constitute a third way between the high social welfare functions in Europe's economies and the cold market-driven American economy. By adopting that third way, America's corporations will have the technical means for reducing work hours, open up more job opportunities through work-sharing, and still make a handsome profit for their firms.

The essential key to that transformation, of course, is the ability of the New Economy to increase its productive capacity through technological innovation even beyond what it now can accomplish. The higher productivity a country has, the more wealth it has, wealth that can be equitably distributed through earnings, income, and wages. Economists know it can be done, and some insightful top executives are already doing it.

> Over any sustained period there are only two ways a country's workers . . . can provide themselves with an increased flow of goods and services: first, and overwhelmingly the most important, the country can increase the *output* . . . that each worker can, on average, produce. [The higher the output, the] more goods and services [the country has] available to enjoy, by using them directly or by trading them abroad to acquire goods and services produced elsewhere. . . . Second . . . the country can improve its terms of trade. It can get more imports for any given quantity of exports.[16] [emphasis added]

Increased output is the real measure of productivity. But we need to view productivity as economists do. For economists, productivity is the "output per unit of labor input."[17] And "unit of labor" is defined as a combination of humans working with any tools that are available. Two complementary inputs are needed to increase productivity: capital, which is the machines and equipment used to produce something, and labor, which is the human power needed to run the machines and do the work peripheral to the machines. The combined cost of capital and labor make up a measure of productivity called *unit labor costs*.[18] The rule used by economists states that "the lower the unit labor costs, the higher the profits and return on investment." Thus the better the tool, the greater the productivity, which is the rationale for more techno-logical applications in the workplace, not less.

A business may increase one side or the other — more capital and less labor or more labor and less capital — in an attempt to gain an increase in productivity. One way to get more efficiency from workers is to pay them more (as Henry Ford did around the turn of the century) and have them work longer hours.[19] Typically, nonindustrial nations have businesses that are "labor intensive." That means they use a large number of people in their factories to get higher productivity; and if productivity slows, they add more people. In industrial countries, especially advanced industrial countries, just the opposite happens; productivity increases with an increase in capital. Industrial countries become "capital inten-sive" — that is, they use more machines — with a sufficient num-ber of workers to tend to those machines.

Obviously, unit labor costs become a factor at some point in both labor-intensive and capital-intensive situations. Add too many workers, and their wages and benefits cut into profits. Or add more labor-saving machines, and the costs are so high that no investor wants to take the chance or the company's debt becomes so large it cannot afford other necessary resources. In either circumstance, shareholder investments may show no returns and the company folds. Traditionally, businesses in industrial nations have sought a balance between capital and labor inputs, providing efficient machines to enable workers to produce goods more efficiently. Machines were seen as extensions of the workers' hands, never as a substitute for those hands.

All that is changing as we approach the 21st century. The balance between capital and labor held until the end of the 1970s. Usually a new era produces more jobs than were eliminated in the old era. However, the New Economy is producing fewer jobs. It is doing so because the traditional balance between capital and labor has been weighted in favor of machines. In the long-run, labor costs more than machines. Thus computer-based manufacturing and informa-tion technologies have resulted in high productivity at lower unit labor costs. As the machines become even more sophisticated, fewer full-time craftworkers will be needed. Even symbolic analysts are in growing over-supply as technology performs some tasks that once were exclusively the domain of human intellects.

There is another way to look at the mix of capital and labor, one that maintains high productivity while expanding job opportunities. But it means scrapping the old way of thinking. It requires redefining a "job" as "a set of tasks." If more of those tasks are assigned to machines, then humans have to spend less time on these tasks. From the old vantage point, increasing technology's "workload" would result in enormous downsizing of the workforce. In the new view, technology is used to reduce the amount of time worked by individual workers. The tasks would be shared among several individuals — work-sharing — so that all workers would be working less hours rather than some working full-time and others being unemployed.

The jobs dilemma will not be resolved by turning back the clock. There will be no return to mass-production industries with millions of routine production workers. The forces of change are inexorable. Instead, Americans should demand even more sophisticated and advanced computer-based manufacturing innovations.

There is no question that America's corporations can increase productivity, increase their global competitive advantage, and still expand the workforce. However, the role of the corporate decision makers will be critical. Not only will they need to develop the intellectual foresight that will enable them to see future opportunities, but they also must have the process skills needed to shepherd their organizations into more effective strategic positions. That will involve four major complementary phases: 1) developing new products and services, 2) developing a more insightful executive cadre, 3) transforming firms into high-performance work organizations, and 4) developing more effective labor/management collaboration.[20]

New Products and Services

Each phase initiates its own set of questions. If increased productivity and market share is contingent on new products and services, the question is *what* new products and services? Do we have any new approaches at all, any new technologies that enable us to access new global markets and to help solve problems the world faces or will face? Mostly, the answers are positive.

If companies in the United States are going to increase their productivity by building the capital side — computer-based advanced manufacturing and electronic information processing — they must have some assurance that there will be customers willing to buy the goods and services produced.[21] Currently, the United States' major trading partners are other advanced industrial nations, such as Japan and Germany. Those nations, along with the growing affluent and middle classes of newly industrializing countries, will form the consumer base for high-technology, high-quality goods.[22]

The customers will come not only from today's advanced economies, but from those newly enriched by the success of the emerging economies.[23] Asian and Latin American workers will demand higher standards of living. They will seek the higher wages and benefits that economic advancement will provide. They will have wealth to spend on the goods and services that America can provide. After that, there will be other countries advancing — such as India, Eastern Europe, Russia, and Indonesia — places that cause other problems for high-performance American corporations to solve.[24] But it is still to America's advantage to see poorer countries enriched. As their middle-class affluence grows, we can expand our market share trade by attending to their demands and needs.

New markets will arise in areas in which U.S. business firms will have notable strength and experience, provided that we continue to graduate high-quality symbolic analysts. Areas in which the United States clearly leads the world include microelectronics and information technology, especially microsystems products that demand smaller sizes and higher quality. Other areas in which the United States still has the lead include optoelectronics, using electric currents and lasers for information compression, increased storage capacity, and instantaneous worldwide information exchange; genetic engineering; materials science, metallurgy, composite materials, ceramics, and the like; environmental clean-up, management, and protection; and pharmaceuticals. Another huge area of growth will be rebuilding the world's decaying infrastructure, both in America and in foreign countries. And the craving for new products among emerging middle-classes in East Asia, China, Latin America, and other newly industrializing nations will be awesome These are technologies we never had before and where world competition is wide open. Although not an exhaustive list, those and other new goods and services will be awaited in the global market place.

Computer-based technologies and America's entrepreneurial values make it possible for U.S. companies to gain *comparative* advantage in those areas and thus increase their market share at the expense of foreign firms. With increased use of technology, America's economy will be able to produce customized goods efficiently and to provide services of the highest quality. Customized products will appeal to the affluent middle classes in Western Europe, Japan, and rapidly developing countries.[25]

As we move into the 21st century, competition will increase both from the other advanced industrial nations and from the newly industrializing countries. To gain a greater market share in that global economy, the United States must be able to do two basic things: produce customized goods and services and expand its technological capacities to respond quickly to changing market demands. On the other hand, old-fashioned management techniques, an emasculated workforce, and short-term planning will be the death knell of corporations in the future.

The key words for future success are *capability* and *competitiveness*. Thus to maintain its competitive advantage, the American economy must accelerate its technological advances and use its symbolic analysts' talents effectively.[26] Therefore American companies must constantly keep upgrading and innovating. American companies will have to invest heavily in research and development, including projects jointly sponsored by government.[27]

American firms also will have to produce goods and services that can compete with goods produced with low-cost labor. We will not be able to prevent lower-level manufacturing to pass to developing countries. Low wages give the emerging countries the advantage on price, so America must pursue an advantage based on quality. But it is stupid to attempt to compete by reducing our own citizens' income and wages, as we have been doing. Even if we were to lower American wages further, we would not be able to match the rates that workers in emerging economies are prepared to accept. Our industries must be able to compete on other grounds.

Managerial Foresight and Job Expansion

A business — even one with sophisticated computer-based manufacturing and electronic information systems — is worth nothing without effective organization. The organization of production systems is the responsibility of top management. How managers set up work flow, how they integrate machine activities with human functions, how they structure decision-making and authority patterns, how they allocate resources, how they organize employees and their tasks, and how they measure the firm's effectiveness all affect the firm's productivity and ultimately its profitability.[28] Because of that enormous responsibility, top managers give a great deal of thought about ideal organizational arrangements. Sometimes those arrangements are based on the authority of expert analysis of tasks and sometimes on the qualitative attributes of the employees performing tasks. That explains why the organization of a hospital made up of doctors and nurses and other professionals is different than the organization of the traditional manufacturing company with executives, supervisors, and front-line workers.

Unfortunately, America's top executives have been tardy in their efforts to reconcile the functions and tasks within a computer-based technological world and the traditional work of mass production. During the 1970s and 1980s in particular, that tardiness caused loss of productivity and a less motivated workforce. On top of that, many executives' first response to technological innovation led to thoughtless organizational re-engineering and the consequent mass downsizing that flowed from re-engineering.[29] The organizations that remained were stripped to their essential core workers — usually a small cadre of symbolic analysts and shop-floor craft-workers — and the elimination of middle managers, supervisors, and redundant clerical and other "white collar" workers.[30]

For more than two decades, the Japanese had shown the superiority of a more progressive organizational model. However, American executives were reluctant to change organizational patterns in response to the impact of technology. For them it was difficult to rise above the familiar, even though the world around them was changing. It appears that some American executives and top managers resisted new patterns because they had an *affective* attachment to the hierarchical business organization model with which they had become familiar.[31] That mode of corporate operation — in sharp contrast to corporate organization and management arising in other countries — usually is associated with the "scientific management" principles of Frederick Taylor.[32]

> [The Taylor] approach emphasized rationality and science. To provide fairness to workers and firms, Taylor applied elements of science to objectively determine standards of piece work and job definition. However, the [workers'] fear of unemployment allowed the efficiency effort in many cases to overwhelm standards of decency. The "drive" system became the dominate way to motivate workers. Foremen had the power to hire and fire and some believed that arbitrary daily firings kept employees in line and productive. Along with arbitrary work rules, job categories and definitions were often narrowed to improve efficiency. Jobs were designed to give workers little or no discretion in their movements and workers were not expected to use their intellect or judgment in performing work. In these situations, management gave little consideration to the idea that efficient use of labor might involve dimensions other than the job process.[33]

Why should corporate executives want to give up the business-as-usual Taylor model and transform their corporation's organizational and management processes into more competitive patterns?

There are many reasons business as usual no longer works, but two in particular are salient. First, firms in newly industrializing countries are competing in price-conscious markets for standardized goods by paying wages that are a fraction of those in the United States. Second, the increased capacity for diversity and customization inherent in microprocessor-based technologies has cut the cost advantages of mass production and increased competition in quality-conscious markets. U.S. companies must now compete on the basis of cost, quality, and customization.[34]

The Taylor model is outmoded; and it is disappearing from manufacturing and processing industries and from high-tech electronic information processing corporations. (However, the Taylor model is holding on much more strongly in school districts.) Those executives with intellectual foresight saw that the industrial world's conditions were changing and that global competitive forces are transforming companies from a Taylorist orientation to more appropriate workplace practices. Foreign competitors whose companies already had reorganized lowered their unit labor costs and were closing the gap between American corporations' competitive edge and their own. Still, most American corporations chose the "low road" to profitability by reducing investments, pushing mass production technologies of the past to the peak of their capacities, and shedding workers.

Some executives chose the "high road" to effective business competition, as the Japanese and Western Europeans were doing; that is, they sought specialty niches and used highly skilled employees who can react quickly and flexibly to rapidly changing technologies and markets. Those executives' companies — especially technology, insurance, and small entrepreneurial businesses firms — are at various stages in their transformation from a Taylorist orientation to more modern management.[35]

If the high road is improving the productivity and profitability of those pioneer companies, why is it that so many corporate executives chose to stop their own transformation after re-engineering and downsizing? Many analysts now believe that not enough creative thought was put to the question of how American business could incorporate new technology without destroying the standard of living of so many millions of Americans.[36] Many business experts are now saying that the goal of expanded job opportunities can be accomplished if more of America's top business executives and political leaders would develop a strategic foresight.

> [Strategic foresight] is based on deep insights into trends in technology, demographics, regulations, and lifestyles, which can be harnessed to rewrite industry rules and create new competitive space. While understanding the potential implications of such trends requires creativity and imagination, any "vision" that is not based on a solid foundation is likely to be fantastical.[37]

In other words, competitive advantage in the new era will be won by the businesses that have smart leaders, those with the foresight to see the strategic potential of newly created demands, then plan for and implement strategies to get a "leg up" on their competitors around the world. With strategic foresight, business executives will see that customer demand, workforce education and training, plus product service and service innovations are forcing change in the competitive climate. For example, mass production techniques (such as assembly lines) are being replaced by more flexible "batch-job high technology manufacturing that competes on the basis of quality and customized service that computers have made economical, and not solely on lowest costs."[38] That new market diversity demands a concomitant major adjustment in structure and organization not only in what is produced but in how it is produced.

Strategic foresight also will help executives understand why simultaneously enhancing technology and producing a larger number of quality American job opportunities will help their business. With those understandings, top executives will serve their corporate needs directly while at the same time indirectly strengthening the country's economic and political future.

In addition, the labor market is changing. Although labor unions have declined severely over the last two decades, dropping from a high of 36% of the labor force in 1955 to only 16% in 1996, they have begun a resurgence.[39] With the election of new AFL-CIO leadership in 1996, there was a growing, more assertive demand within the labor movement for greater job security, control of runaway overtime, and participation in decision making, as well as wage issues.[40] Several recent contract settlements reflect the growing influence of unions and the nature of their demands.[41]

The labor market also is changing in other ways. As a result of educators' efforts, workers are developing higher-level skills and cognitive abilities on which Corporate America is coming to depend. If management continues to use traditional Taylorist techniques to supervise such high-skilled craftworkers, they will find resistance and worker-management cooperation will deteriorate. However, when the behavior is more congruent with the new worker expectations, they know that:

> the new computerized technologies used in expanding markets. . . require continual responsiveness of flow of data by workers and management. This has resulted in heightened responsibility, an increased demand for cognitive skills, closer integration of the tasks of management and workers. Organizations that respond to the new technology by creating a learning environment through management-labor cooperation, integration, and involvement are more successful in using technology to its fullest potential.[42]

Many analysts believe that top executives did not understand the long-range implications of using technological innovation merely to downsize. They never figured out how to incorporate new technology into their corporations in ways that would not destroy the standard of living of so many millions of Americans.[43] If more executives had developed strategic foresight, they would have seen what their colleagues in high performance companies have seen:

> We are standing on the verge . . . of a revolution so profound as that which gave birth to modern industry. It will be an environmental revolution, the genetic revolution, the materials revolution, the digital revolution, and, most of all, the information revolution.[44]

For educators that revolution will mean advanced computers, electronic books, interactive audiovisual distance learning, personally tailored multimedia curricula, and a host of other technological marvels that will profoundly transform America's schools. For the world there will be further changes, all of which will both affect our economy and provide expanded opportunities for work:

> Entirely new industries, now in their gestation phase, will be born. Such prenatal industries include microbiotics — the miniature robots built from atomic particles that could, among other things, unclog sclerotic arteries; machine translation between people conversing in different languages; digital highways into [schools and] the home that will offer instant access to the world's store of knowledge and entertainment; urban underground automated distribution systems that will reduce traffic congestion; "virtual" meeting rooms that will save people the wear and tear of air travel; biometrics materials that will duplicate the wondrous properties of material found in the living world; satellite-based personal communicators that will allow one to "phone home" from anywhere on the planet; machines capable of emotion, inference, and learning that will interact with human beings in entirely new ways; and bioremediation — custom designed organisms — that will help clean up the earth's environment.[45]

All of those markets, plus the thousands others that will appear, are areas that will drive the industry and services of the techno-information economy. They are areas in which competitive advantage may be gained and growth rates increased.[46] More important for our purposes, those markets could create the demand for millions more craftworkers and symbolic analysts. There is work to do in the future, work that will increase the demand for human labor.

To reach those new markets and create that workforce demand, America's businesses must be the first to introduce new products and services. The payoff for being first is increased market share.[47] And to develop those products and services, business must join with government to boost research and development efforts right now. However, research and development gives an advantage only when combined with the strategic foresight of top management. Executives who fail to see potential in even the most novel proposals can make terrible decisions. For example, RCA Corporation invented the liquid crystal display now used in hundreds of applications. Yet RCA executives did not pursue the discovery, and now almost all LCDs are manufactured in Japan. Xerox invented much of the technology that makes computers work well — computer workstations, networks, and graphical user interfaces — but managers passed on them to concentrate on its paper machines.[48]

When executives have that foresight, even dismal business prospects can be turned around. For example, Hughes Corporation used to be almost totally dependent on defense contracts. Its executives anticipated the end of the Cold War and decided to use the technological expertise the company had gained from defense work. Now Hughes is a leader in direct-satellite television, and the company's profits jumped 32%.

Many executives are beginning to question the wisdom of mindless re-engineering and downsizing. They still believe that re-engineering was necessary to weed out redundant tasks and make sure processes within the firm were geared toward customer satisfaction, reduced cycle time, and assurance of total quality. But re-engineering processes by themselves are not sufficient if the intent is to build and maintain a firm's future competitive advantage. Stopping the transformation processes after re-engineering actually may be a sign of senior management's ineffectiveness:

> Far from being a tribute to senior management's steely resolve or far-sightedness, [the cost of] a large restructuring and reengineering [effort] is simply a penalty that a company must pay for not having anticipated the future.[49]

Restructuring a company merely through simple-minded re-engineering techniques may, in fact, not do the company nor its shareholders any long-term good. A recent study of 16 large American corporations with at least three years of restructuring experience found that while share prices did increase, the increase was temporary. After three years, those same companies were *further* behind on growth index rates than they were when they started restructuring.[50] Simply cutting capital investment and shedding workers — what economists call a "harvest strategy"— is a dead-end street for the modern company.

Even those companies that jumped on the downsizing bandwagon seemed to be hurt by long-range trends. For example, AT&T, which had fired hundreds of thousands of their high-tech workers plus 40,000 middle managers and supervisors, experienced a stock price drop from $67 to $66. On the other hand, such corporations as Boeing that, after union protests, were forced to hire more craftworkers (5,000 more in Boeing's case) actually saw their stock prices increase — Boeing's went from $76 to $83 since the new hires.[51] Apparently even Wall Street is beginning to realize that continuation of rampant downsizing will prove self-defeating for shareholders over the long term.

The Third Way

The American jobs dilemma is growing worse. The economy continues to fail to produce new decent job opportunities for qualified craftworkers, university graduates, and symbolic analysts. Soon Corporate America will have taken downsizing too far, causing such disastrous social and economic problems that the only recourse for citizens will be political. Even now some social commentators and concerned public officials are asking: Isn't it possible for corporations to take some responsibility for the well-being of the nation? Even if only on a small scale, some American companies have already demonstrated that they can make a handsome profit while still being socially responsible.

> Is it possible for corporations to make money and still have a social conscience? Ben & Jerry's, Patagonia, and Starbucks are all small but growing corporations, but each has made an effort to respect the environment, give its workers a fair deal

by profit sharing stock options and decent wages and humane benefits, and still make a profit by emphasizing *quality* and *uniqueness*. These corporations also treat their suppliers fairly. The CEOs make reasonable salaries and are still fiercely competitive and won't hesitate to drive competitors out of business or engulf them — but that's capitalism. Better to have them rapaciously focused on competitors than on screwing workers and farmers.[52]

There is no reason, aside from unbridled greed and lack of foresight, that corporations in the United States could not practice more social responsibility. A first step would be for America's major corporations to face the fact that they should be a major part of the *solution*, just as they are part of the problem. Socially responsible corporate executives need to go beyond re-engineering and downsizing. They need to change their corporate attitude.

Notes

1. Alice M. Rivlin, *Reviving the American Dream* (Washington, D.C.: Brookings Institution, 1992), pp. 35-41.
2. Warren Bennis, "Distrust Is Fueling Workers' Rage," *Los Angeles Times*, 20 February 1996, p. B7.
3. Gary Hamel and C.K. Prahalad. *Competing for the Future* (Boston: Harvard Business School Press, 1994), pp. 73-106, 177-96.
4. Paul S. Adler, ed. *Technology and the Future of Work* (New York: Oxford University Press, 1992), pp. 5-8.
5. James Fallows, "What Is an Economy For?" *Atlantic Monthly* (January 1994): 76-92. Much of the discussion that immediately follows is based on Fallows' more extensive analysis in this article.
6. Ibid., p. 77.
7. Alfred Herrhausen Society, *Work in the Future, The Future of Work*, the Second Annual Colloquium of the Alfred Herrhausen Society for International Dialog (Stuttgart, Germany: Schaffer-Poeschel Verlag, 1994), passim.
8. Gary Bloom and Arthur Pearl, "Challenging the Assumptions About the Future World of Work," *Thrust for Educational Leadership* (February/March 1994): 12.

9. Lewis J. Perelman, *School's Out* (New York: Avon, 1992), passim.

10. Stanley Aronowitz and William DiFazio, *The Jobless Future: Sci-Tech and the Dogma of Work* (Minneapolis: University of Minnesota Press, 1994), passim.

11. Bennis, op. cit. Bennis has been a leading academic analyst of business corporations for three decades.

12. Robert A. Levy, Matianne Bowes, and James M. Jondrow, "Technological Advance and Other Sources of Employment Change in Basic Industry," in *American Jobs and the Changing Industrial Base*, edited by Eileen L. Collins and Lucretia Dewey Tanner, (Cambridge, Mass.: Ballinger, 1984), pp. 77-95.

13. Ibid., p. 94.

14. James Fallows, "Looking at the Sun: A Case of Japanese Industrial Success and American Failures that Can't Be Explained by American Economic Rules," *Atlantic Monthly* (November 1993): 69-100.

15. Eileen Applebaum and Rosemary Batt, *The New American Workplace: Transforming Work Systems in the United States* (Ithaca, N.Y.: ILR Press, 1994).

16. Charles L. Schultze, *Memos to the President: A Guide Through Macroeconomics for the Busy Policymaker* (Washington, D.C.: Brookings Institution, 1992), p. 223.

17. Ibid.

18. This term — unit labor costs — is often assumed to mean how much workers' salaries and benefits cost a company. Actually, it is the cost of capital — machinery, equipment, and the like — plus the cost of workers' wages and benefits that make up the total concept of unit labor costs.

19. Ford paid his workers $5.00 a day when other automobile companies were paying only $3.00 a day. Ford explained the difference by saying that he wanted the best workers, loyal to his company, and who would also one day be good customers — including being able to afford his cars. That attitude seems to have been lost among too many of today's executives, who feel they can shed workers with no long-range effects on consumer behavior. They are wrong, as events in 1996 have shown.

20. These areas are a paraphrase of Hamel and Prahalad's model, called "Three Phases of Competition for the Future," in Hamel and Prahalad, *Competing for the Future*, p. 47.

21. Alan W.H. Grant and Leonard A. Schlesinger, "Realize Your Customers' Full Profit Potential," *Harvard Business Review* (September-October 1995): 59-72.

22. Paul Krugman, "Does Third World Growth Hurt First World Prosperity?" *Harvard Business Review* (July-August 1994): 113-21.

23. Grant and Schlesinger, op. cit.

24. Paul Krugman, "The Myth of Asia's Miracle," *Foreign Affairs* (November-December 1994): 62-78.

25. Hamel and Prahalad, op. cit., pp. 27-48.

26. Krugman, op. cit.

27. *Business Week Special Edition* (December 1992): 164-71.

28. John P. Kotter, "Leading Change: Why Transformation Efforts Fail," *Harvard Business Review* (March-April 1995): 59-67.

29. Even though the pioneers of re-engineering, Hammer and Champy, warned against using the process simply to downsize, thousands of corporate executives ignored the message. The authors devoted several pages in the paperback edition of their book to warning executives about such practices and giving horror stories about those who ignored their advice and disrupted their businesses. See Michael Hammer and James Champy, *Reengineering the Corporation: A Manifesto for Business Revolution* (New York: Harper Business, 1993).

30. Bennett Harrison, "The Dark Side of Flexible Production," *Technology Review* (May-June 1994): 39-45.

31. Kotter, op. cit., pp. 59-67.

32. Fremont E. Kast and James E. Rosenzweig, *Organizations and Management: A Systems Approach* (New York: McGraw-Hill, 1970), pp. 60-64.

33. Susan Parks, "Improving Workplace Performance: Historical and Theoretical Context," *Monthly Labor Review* (May 1995): 21.

34. Applebaum and Batt, op. cit., p. 3.

35. "Knowledge at Work: Companies That Know How to Manage Employee Know-How," *Los Angeles Times*, 17 December 1995, pp. D1, D3.

36. Harrison, op. cit., pp. 39-45.

37. Hamel and Prahalad, op. cit., p. 128.

38. Krugman, op. cit., pp. 40-51.

39. David Moberg, "Heeding the Call," *In These Times*, 13 November 1995, pp. 20-22.

40. Joel Rogers, "Talking Union," *The Nation*, 26 December 1994, pp. 784-85.

41. A strike occurred in October-November 1995 at Boeing Corporation. The union had three major demands: a hefty wage increase (Boeing had signed three multi-billion-dollar contracts in that year); no shifting of benefit payments to workers (the company had traditionally paid for benefits); and no shifting of jobs to foreign contractors if they could be done by Boeing workers. The union won all three points, with workers getting a 6% wage increase. See "Labor Winning Some: Contract With Boeing Helps Save Aerospace Jobs in U.S.," *Los Angeles Times*, 13 December 1995, pp. D1, D3. The wisdom of that strike demand and victory was later proven when Boeing announced it was hiring 5,000 new high-tech American employees. See "Boeing Will Reportedly Add 5,000 Jobs in '96," *Los Angeles Times*, 29 January 1996, p. D4.

42. Parks, op. cit., p. 22.

43. Harrison, op. cit., pp. 39-45.

44. Hamel and Prahalad, op. cit., pp. 27-28.

45. Ibid.

46. Heinz Riesenhuber, "New Products — New Work: What Opportunities Do Research and Technology Present?" in *Work in the Future, The Future of Work*, the Second Annual Colloquium of the Alfred Herrhausen Society for International Dialog (Stuttgart, Germany: Schaffer-Poeschel Verlag, 1994), pp. 49-64.

47. Gary P. Pisano and Steven C. Wheelwright, "The New Logic of High-Tech R&D," *Harvard Business Review* (September-October 1995): 93-105.

48. "Basic Research Can Bring a Company Profit in Unexpected Ways," *Los Angeles Times*, 20 July 1995, p. D3.

49. Hamel and Prahalad, op. cit., pp. 11-12.

50. Ibid., pp. 125-26.

51. "The Layoffs Love Affair Is Cooling," *Washington Post Weekend Edition*, 4-10 March 1996, p. 21.

52. Peter Carlin, "Pure Profit," *Los Angeles Times Magazine*, 5 February 1995, pp. 12-15, 30.

Chapter Six

Work Will
Never Be the Same

The only certainty regarding the future is that it is ahead of us. All the rest is uncertainty, which applies to job projections by futurists. Futurists have had a mixed track record in predicting future jobs; generally they have been unrealistic, have extrapolated using assumptions that are too broad, or have been just plain wrong. But some futurists' prognostications, those not projecting too far into the future, provide more useful scenarios than others. For example, some futurists have realistically portrayed the influence of computer-based and information technology in the workplace, what they like to call "infotech."[1]

Futurists predict that four information technologies — computer networks, imaging technology, massive data storage, and artificial intelligence — will reshape today's occupations, become essential tools for workers, and provide the basis for work-sharing and job expansion in the next century. The best of those prognosticators also project the kind of future our students are likely to face in the 21st century. The following does not seem so fanciful an extrapolation:

> *Networks* will become indispensable for sharing and communicating information. National information highways of computer networks are in the early stages [of development]. The final step will be linking national networks to create the

global village of electronic networks, making it possible to communicate with anyone, anywhere, anytime. . . . *Imaging technology* will make information more user-friendly and will enable the rapid transmission of images, which is still a bottleneck today. . . . *Massive data storage systems* will handle the expansion of information, which will be stored electronically in readily accessible, attractive, and concise formats. This will help workers to deal with the problem of information overload. . . . *Artificial-intelligence systems*, including expert systems, knowbots, and machine vision, will become partners with workers, although sometimes they will replace workers.[2]

Infotech combines telecommunications and networking, plus the use of expert systems, imaging automation, robotics, sensing technologies, and microprocessor-embedded devices. Many of those technologies already are important today, but they will become pervasive in the 21st century world of work as businesses learn to use them more effectively. They also will become more important in our daily lives. Infotech will have even more of an effect on the future of work than it does now. It will change the nature of jobs and how workers do their jobs, affecting probably 90% of the workforce by 2010.

The influence of information technologies will not be confined to the office, where their primary effects are being felt today. Infotech is spreading across the full spectrum of workplaces. Most workers in 2010 will be primarily information workers who incidentally make widgets, sell clothes, and grow corn. The worker's primary activities will be gathering, creating, manipulating, storing, and distributing information related to products, services, and customer needs.[3]

The speculations of the futurists are interesting. Unfortunately, many educators look to these speculations as answers for the future job market. They want to believe that the positive predictions will actually happen, and their hope is that reality will not intrude on these rosy projections.

But more important questions are whether top executives believe in these predictions and, even if they do, whether their corporations will use the technology to generate sufficient numbers of decent jobs for our graduates. Put that way, the issue is not what kind of nifty futuristic occupations will replace those we have today, but *how many of them there will be*. Work-sharing and gain-sharing programs could, in theory, expand the number of decent jobs far beyond current projections. The key question is whether Corporate America can be organized so that increased productivity will make it possible for them to *afford* to hire millions more workers.

The speculations of futurists lack detail regarding how that can happen. That is the job of economists, who, in this case, are more apt predictors. What do economists see in our immediate future? Can corporations afford job expansion? Can business organizations change sufficiently to create more decent jobs? As with a lot of things, there is good news and bad news.

What Goes Down Must Come Up

Economists know that the benefits of the old economy are gone forever. In the New Economy, computer-based technology is making it possible to replace standardized, mass-produced products with high-quality, customized products. The low production costs that had driven mass production in the past depended on labor-intensive manufacturing, which can now be replicated with computer-based manufacturing. As a result, millions of jobs for unskilled workers have been eliminated by American corporations.

Through computer-aided design, engineering, and fabrication, products can be tailored to the wants of small groups of customers without much additional cost. Automobiles, magazines, even computer chips can be made to order. The real value lies in discovering who wants what and getting it to them quickly. Good jobs go to people who continuously identify unmet needs and then figure out profitable ways to meet them.[4]

> Customized products will be made as fast and as cheaply as mass-produced products. . . . The price of products will be determined not by adding up the costs of all the parts in a fin-

ished product, but by the value of the know-how and services that a company musters to assure utmost customer satisfaction. Once customers realize that agile suppliers can provide exactly what's needed on a tight schedule and eliminate the costs of maintaining inventories of parts, "price is no longer a factor, . . . It is literally the last thing discussed."[5]

In such a market, only the most informed, strategic judgments of corporate executives can identify solid trends and needs. And only the innovations of the most creative symbolic analysts and most skilled craftworkers can add the kind of value to products and services that will make them prized by businesses and individual customers around the globe.

As computer-based technology plays a larger role in the American workplace, even larger numbers of unskilled and semi-skilled workers will become redundant. Corporations intend to use technology to reduce their workforce even further, retaining a mere handful of core craftworkers.[6]

As mass production disappears and high-paying, low-skilled jobs vanish, the old middle class is following in its path.[7] Well-educated symbolic analysts — system designers, engineers, computer scientists, advertising executives, film makers, management consultants, and the like — and many craftworkers are doing reasonably well. But those with only a high-school diploma or less are hurting. Only the most menial jobs are open to them; and their real wages have been shrinking for years, with no end in sight. Even high school graduates who have no community college or vocational education are three times more likely to be unemployed than are people with college degrees.[8]

In addition, the transformation of American businesses is being accelerated by the growing economic prowess of newly industrializing countries — especially China, India, Indonesia, Korea, Malaysia, the Philippines, and Singapore. One of the most radical changes brought about by the techno-information revolution is the democratization of ideas, techniques, and processes and the instantaneous dispersal of information everywhere, including to Third World countries.[9]

Third World countries have undergone an interesting transformation over the last 50 years. Immediately after World War II, their struggle was to throw off colonial controls. Next, from 1970 to 1985, they became the source of cheap labor for labor-intensive manufacturing. However, during that same period they sent millions of their best and brightest to American, German, French, and Canadian universities to learn the latest about computer sciences, information technologies, modern manufacturing techniques, and business sciences. The small elite who had been selected for such learning returned home to become school and university teachers, training millions more of their fellow citizens. The latest phase of the radical transformation of Third World countries has been their entrance into the world of computer-based mass production. They are using their own cadres of craftworkers and the technologies from advanced industrial nations to challenge our supremacy.[10]

American companies will be able to maintain and extend their global competitive position only if they produce higher quality goods and services and use computer-based technologies and info-tech services.

The competition of Third World and other advanced industrial nations to get a piece of the global market has an enormous effect on the nature and number of American jobs.[11] For example, it is extremely unlikely that the United States will ever see the return of routine mass-production jobs, because Third World countries will be in a better competitive position for producing standardized goods; the Third World countries have both low wages and modern facilities, making them the clear winners for routine mass production. In addition, many Third World countries have developed their own cadre of symbolic analysts, who are in direct competition with those in advanced industrial nations. Even those countries as impoverished as Bangladesh now boast certain kinds of symbolic analysts — programmers, for instance — who work at a twentieth of the wages of an American doing the same job.[12] Even with America's depressed wages, they are princely sums when compared to what workers in Third World countries get.

Thus there is no chance that American businesses could compete with such low-wage, high-tech challenges in the global marketplace, nor that unskilled jobs will ever again be plentiful here. Instead, corporations will need creative symbolic analysts and high-tech craftworkers. These highly skilled knowledge workers are the hope of the future for the United States. Still, how many of them will be needed to run a high-tech economy?

While the Third World's wage/technology advantage explains part of why the remaining low-tech workers in the United States have not had a decent wage increase for more than a decade, the major reason for poorly paying jobs in the United States is the decline of labor unions. Traditionally, most business executives viewed unions as the enemy. More recently, executives have seen unions as a countervailing power bent on exposing economic inequities and resisting the transition to a New Economy. As a result, labor unions came under attack from corporate managers. Even the federal government got into the act during the 1980s, most obviously when the federal administration summarily replaced striking air controllers with nonunion people. Since then, labor unions have been fair game; and the safety net and laws that once gave labor a "level playing field" in collective bargaining collapsed. American unions peaked in the mid-1950s at nearly 40%; since then they have steadily declined. Today, only 16% of all employees are covered by collective bargaining, with 12% of them in the private sector. The United States now has the lowest union-to-nonunion ratio of any industrialized nation. Indeed, unions today represent a smaller share of American workers than before the passage of the National Labor Relations Act in 1935, the law that helped union membership soar.[13] If the current resurgence in union growth cannot stem the decline, at the current rate of decline unions may represent only 5% of private-sector workers by the year 2000.

That would not bother some business executives, those who assume that weakened unions will help stimulate economic growth. Emasculated unions, they maintain, will let them control "spiraling wages." That, they argue further, will leave more profits to invest, which will create more jobs. The argument has been that lifting the restraints of collective bargaining obligations will allow

Corporate America to move into new markets and beat companies from other industrial countries, whose workers are paid higher wages.[14] As we have seen, Corporate America did not even come close to attaining those goals. Indeed, the reverse occurred; without unions, American workers saw their wages stagnate while corporate profits soared.

Some educators, especially school administrators, do not value unions. Until the advent of interest bargaining, education administrators often were forced into adversarial bargaining roles with teacher unions and classified associations. For some, that process fostered antagonism between administrators and teachers. However, it is important for educators, as well as other Americans, to understand that labor unions were essential to maintaining a decent wage structure in the United States. There is a very close parallel between the decline of union influence and the overall decline in everyone's wages, that is, everyone except the super-rich and top executives.

During the same period in which America's corporations and government were working to reduce union influence, union membership in other advanced nations increased. With strong unions, the economies of most of those other advanced nations showed rapid economic growth — 2.7% in Germany and 3.3% in Canada, for example — while growth remained marginal at only 1.9% in the United States.[15] Instead of more jobs and new markets, Americans got de-unionization and slower growth. While other advanced industrial nations maintained their virtuous circle through high productivity and good wages, wages in the United States began to spiral downward. In addition, weak unions have been unable to counterbalance the political influence of business, which meant that the government ignored or resisted creative ways for dealing with the jobs dilemma. For the nation as a whole, the plight of the unions also turned out to be the decline of middle-class prosperity.[16]

An unanticipated consequence of the decline of unions may be *reduced* corporate productivity. According to economic analysts, unionized establishments have greater labor discipline and lower turnover, which result in more experienced and loyal workers, factors that correlate with increases in productivity. Even high-performance work organizations that purposefully initiate worker-participation programs experience greater productivity when unions are involved. Studies have shown that workers in union shops feel more free to make suggestions that challenge established ways of doing things. The evidence of attempts to involve employees and implement quality-of-life programs in even the most socially committed organizations demonstrates that those programs do not work well without workers having an independent source of power.[17]

Thus there have been a number of factors that wrecked the virtuous circle processes and caused the vast economic inequalities found in America today. But why should educators be concerned with that? Isn't that out of their bailiwick? Not really. The jobs dilemma stems in part from the educators' commitment to develop a world-class workforce. Billions are being spent and vast changes in curriculum and instruction are under way to accomplish that goal. Unfortunately, most of the graduates from our universities will be overqualified for the low-wage jobs that will be available to them. They will be overqualified simply because we pushed them to get educated for high-tech and symbolic analyst jobs. In that situation, education is certainly not an advantage for these graduates. If that is the future, educators may have to revisit their own mission. More than that, as part of their moral commitment to students and their own professional values, educators should challenge businesses and government to back up demands for world-class graduates by providing the jobs for those graduates.

Can that challenge be met? Can we expand the number of decent, well-paying jobs sufficiently to rebuild an affluent middle class, one that can fuel a renewed virtuous circle and avoid dysfunctional socioeconomic outcomes for America's youth? We already have seen that there are viable job-expansion techniques. But can business afford them? Are there really models of business organizations that need a high-quality workforce and can be productive enough to afford job-expansion programs?

The answer to those questions is an unqualified *yes*. Economists tell us that the *high-performance work organization* (HPWO) is that model. Even better, those organizations may be the real future of American business. For educators, HPWOs will affect the future workforce in two critical ways: 1) they will increase the demand for higher levels of instrumental and interpersonal competence from their workforce, and 2) they will provide millions of expanded job opportunities because they will be so productive. Those two features provide the hope and the mission for education.

And that is the good news. All we need is the commitment of business executives to the concept and a government willing to produce the scaffold both business and labor will need to accomplish job expansion, as outlined in Chapter 5. Transforming into high-performance work organizations will allow American core corporations and their business networks not only to meet global challenges but, even more important, to produce the kind of jobs here at home that will keep America prosperous for all of us.

High-Performance Work Organizations

America does not have to wait until some visionary technology is invented to begin the process of job expansion. That can be done with the technological capabilities available to Corporate America right now. Over the past decade, smart U.S. businesses have invested more than $1 trillion in the modern tools of computers and communication systems.[18] When those companies also employ high-tech craftworkers, along with the usual symbolic analysts, and make appropriate changes in how management decisions are made, they become high-performance work organizations.

Other companies will not become high-performance work organizations simply as a means for expanding job opportunities. Nor will their top management show interest because they suddenly develop foresight or strategic analysis. Instead, international competition and sagging competitive advantage will motivate corporate executives to take advantage of the strength of computers and information technology to restructure their companies and make them profitable.

211

Sharply rising competition in world and domestic markets during the past two decades put increasing pressure on U.S. firms to undertake innovations in their work systems. Management practices in some countries whose firms compete successfully against American producers differ markedly from the post-World War II organization of production in the United States. Among the alternative approaches to organizing and managing work, several are being used with apparent success: quality circles and continuous improvement in Japanese firms, worker participation in plant-level and strategic-management decisions in German companies, autonomous teams of workers who are responsible for making decisions in Swedish operations, and inter-firm networks, which are responsive to changing market conditions, in Italian and German industrial districts.[19]

Foreign firms, which had begun to transform their production systems in the 1970s and early 1980s, had by the mid-1980s gained competitive advantage in several key industries — automobiles being the most obvious. That challenge showed the ineffectiveness of the Taylor model and the limits of re-engineering. Realizing their disadvantage, some American executives initiated changes in their own companies — especially in such high-tech companies as Xerox, Hewlett Packard, and a number of others — which led to the development of high performance work organizations. In the last decade, a wide variety of other U.S. firms have borrowed organizational and process techniques from successful competitors abroad and from America's own cutting-edge companies.

The HPWO model, in distinct contrast to the Taylor model, integrates technological capability, management processes, and worker empowerment into a functional, process-oriented business organization. Since the principle of *enhanced technology* underlies their operation, HPWOs' productive strength comes from the emphasis they place on the *value-added* contributions of symbolic analysts and high-skill craftworkers.

There are 10 characteristics that distinguish an HPWO from the traditional Taylor business organizations. Preparing students to work in organizations with those characteristics should be the real aim of schools and colleges as they consider transforming their traditional programs into ones more amenable to world-class expectations:

- Technology intensiveness
- Lean production processes
- Flattened hierarchical decision-making
- Fewer middle managers/supervisors
- Multiskilled workforce
- Incentive pay, such as profit-sharing and gain-sharing
- Worker participation in decisions
- Increased workforce training
- Increased employment security
- Greater flexibility in job definition and organizational structure

The modern HPWO combines America's traditional "human resource model" and the characteristics of "lean, flexible production" to form a sociotechnical system. It is called "sociotechnical" because it combines a sensitivity toward worker needs and contributions with the most efficient computer-driven techniques — so-called lean production techniques — to achieve high productivity.[20] The key features of lean processes include computer-based technology and information systems, "just-in-time production, small inventories, short production runs, work standardization to enable multiskilled workers to do a variety of jobs, good communication between work groups, strict engineering schedules, and an expert project manager to bring closure when the work-team makes a proposal."[21] These efficiencies allow HPWOs to become very cost-competitive in both global and domestic markets.

Education is critical for HPWOs because their strengths derive from the abilities of highly skilled employees and teamwork, in addition to lean engineering and technology factors. Top executives in HPWOs know that their symbolic analysts and craft-workers are key players, adding value to products and services over and above what technology may accomplish. Obviously, symbolic analysts are important for creativity, innovation, and design;

but frontline craftworkers are critical for team production processes, converting designs into real products. They can program and run computer-based machines as well as oversee production processes, maintain quality control, and identify and solve problems. They work to focus resources, to make decisions that ensure continuous improvement, and to maintain quality control that goes far beyond the capabilities of even the most sophisticated computers.

The knowledge, skills, and attitudes it takes to be an effective worker within an HPWO should have a direct effect on how educators design and deliver curriculum and instruction in both high school and college. This is the kind of worker that our schools and colleges should be aiming to educate as we approach the 21st century.

Interestingly, two of the practices on which HPWOs are based — the human resources and lean production models — are American management innovations devised in the 1930s and 1950s. Other features were adapted from foreign models. Total quality management (TQM) and statistical control processes originated in the United States in the 1920s at Bell Labs and were a central feature of war production in U.S. companies during World War II. Others strategies, such as self-managed teams, came from Great Britain and Sweden and spread to other countries as early as the 1950s.[22]

Corporate America failed to follow up on human resource and lean production practices because Taylorist principles became the dominant theory of production and continued to dominate up through the 1970s, in spite of a number of warning signs of growing inefficiencies. However, both human resource and lean production practices were adopted and expanded by Japanese and European corporations, which still use them today.[23]

Corporate America is poised to reclaim its organizational innovations for itself. As it does, the workplace and the workforce will change radically, but not so radically that perceptive educators cannot be ahead of the learning curve. Educators can do that by preparing students for the opportunities offered by HPWOs. That means offering meaning-centered curriculum and instruction in high school. Such instruction should focus on high-order thinking processes and on other personal competencies that graduates will need to participate successfully in a high-tech society and as the foundation for further education to at least the community college level. Those competencies will be essential work skills for employees of high-performance work organizations.

Working in a High-Performance Work Organization

It will be next to impossible to get a job in an HPWO, even with job-expansion policies in place, without at least a two-year community college degree for craftworkers and, at minimum, a bachelor's degree for symbolic analysts. The demands and expectations are simply too high for those who are undereducated. Combining high technology with high-skill craftworkers and advanced management operations, for example, produces an environment that changes the nature of work and the tasks of craftworkers. Multiple tasks become the norm. Craftworkers will be expected to be lifelong learners, broadening their knowledge base as their job requirements expand. Databases for operating the new technology will expand continuously and become more complicated, often beyond even management's comprehension. Because of that, high-tech craftworkers will be empowered to decide and act independent of cumbersome chains-of-commands. In that sense, craftworkers will be given more control over their work and will gain more authority. Information, formally the exclusive domain of managers, will be readily available to all frontline craftworkers, enabling them to act on their own and take immediate action when problems arise.[24] Because of these changes, schools and colleges that do not focus instruction more clearly on higher-order thinking skills and collaborative teams, as well as basic interdisciplinary processes, will do their students a disservice.

Involving frontline craftworkers in decisions and expanding the scope of their jobs will change the relationships between supervisors and workers. The more highly automated facilities become, the more need there will be for integration and coordination of work at lower levels, pushing decision making downward to the

215

front line. Top-down decisions cannot be effective in organizations where quickness of response to market conditions makes the difference between success and failure. Thus companies will organize, as some already have, along horizontal lines of communication and decision making — a process known as "flattening the organization." A flat organization has fewer layers of management and supervision, and decision making is decentralized. In fact, to ensure continued and meaningful involvement of their high-skill workers, HPWOs will have formal "structures for the representation of workers' interests at several levels of the organization: the work unit or shop floor; intermediate levels, such as the department or establishment level; and in many instances, the strategic or corporate level."[25]

Again, for schools and colleges that means greater effort to involve students in meaningful cooperative learning and real experiences that develop interpersonal decision making and *creative* problem-solving skills. Democratic decision making, involving frontline workers along with management, will necessitate further effort by schools to have students experience such processes themselves.

While progressive high schools and postsecondary education builds a solid foundation, the education of a craftworker does not stop there. Ever-changing new technology creates situations in which highly skilled craftworkers must be ready to learn and adapt to new production conditions as they emerge. Indeed, HPWOs stay on the cutting edge by consciously becoming "learning organizations."[26] That means they have:

> the capacity or process within [their] organization to maintain or improve performance based upon experience. Learning is a systems-level phenomenon because it stays within the organization, even if individuals change.[27]

Such companies purposefully change themselves by trying out new ideas, cultivating new capabilities, and taking risks. The craftworkers and symbolic analysts within such organizations are expected to do the same so that they can produce creative solutions to newly perceived or created customer needs. Those expectations alone should have a profound effect on how we organize and present high school and college education to students. Where better than in school can students find a safe environment for trying out new ideas, conducting experiments, and developing their critical-thinking and problem-solving skills?

Finally, the income levels and wages in HPWOs are better than in other, more traditional companies. Many use ESOPs, but others simply give workers bonuses proportional to those that managers get. HPWOs get a higher return on equity than do regular companies, more than 16%; and their top executives are moving rapidly to implement more equitable bonus and other incentive programs for all employees. As one management firm said, that drive for equitable distribution of higher productivity comes in part because executives trust and value their employees more than executives do in traditional companies. That analyst said: "The key to success at high-performance companies is engaging employees in a business partnership. It will improve a company's bottom line."[28]

High-Performance Networks and Job Expansion

As America's core corporations transform themselves — or to use Mr. Gerstner's term, "re-invent" themselves — to become HPWOs, their productivity increases significantly.[29] If that same productivity is used to help defray the costs of work-sharing, it would mean adding millions of additional high-wage job opportunities for college and high school graduates.

Large companies often build alliances with smaller firms, and those alliances are a source for additional jobs. It is possible that another million jobs or so can become available through alliances formed with core corporations, or what are more accurately called *networks*.[30] The "network model"— companies with common purposes but with differing technical capabilities coming together to form mutual support groups — was a Japanese idea, the *keiretsu*.[31] Today's networks are:

> clusters, constellations, or virtual corporations, these groups
> consist of companies joined together in a large overarching

217

relationship. The individual companies in any group may differ in size and focus, but they fulfill specific roles within their group. Within their group companies may be linked to one another through various kinds of alliances, ranging from the formality of an equity joint venture to the informality of a loose collaboration.[32]

Formal network organizations are similar to a wheel, with a core corporation as the hub and the suppliers or creative firms forming the spokes. Informal networks are temporary or virtual organizations that come together to work jointly on a specific project — such as a film or the construction of a new office building — and then disband, each participating firm taking its cut of the profits.

Each of the companies forming the wheel around the hub company has a collaborative agreement for either a short-term, specific project or for a longer relationship when the product or services sold by the hub company needs the continuous creative input, specialization, or parts supplied by firms in its network.[33]

> Networks grew out a need to gain competitive advantage. In the 1950-60s U.S. companies were unchallenged in their technology, marketing skills, and ability to manage large-scale businesses. In the global environment of the 1980-90s companies all over the world have matched or approximated the achievements of those U.S. based companies. New challengers can ride the wave of new technologies and thus adapt more readily to changing market demands. It is now essential for U.S. companies to develop relationships with peers abroad — if only to remain abreast of important external developments and perhaps to influence them.[34]

All members of the network benefit through joint volume control, just-in-time production, specialization, and being able to cope with the many changes in the market. American corporate networks give HPWOs the nimbleness to compete in the global economy.[35] There also are pragmatic reasons for American business firms to be joining together into networks: the growing complexities involved in design, production, and delivery of products and services.

218

It is the rare product today that doesn't contain components incorporating wholly distinct and specialized technologies. It's the rare service today whose performance doesn't combine several specialized skills. And it is the rare business today that doesn't rely for its raw materials, marketing, or distribution on people with diverse technological or market specific skills. Finding and assembling all those assets under one roof is difficult and in some cases undesirable. Because the greatest advantages of specialization and of scale are often realized at the component rather than at the system level, companies may do best to focus on the component level while forming ties to one another in order to manage system-level interdependence.[36]

Strategic outsourcing is the practice of letting network subcontractors do part of the job involved in producing goods or services. A major reason for doing that is to shorten the time it takes to get a new product on the market. For example, an HPWO may concentrate on designing the specs for a new product and ask one subcontractor to mass produce it and another subcontractor to market it.[37] Outsourcing lets HPWOs focus on using their workers' core competencies while other expert companies contribute to their success using their own core of highly skilled craftworkers. In addition, networked companies can emulate economies of scale, an advantage that had been lost to low-wage Third World nations. That advantage is driving many companies — such as Sun Microsystems Tandom, CompuAdd, Phillips, AT&T, Prime, Matsushita, Goldstar, Hewlett Packard, and others — into mutual support alliances.

Strategic outsourcing often is supported by a concentration of businesses in a region. At the University of California at Los Angeles' Lewis Center for Regional Policy Studies, researchers are studying the means by which such industrial districts as Silicon Valley, the Southern California aerospace industry, or the agglomeration of textile firms near Florence (known as the Third Italy) achieve "external" economies of scale. Once a regional industry has begun to grow, it attracts a skilled labor force and a supporting infrastructure of city streets, expressways, and airports. Small specialty firms then may coexist with giant production houses. The scale factors can involve hundreds of thousands of workers spread over a few square miles, rather than single plants or pipelines.[38]

Networks and strategic outsourcing add to an HPWO's potential to expand jobs. The networked firms employ a great number of symbolic analysts and craftworkers to provide specialized professional capabilities that otherwise would be unavailable to the hub company or too expensive to replicate. As they grow from their association with hub corporations, their capacity to hire more craftworkers and symbolic analysts grows. Programmers, computer repair and servicing, systems analysis, unique technical skills, design work, precision assembly, and a host of other job opportunities can be created within the core corporations' networked firms. And if they also institute work-sharing and gain-sharing programs, an even greater source for job expansion is developed.

However, outsourcing to foreign networks can be a danger to America's potential for job expansion. Unfavorable transfers of technology as part of an outsource contract — such as the Boeing Corporation's recent attempt to transfer jobs to China as part of a trade agreement — not only hurts the American job situation but provides other countries with a technological edge.[39] There is also a problem with the potential "hollowing out" of American jobs as skilled, technical work is shifted to other countries, leaving only low-skilled work for Americans. For example, by not developing the light manufacturing associated with parts supply — a multi-billion dollar business — America loses a good source for job expansion. If U.S. companies bought parts from American suppliers, domestic job opportunities would open up. It is estimated that 90,000 jobs in the electronics industry alone would open in the United States if newly industrializing countries increased their purchases from the United States by just 12%.[40]

Companies in Japan and Germany provide extensive support for their local suppliers, and their governments hold them accountable for nurturing local suppliers. Hub firms in both countries are expected to buy their supplies from their network suppliers regardless of costs. In that way, the industry is strengthened. More important, network suppliers are additional sources of high-tech jobs for Japanese and German craftworkers.[41]

Corporations that become HPWOs can restore some elements of the social contract between companies and workers.[42] As the obvious productive and money-making strengths of high performance work organizations spread and more American companies transform themselves, high-skill craftworkers — professional-technical workers, machine operators, repairers, skilled troubleshooters, and similar occupations — will be especially valued. Many existing HPWOs already have established an unspoken "no layoff" policy to protect their craftworker cadre. They find ways to maintain their employees even when demand for their products or services slows temporarily. When demand exceeds normal levels, these companies often use temporary workers, but that practice could be replaced by work-sharing programs.[43]

That is just one more reason labor unions have joined the chorus of voices calling for the establishment of HPWOs. Unions see HPWOs as an opportunity to humanize the workplace and save jobs.

> There is no logical or inevitable tradeoff to be made between technological progress and the welfare of workers. But if such a choice is forced on American workers, it should come as no surprise that workers and their unions will make every possible effort to humanize technological change, to ensure that people get priority over technology and productivity and efficiency, and to make human values prevail.
>
> The long-run benefits of progress and the long-run necessity of change are easier for workers to accept if the workers know that job security and income security are protected. Workers want to share in the benefits of technological change and technological progress.[44]

If so many virtues are found in HPWOS, and they are even supported by unions, why haven't more companies transformed themselves into HPWOs? The simple answer is that harvest strategies — using computer-based technologies to shed workers and making those that remain worker harder and longer — are still being used today to make quick profits. Too often, executive myopia prevents them from understanding the long-run implications of a reduced American consumer base that will result from the impoverishment of American workers. Those same executives also apparently refuse to understand that other advanced industrial and emerging industrial nations are rapidly modernizing to steal away global customers from U.S. companies. But it is only a matter of time before either political action or economic factors, more likely both, will impel those executives to realize that traditional practices need to change.

When the decision is made, the transformation into a high performance work system will call for changes in five segments of corporate life:

1. Incorporation of technological innovation, automation robotics, and lean production techniques into all phases of production.
2. Implementation of new "flat" organizational patterns based on re-engineered organizational, operational, and management processes.
3. Participation of high-skill craftworkers and symbolic analysts in teams and in decision making.
4. Commitment to organizational learning, research and development, and continuous innovation.
5. Establishment of alliances and networks with those firms that can provide needed services and goods for the mutual support of all.

A sixth characteristic, work-sharing, has yet to be fully accepted by America's corporate executives; but such gain-sharing practices as profit-sharing and employee stock-ownership programs are a growing feature of today's medium and small businesses. Many analysts expect work-sharing to become a standard practice in the near future as unemployment and underemployment pressures build.

The 21st Century Workforce

A new workforce is emerging. The shift from routine manufacturing to HPWOs is profoundly changing how work is done. Routine production jobs are moving to other nations, and the U.S. workforce is shifting from unskilled workers in mass production to highly skilled workers in a technology-driven economy.[45]

A new workplace also is emerging. It will maximize the efficient use of computer-based technologies and information systems by skillful knowledge workers.[46] As a result, it will force workers to acquire sophisticated skills. If job-expansion practices are instituted, the need for such workers will increase by millions over the current projections of the Bureau of Labor Statistics. Unless the curricula and instruction in most schools and colleges change to meet those needs, our education system will have difficulty producing enough graduates with the required skills.

Both corporate executives and academic scholars agree that the future success of America's economy will depend on the education and skills provided to the forthcoming workforce by America's schools and colleges. As a matter of fact, business has known for some time what generic competencies will be needed. For example, a 1990 international conference at Stanford University brought together 200 business leaders and 50 researchers to study the issue of technology and work. The participants agreed that the need for "higher-skill jobs, and jobs requiring the most education and training, [is] expected to grow more rapidly than the workforce as a whole through the end of the century."[47]

The experts participating in the Stanford working conference developed a hierarchy of competencies — *doing, controlling, learning, designing, and valuing* — that sound suspiciously like the continua of knowledge and abilities that future-oriented educators advocate as the outcome of the school experience:

> The [first] layer, closest to the work itself, is "doing," the actual performance of the work task. But the performance of any task needs always to be informed by a second, higher-order layer of skill — "controlling." Some examples of con-

trolling skills are techniques like . . . SPC [statistical process control, a process demanding creative application of mathematical and computer techniques]. The third layer of skill is "learning" — the experience of stepping back from the task to reflect on it and to improve performance over time. Controlling a task is a resource for learning; it provides the data that allows the worker to recognize pattern. The true value of . . . SPC . . . is in driving this continuous learning. The fourth layer of skill is "design" — the process of innovation, or designing new systems. And, finally, the fifth layer is "valuing" — understanding how to evaluate alternative designs.[48]

The implications of the Stanford group's conclusions were clear. With the shift from mechanical equipment to computer-based and information technology, corporations needed qualitatively different workers; the unskilled and semi-skilled are out, high-tech craftworkers are in. The demands on workers in high-performance organizations contrast markedly with what traditionally has been expected of workers. For example, instead of being able to manipulate parts of a machine, the worker now must interact with symbols on a computer. Most computer-based manufacturing companies use numerically controlled machines that demand higher skills than were possessed by the traditional workforce. Today's workers must know how statistical numerical controls work and must understand other advanced technological applications, most of which involve knowledge of statistics, logic, probability, measurement systems, and even applied physics. Higher-order language arts and thinking skills also are required to enable craftworkers to analyze printed and telecommunicated information.[49] And because they will be involved more directly in teams, solving problems and participating in decisions, workers will need more sophisticated communication skills.

Unfortunately, many adult Americans are finding the implications of the move to knowledge work to be a challenge. During the Industrial Revolution, uprooted farmers were able to learn to operate machinery in factories with little trouble. But the current infusion of technology has resulted in deskilling the current crop of workers. The hundreds of thousands of industrial workers who have been laid off by giant corporations cannot move easily into new jobs without first acquiring the necessary education and skills. Even skilled workers who currently are employed will have less job security as technology changes rapidly. Indeed, constant job retraining will be as important to keeping one's job as it will be to getting a job.[50] Nevertheless, as the transformation to HPWOs proceeds, the demand for an American "world-class workforce" will be amplified even more. And that will modify the traditional configuration of the workforce.

The proportions of various occupations in the workforce also will shift by 2005. However, what that shift will entail is based on several conditions. For example, if productivity declines and companies continue to downsize, the growth in decent jobs would barely match population growth.[51] On the other hand, if job-expansion practices gain legitimacy, many more Americans, 21% of the workforce is the estimate, will be able to find jobs as craftworkers, which is more than the best projections from the Bureau of Labor Statistics. Another 25% will find work as symbolic analysts, and 10% will be executives and administrators. That means, with job-expansion policies in place, more than half the jobs in the United States by 2005 could be decent, well-paying, and stimulating jobs.

Still, even with the high-end projection, there will be many other kinds of work. In-person service workers, which traditionally have been low-wage jobs, will constitute 35% of the workforce. However, a better wage structure may emerge for these workers if gain-sharing practices, such as profit sharing and stock ownership programs, continue to grow in favor.

Finally, those who work as semi-skilled production workers, mostly in contingent, part-time jobs, will make up another 9%. The chronically unemployed and the retired will make up the rest of the adult population.[52]

It also could be that as technology does more and more intelligent work, service work may be all that is left, as Krugman only half-facetiously suggests:

It will be a very long time before we know how to build a machine equipped with the ordinary human common sense to do what we usually regard as simple tasks. So here is a speculation: The time may come when most tax lawyers are replaced by expert systems software, but human beings are still needed — and well paid — for such truly difficult occupations as gardening, house cleaning, and the thousands of other services that will receive an ever-growing share of our expenditure as mere consumer goods become steadily cheaper. The high-skill professions whose members have done so well during the last 20 years may turn out to be the modern counterpart of early 19th-century weavers, whose incomes soared after the mechanization of spinning, only to crash when the technological revolution reached their own craft.[53]

For the skilled craftworkers, education will mean more than just a high school education. Essentially, high school will be the place for developing basic, personal competencies for participating effectively in the social and civic life of the 21st century, much as an elementary education was sufficient for most people earlier in this century. However, the economic competencies needed by craftworkers will demand additional education and training in community colleges and through apprentice programs.

The education of symbolic analysts most assuredly will require not only university-level work in pragmatic areas — such as systems analyst, computer science, psychology, film production, medicine, etc. — but also wide experience before they can reach higher income levels. As the skills needed for operating new technology increase, the lifelong learning demand on high-skilled craftworkers and symbolic analysts will expand commensurately.

The transformation of manufacturing and service industries is changing the very nature of work tasks and, consequently, the skills and knowledge needed to perform those tasks. Under the old mass-production system, machinery performed a single function. Single-function machinery gave rise to single-purpose jobs. But today, computer-based technology allows business organizations to program and reprogram their machines to perform different and sometimes multiple tasks. Since processes are highly integrated and coordination of work is increasingly found at frontline levels, jobs become more general and frontline workers become more broadly skilled. Rigid craft demarcations thus are giving way to multiskilled jobs and the rise of craftworkers.[54]

Craftworker Competencies

Job-expansion programs are likely to make craftworker jobs the largest single occupational group. Thus it is important to identify the competencies that students will need to develop to get a decent job. Those competencies relate directly to the technological transformation of American corporations into high-performance work organizations. Competencies in the future will arise mostly from the high levels of responsibility and autonomy that workers will have. Workers will be responsible for managing their work stations and will need to be flexible enough to perform several tasks. Because high-performance organizations are decentralized, more emphasis will be placed on workers' frontline problem-solving and decision-making skills. They will need to adapt to new situations and respond by increasing the breadth of the skills they bring to the job. Thus self-direction will be required. And because teams will be the dominant mode for accomplishing work, workers will need to be effective team members. Thus collaborative problem solving, participative decision making, and effective group communication will be critical skills.

Computers will perform most processing functions, so craftworkers will have to be able to program and reprogram software and must be master diagnosticians. They must be able to reason and solve problems logically, since the operations of a computer, unlike those of traditional machines, are invisible.

> Workings of machines are becoming less observable. As more parts of devices become controlled by digital — as opposed to mechanical — components (thermostats, ignition systems, timers), there is less possibility to understand the

227

operation of a new device by taking it apart or observing it. For example, it is a very different task to diagnose and repair a computerized automotive ignition system than it is a mechanical one. Workers cannot view the components that are moving or being adjusted. They need to have a "mental model" of the electronic interconnections to be able to reason about the system being repaired and to carry out all but rudimentary diagnostics.[55]

Perhaps the major change will be the expectation that craftworkers participate in organizational matters usually reserved for management: quality control and organizational awareness. Craftworkers' primary charge will be to produce quality goods and services, so quality control will be their paramount focus. However, they also will be expected to learn about general corporate functioning.

Educators often hear the shrill cry that "basic skills" are what is most needed. This cry usually comes from local merchants who are fed up by the poor skills that local high school students allegedly have. But in the age of high-performance organizations, a different message should be heard. For example, unexpected priorities are revealed in some top-management focus groups.[56] When asked what competencies would make the difference between hiring, firing, or promoting an employee, the first concept mentioned by top managers was "creativity." Then came problem solving, skill in dealing with people, adaptability, innovation, and the capacity to change. Next came the typical competencies often stressed by small-business people: responsibility, teamwork, loyalty, good work habits. Only after all those other competencies were identified were "basic skills" even mentioned.

Most other research corroborates what was learned from those focus groups. The National Jobs Analysis Study, a major survey involving 12,000 workers employed in the fastest-growing occupations, was conducted by American College Testing under the aegis of the U.S. Departments of Labor and Education. That study identifies what *current employees* say are the most frequent task requirements in their daily work. Thus, rather than simply having

228

a group of experts conjure up a list of needed workforce skills, the survey's data reflect the daily experience of real employees when asked, "what do you actually do," rather than, "what do you require." Knowledge of computers, collaboration skills, and the ability to process and safeguard information were at the top of the list. Those skills involve being able to use a computer to locate, process, or communicate information; to determine priority of tasks; to collaborate with people in other departments; to judge the importance, quality, and accuracy of information; and to coordinate individual work with the activities of other workers.[57]

Many of the competencies identified for the world-class workforce have direct effects on classroom instruction. They suggest that students must learn how to "be proficient at accessing, evaluating and communicating information. . . . [Students need] to raise searching questions, enter debates, formulate opinions, engage in problem solving and critical thinking."[58] The emphasis on thinking and reasoning skills is a major requirement. Some reports advocate constructivist teaching, though they do not call it that:

> High-level process skills cannot be "taught" in the traditional sense; they cannot be transferred directly from the teacher to the learner. Students need to develop these skills for themselves, with appropriate guidance. They need to struggle with questions they have posed and search out their own answers.[59]

Craftworkers will need more than a set of narrow, situationally specific skills.[60] Instead, the workers who will be most desirable to high-performance organizations will be those with higher level, more "generic" skills and an aptitude for acquiring new skills. According to the Michigan Employability Skills Task Force:

> The changes in the social organization of work, the changing technologies used in the workplace . . . argue for increasingly stronger general or "generic" skills than have traditionally been the targets of instruction in vocational education. The generic skills referred to here are complex reasoning skills, such as the abilities to define and solve

problems, think critically, acquire new knowledge, and evaluate problem solutions. These are different from "well-defined" skills, such as memorizing the specific facts or algorithms surrounding a job.[61]

Of course, there are still the traditional personal characteristics that count in any situation, such as a strong work ethic and a willingness to take responsibility. But these are more ephemeral and do not lend themselves to training. Indeed, it would appear that work ethic, loyalty, responsibility, and such, are derived from the degree of trust workers have in their companies. The downsizing frenzy of the 1990s led many workers to the point of "working to the standard" and no more. They assumed their time would come, so why break their backs for a company that did not care about them? In high-performance work organizations, however, motivation, work ethic, and loyalty are encouraged when the firms not only "talk" employee empowerment but actually establish organizational means that guarantee worker empowerment.

Regardless of those new responsibilities, computer skills remain at the heart of the new craftworker competencies. Frontline high-skill workers are taking responsibility for programming or reprogramming computer-controlled machines.

> Since programming a robot is not difficult, many companies find it makes sense to retrain production workers as programmers. This is particularly true in walk-through teaching of robots, but even off-line programming may be within the ability of workers. Their knowledge of the operation . . . may make them better on the job. Similarly, many robot technicians are being trained in two-year colleges [but even then] companies are finding it more expedient to retrain present workers.[62]

Craftworkers are also involved with the repair and maintenance of computers, a skill they need because computer technology is complex and subject to breakdown. When out of commission, trained workers can make repairs or adjustments themselves, thus maintaining more efficiency and less downtime when something goes wrong. Those workers also are trained to diagnose problems and do preventive maintenance. As a matter of fact, a new craft-worker category — operator-maintenance — increasingly is found in companies. Quality circles help teams of workers identify ongoing maintenance problems and work to eliminate them.[63]

From whatever angle one views it, the defined needs of craft-workers fit what leading education spokespersons and practitioners have been advocating for today's classrooms: a primary focus on thinking and problem solving, a learning environment that is infused with technology so that students are genuinely and actively involved in learning, and instruction that is responsive to the multiple learning styles of students.[64] For teachers, it means a classroom that uses authentic assessment methods, integrates disciplines, has a curriculum that is project-based, and employs constructivist pedagogy.[65] Further analysis of work tasks in high-performance organizations will help educators incorporate more specific knowledge and skill elements into high school and university curricula.

Most proposals for the new workplace separate competencies into two or three groups, primarily because that is the way SCANS did it. "Basic" skills are fundamentals, learnings any graduate should have — reading, writing, mathematics — but in this case the stress is on *application* of those skills, not concepts or rote. Most academics agree that to be successful in the new workplace, workers will need to move beyond mastery of the basics to "complex reasoning" skills. If workers are expected to identify and solve problems, they need reasoning and problem-solving skills. If they are going to program and reprogram numerically controlled machines, they will need logic, geometry, and arithmetic applications. If they are going to be effective members of teams, they will need good communication and planning skills. If they are going to be involved in quality control and assessment, they will need to know how to apply benchmarks and use evaluation skills. In addition to those generic skills and abilities, workers will need domain-specific skills appropriate to the specific responsibilities of their jobs. But even those will be interpreted broadly, so that workers will be multiskilled, able to cover many different phases of an operation and to fill in as a team member.

To stay competitive, workers will be required to adapt to new working conditions that demand much higher levels of involvement in setting goals and organizing work. Craftworkers will need to cooperate with both fellow workers and management, to communicate effectively, to identify problems and formulate effective solutions, and to think critically about decisions that will affect the operations of their companies. These skills once were thought to be the domain of only white-collar supervisory employees.

Tomorrow's Workforce

An article in a leading business magazine reflects the growing awareness of the technological revolution:

> Technology's starkest feature is its [rapid growth]: Today, the power of a personal-computer microchip doubles every 18 months. Our ability, as a nation, to maintain and build wealth depends in large part on the speed and effectiveness with which we invent and adopt machines that lift productivity. Such a relationship has been a given throughout the Industrial Age.[66]

Most analysts agree. Change will continue into the future. Technological innovations will further the trend toward fewer humans and more machines doing the work. There will be a closer symbiosis between machine and worker. Technology also will affect how managers do their jobs. Over the next decade, managerial performance will be based less on the ability to direct and coordinate work functions and more on improving key work processes.

> The dynamic organization recognizes the need for continuous improvement to meet changing customer requirements and competitor actions. In such organizations, managers will be increasingly judged on their ability to identify and implement improvements and to encourage innovative thinking from team members, while professionals will be judged on their ability to adapt quickly to widely different work environments.[67]

As symbolic analysts, teachers' roles will be transformed by information technology. They will help students tap into educational programs customized for their particular needs. The teacher will design databases for students that incorporate computers, interactive software, distance learning, video, educational television programs, and artificial intelligence. Teachers will facilitate learning. Teachers will act as intermediaries between students and the world of information, helping students draw on resources around the globe. Using those technologies, teachers will design learning environments that will personalize instruction and accommodate wide variations in learning styles and interests.[68]

As technology allows Americans — and people from other advanced industrial nations — more leisure time and relief from work, service jobs will grow more important in their lives. There will be a constantly growing demand for all services connected to vacations and holidays — travel agents, hotel employees, waiters, trainers, recreation personnel, and the like. As the public and private infrastructure is rebuilt, hundreds of thousands of construction workers will be needed; and they, in turn, will need more fast-food outlets, gasoline stations, retail stores, and other support services, which employ cooks, servers, attendants, clerks, and a host of other in-person services. Retirees not only will be seeking retirement services but also will be developing new avocational interests that will expand the need for consultant and expert services. As the population ages, the elderly will need more health aides and other health service workers. Even moderate projections by the Bureau of Labor Statistics show an increase of more than 6.4 million *new* service jobs by 2005.[69] With gain-sharing and other job-expansion programs in place, that number of service workers could easily double.

The increasing demand for in-person services could increase wages for those workers, especially if unions succeed in organizing service workers. Some of that increase will come from profit-sharing plans, which reward service employees for increased productivity. Productivity, in this case, is measured almost strictly by indicators of consumer satisfaction, such as increased patronage of the service.

Take, for example, one service area: resort hotels. When a vacation resort employs a large number of service workers to provide the most exquisite personal experiences — the best food, the most well-kept rooms, etc. — patronage will increase. As it does, profits will increase; employers who realize their dependence on their service workers will institute generous profit-sharing plans. Indeed, as any service improves, patronage will increase; and the resultant profits can be shared. In that way, all wages for service jobs will increase, making those workers part of the new middle class who regenerate a new virtuous cycle in the economy.

The key to it all will be an education broadly defined to attend to the multiple personal and social needs of high school and university students. Assuming that schools and teachers will continue to perform their primary mission of educating the whole child, not simply the economic child, how will those expectations be filled by schools? Must schools be transformed further to meet the ever-increasing task of educating young people? Those issues are explored next.

Notes

1. For example, a contemporary automobile is filled with microchips, monitoring its functions. These become the source of information for mechanics when the car is in the shop for service. Microprocessors also are found in most modern appliances, as well as in sophisticated numerically controlled machines.
2. Andy Hines, "Jobs and InfoTech: Work in the Information Society," presentation to World Future Society, General Assembly, Washington, D.C., 27 June - 1 July 1993.
3. Ibid.; see also *The Futurist* (January-February 1994): 9-13.
4. Robert B. Reich, "Meet the New Middle Class," *Los Angeles Times*, 27 March 1994, p. M5.
5. Ottis Port, "Custom-Made Direct from the Plant," *Business Week Special Edition*, 18 November 1994, p. 158.
6. "March Layoffs Up 11% Even as More Jobs Created," *Los Angeles Times*, 9 April 1996, pp. D1, D12.
7. Richard Rothstein, "New Bargain or No Bargain?" *The American Prospect* (Summer 1993): 32-47.

8. Lawrence Mishel and Jared Bernstein, *The State of Working America, 1994-95* (Armonk, N.Y.: M.E. Sharpe, 1994), pp. 140-44.

9. Paul Krugman, "Technology's Revenge," *Wilson Quarterly* 18 (Autumn 1994): 56-64.

10. Ibid.

11. Ibid.

12. "The New World of Work," *Business Week*, 17 October 1994, pp. 76-93.

13. Commission on the Future of Worker-Management Relations, *Fact Finding Report* (Washington, D.C.: U.S. Departments of Labor and Commerce, May 1994), pp. 2-24.

14. Rothstein, op. cit.

15. Organisation for Economic Cooperation and Development, *Employment Outlook* (July 1994), p. 8.

16. Rebecca Blank, "Does a Larger Social Safety Net Mean Less Economic Flexibility?" in *Working Under Different Rules*, edited by Richard B. Freeman (New York: Russell Sage Foundation, 1994), pp. 157-87.

17. Richard Rothstein, "Productivity Forever," *The American Prospect* (Summer 1993): 35-37.

18. Roy B. Helfgott, *Computerized Manufacturing and Human Resources* (Washington, D.C.: Industrial Relations Counselors, 1988), pp. xvii-xviii, 1-10.

19. Eileen Applebaum and Rosemary Batt, *The New American Workplace: Transforming Work Systems in the United States* (Ithaca, N.Y.: ILR Press, 1994), p. 12.

20. Ibid., pp. 6-8, 123-45.

21. Michael A Cusumano, "The Limits of Lean," *Sloan Management Review* (Summer 1994): 27-32.

22. Applebaum and Batt, op. cit., pp. 3-13.

23. Ibid., pp. 123-45.

24. Helfgott, op. cit., pp. 68-69. It appears that some managers resist this change. They believe that "information" is a way to control a situation and are reluctant to relinquish it to high-tech workers.

25. Applebaum and Batt, op. cit., 3-13.

26. For more on learning organizations, see Anne G. Perkins, "The Learning Organization," *Harvard Business Review* (March-April 1995): 10; and Edwin C. Nevis, Anthony J. DiBella, and Janet M. Gould, "Understanding Organizations as Learning Systems," *Sloan Management Review* (Winter 1995): 73-85.

27. Nevis, DiBella, and Gould, op. cit.

28. These data came from a survey of corporations that recently had redesigned themselves to match the attributes of HPWOs. See "Corporate America Is Changing How It Thinks About Pay, Survey Finds," *Los Angeles Times*, 24 August 1996, p. D3.

29. Two-thirds of those corporations that recently have converted report higher profits and productivity than before "re-invention." See *Los Angeles Times*, 24 August 1996, p. D3.

30. Rosabeth Moss Kantor, "Collaborative Advantage: The Art of Alliance," *Harvard Business Review* (July-August 1994): 96-108.

31. "Keiretsu Connections," *Business Week*, 22 July 1996, pp. 52-54.

32. Benjamin Gomes-Casseres, "Group Versus Group: How Alliance Networks Compete," *Harvard Business Review* (July/August 1994): 63.

33. Kantor, op. cit., pp. 96-108.

34. Gomes-Casseres, op. cit., pp. 62-74.

35. "The Agile Factory: Custom-Direct from the Factory," *Business Week Special Edition*, 18 November 1994, pp. 158-59.

36. Gomes-Casseres, op. cit., pp. 63.

37. James Brian Quinn and Frederick G. Hunter, "Strategic Outsourcing," *Sloan Management Review* (Summer 1994): 43-55.

38. Gary Stix and Paul Wallich, "Is Bigger Better?" *Scientific American* (March 1994): 109.

39. *Business Week*, 27 November 1995, p. 46.

40. David Friedman, "America's Industry Being Hollowed Out," *Los Angeles Times*, 30 April 1995, pp. M1, M6.

41. Ibid.

42. One popular economic writer predicts that craftworker wages will shortly grow larger, because demand for their services will be increasing as companies find it necessary to "up-size." James Flanigan, "An Economy Pushed Along by Boomers," *Los Angeles Times*, 31 March 1996, pp. D1, D4.

43. Helfgott, op. cit., pp. 51-53, 68-69.

44. Markley Roberts, "A Labor Perspective on Technological Change," in *American Jobs and the Changing Industrial Base*, edited by Eileen L. Collins and Lucretia Dewey Tanner (Cambridge, Mass.: Ballinger, 1984), p. 197.

45. Willard Daggett, "The Skills Students Need for Success in the Workplace," *California Catalyst* (Fall 1993): 4-13.

46. *The EQW National Employer Survey, First Findings* (Philadelphia: Center on the Quality of the Workforce, University of Pennsylvania, nd), pp. 1-3. The survey data indicate that 56% of firms participating have increased skill demands as a result of technological innovation.

47. Larry Hirschhorn and Joan Morkay, "Automation and Competency Requirements in Manufacturing: A Case Study" in *Technology and the Future of Work*, edited by Paul A. Adler (New York: Oxford University Press, 1991), p. 24.

48. Paul Attewell, "Skill and Occupational Changes in U.S. Manufacturing," in *Technology and the Future of Work*, edited by Paul A. Adler (New York: Oxford University Press, 1991), p. 80.

49. Daggett, op. cit., pp. 4-13.

50. *Los Angeles Times*, 10 December 1995, pp. D1, D11.

51. George T. Silvestri, "Occupational Employment: Wide Variations in Growth," *Monthly Labor Review* (November 1993): 59.

52. These figures are adapted from estimates in Fred Best, *Reducing Workweeks to Prevent Layoffs* (Philadelphia: Temple University Press, 1988); George T. Silvestri, "Occupational Employment: Wide Variations in Growth," *Monthly Labor Review* (November 1993): 59; and the more pessimistic numbers from Robert B. Reich, *The Work of Nations* (New York: Vintage, 1991), pp. 171-84.

53. Paul Krugman, "Technology's Revenge," *Wilson Quarterly* (Autumn 1994): 64.

54. Helfgott, op. cit., pp. 68-69.

55. Matthew W. Lewis, "Emerging Uses of Computers for Education: An Overview of Tools and Issues for Vocational Educators," National Center for Research in Vocational Education, University of California-Berkeley (Santa Monica, Calif.: RAND, 1992), pp. 1-66.

56. Ibid.

57. Peter West, "Skills Needed to Succeed in Workplace Outlined," *Education Week*, 15 November 1995, p. 9.

58. Lewis, op. cit.

59. Kyle L. Peck and Denise Dorricott, "Why Use Technology?" *Educational Leadership* (April 1994): 12.

60. Sandra L. Miller, "A Delphi Study of the Trends or Events that Will Influence the Content of Curriculum and the Technological Delivery of Instruction in the Public Elementary School in the Year

2005," Doctoral dissertation, University of Michigan, Ann Arbor, 1995.

61. Lewis, op. cit., p. 2.
62. Helfgott, op. cit., 71.
63. Ibid., p. 74.
64. Daggett, op. cit., pp. 4-13.
65. Terrence R. Cannings and LeRoy Finkel, eds. *The Technology Age Classroom* (Wilsonville, Ore.: Franklin, Beedle & Associates, 1993), pp. 88-89.
66. "The New World of Work," *Business Week*, 17 October 1994, pp. 76-93.
67. Robert Barner, "The New Millennium Workplace: Seven Changes that Will Challenge Managers and Workers," *The Futurist* (March-April 1996): 16.
68. Robert Barner, "The New Career Strategist," *The Futurist* (September-October 1994): 10.
69. Silvestri, op. cit., pp. 56-84.

Chapter Seven

The Schools We Have

Universities already are adapting their areas of study and majors to meet the requirements for many symbolic-analyst positions — systems analysts, computer scientists, financial analysts, computer engineers, technology-smart business managers, and other jobs. But if job-expansion practices are instituted, the highest demand in the workforce will be for craftworkers. Thus schools must graduate men and women with higher-level thinking skills who can program and reprogram computer-driven machines, address sophisticated problems, and come up with creative solutions. These graduates also must be good communicators, team members, and participants in critical decisions.

For some high school educators, the increased demand for craftworkers presents an exciting challenge, one they are eager to confront. For some others, however, there is trepidation, either because they see potential institutional inadequacies or because they are themselves reluctant to do something new. But perhaps the majority of high school educators are blasé; they believe that the high schools we have now are doing the job or, at most, that any weaknesses can be easily remedied.

Not many independent analysts believe that today's high schools have the curricula, instruction, and organizational patterns that fit the educational needs of future symbolic analysts and craftworkers. These critics argue that the traditional patterns of programs, schedules, courses, and tests — as well as a singularly pervasive mode of teaching — in most high schools today are inappropriate for our future needs. The apparent mission of those schools is to process students through those patterns until they have accumulated sufficient seat time and test scores to pass to other experiences — college and work. Successful students are those who perform the rituals expected of them by that system and, depending on their native talent, can be graduated with their dignity intact.

Teachers in the system have mixed feelings. Teachers typically are divided between those who find little problem with lengthy textbooks, curriculum guides, lists of objectives (many of which never get met), course outlines, and multiple-choice tests, and those who try to do something about the boredom and rote behavior of even the brightest of students. The more creative teachers try to use interesting material, have more teen-related assignments, use multimedia presentations, and otherwise try to liven up a deadening (at least for teenagers, whose body juices are running hot much of the time) textbook and lecture approach. When these patterns do not work, the solution is usually to do more of it — more time in a day, more days in the year, more core courses, more difficult texts, more repetition of coursework (for example, U.S. history in grades 5, 8, and 11), more homework, more finite division of students into "advanced," "honors," "general," and "special" or "continuation." As Linda Darling-Hammond puts it, "There are no problems of practice in this view. There are only problems of implementation."[1]

A small cadre of dissident teachers has learned that most of the basic pedagogy that passes for high school teaching is little different — except in the size of the textbooks and the use of movies — from that which scholastics offered students in medieval times. Many of those teachers are attempting to buck the system or are joining the faculties of private alternative schools or the few progressive public high schools found scattered throughout the United States. That may gain them some personal relief from the basic anti-intellectual atmosphere of traditional high schools, but it does little to relieve the disengagement and alienation that many high school students experience as they pass through their four years. In a large sense, almost no one really wants to rock the boat — except for a few thoughtful principals, teachers, concerned university educators, and district-level professionals who know full well the discrepancies between what is and what should be. And certain business leaders see the gap between what high school graduates can do and what businesses need them to do.

Despite many of the charges leveled against high schools, there is little problem with their academic outcomes. And amazingly, most parents are satisfied with their child's high school experience, as long as they feel that the school is moving their child through the process and onto bigger objectives — such as work and college. Many parents also enjoy the vicarious reliving of their own high school experiences — since they do not have to put up with the drudge part of it — and often are active participants in high school activities. Students, too, at least those who come from supportive middle-class families and are fairly successful at getting decent grades, blithely move through their paces.

But there is something wrong with today's high schools and that wrongness clearly relates to the huge discrepancy between what is taught and how it is taught. What is taught is often irrelevant for anything except earning credits toward graduation. How it is taught too often has little to do with how humans actually come to know something.

This chapter explores what is going on in high schools today. The next chapter examines what they should be doing. This critique of the schools is not a facile repetition of their supposed academic failures. Instead, it focuses on their meaninglessness — except for extracurricular activities — in the lives of students and their preparation for the exigencies of 21st century living. Consider Sara and Bill Jacobson.

A Day in the Life

Sara Jacobson is 17 years old; Bill Jacobson is 15. Both are in high school. Sara is a senior; Bill is a sophomore. Both come from a family that lives in a modest tract house in the suburbs. Their mother and father both work and earn a comfortable income as skilled craftworkers. They are not pinching pennies, but they are not so affluent that they can engage in frivolities. Both Sara and Bill are planning to attend college, probably a state college; but Sara has been frantically applying to private universities, especially in the Northwest, hoping she will get a scholarship in music. Just now, Sara and Bill are off to school and have just climbed onto the school bus for the five-mile ride to Emerald High School.

Emerald High is a Blue Ribbon School. That means it has been recognized for high achievement resulting from its forward-looking curriculum and instruction. It has a number of Advanced Placement classes, even more honors classes, and a full tech-prep program for those not bound (at least not directly) for a four-year college. For the occasional nonconformist student, a small continuation high school is just two miles away, tucked into a corner of the district office's parcel. The faculty at Emerald is stable, with an average tenure of 16 years; and most of the teaching staff have master's degrees. The principal, Dr. Rebecca Taylor, has been an administrator in the district for 14 years and was a teacher for seven years before that. She is a firm disciplinarian, but her amiability with students makes them comfortable with her, especially during sports events when she is dressed in casual clothes. As is her usual practice, this morning she is on duty, monitoring the arrival of the bused students.

Sara and Bill do not sit near each other on the bus, nor do they even acknowledge each other's presence. Being different ages is a yawning social chasm between them when they are in public. In the noisy bus, Bill is talking loudly to a friend from his chemistry class: "Did you get the homework done, Tim? I got dragged to a party last night and, as usual, I didn't get it done. It was lame, anyway. So whatcha got?" Tim is the reluctant resident scholar in chemistry, because he seems to have a knack for it.

"What's it worth to ya, dude?" he smiled and waved a sheaf of notebook papers in his hand.

"Whoa, you mean you want something! Didn't I fix you up with Barbara for the homecoming dance? Come on, you owe me,"

Bill replied. And after some more jocular remarks, Tim hands him the homework, which Bill proceeds to copy furiously. By the time he is finished, the bus is pulling into the drive and the students are standing, ready to jump off as soon as the bus doors open, regardless of the driver's protest not to stand while the bus is moving.

Patrolling just near the bus, Dr. Taylor passes by the bus door as the rowdy students pile off. "Hold it right there, Mike," she commands to one of them. "Try walking like a decent human rather than an orangutan in heat." The other kids laugh as Mike slows to a more leisurely pace. Dr. Taylor then spots Sara as she is exiting the bus and calls to her, "Sara, please come here for a moment." And Sara walks up to her.

"Yes, Dr. Taylor?"

"I talked with Miss Hennessey this morning and she wanted to remind you that cheerleader practice is at 3:00 today, not 2:30. She has a short faculty meeting to go to first," Taylor informed Sara.

"Thanks, Mrs., I mean, Dr. Taylor," Sara said as she hurried off to catch up with her friends, who had walked ahead. The homeroom period chime (no bells) had just sounded.

Homeroom is just a holding tank for taking attendance and listening to announcements over the public address system. Emerald had received a grant to install closed-circuit televisions, so announcements were beamed into each classroom. First, a nervous-looking student leads everyone with the pledge of allegiance.

Afterward, a girl in a funny costume does a hip-hop routine while reminding everyone that the sophomore dance is coming soon. She is followed by an enormous boy, who haltingly announces the scores and standing of the Northrup League basketball teams. When he reports that the "Green Devils" (Emerald's nickname) trounced a rival team, shouts of pleasure can be heard filtering out of each of the classes.

Next comes a neatly dressed man that everyone recognizes as the activities director. He is so gushingly pleasant with students that some of his colleagues accuse him of never having mentally left high school. He proceeds to describe the pep rally to be held later and reminds students to wear the green ribbons passed out earlier in the morning.

"What green ribbons?" a girl yells. "I didn't get a ribbon. Did you, Marsha?"

"Who cares," several students reply.

"Hold on there," says the homeroom teacher, Mr. Holmes, who also is the chemistry teacher. He takes a bunch of green ribbons from his desk and hands them to a girl in the front row to pass around. A few students take a ribbon, the rest ignore them.

The final announcement comes from the head counselor. "All seniors who have requested transcripts for college applications must see me today or tomorrow. I have some important information for you. Also, remember that the first round of the SATs is Saturday. If you have signed up and paid your fees, make sure you arrive at 7:30, because they will start without you if you're not on time."

With that, the screen goes blank, the chimes sound, and everyone traipses to their first-period class. Bill stays, because chemistry is his first class. After everything settles down, Mr. Holmes calls for silence and proceeds to give a lecture on the composition of the atom. As he lectures, he occasionally pops a question to the class.

"What did I say made up the nucleus, Dave?" When Dave does not reply quickly enough, Holmes says, "Anyone?" and looks around the room. When no one volunteers, Holmes starts re-explaining electrons and protons, making squiggly circles and drawing on the blackboard to illustrate his point. Near the end of the period, he announces that the test is on Friday and asks the students to take out their homework for review. Bill was hoping he would not be called on, since he has not memorized the homework he copied from Tim.

But Holmes never gets the chance to ask anyone beyond the first student. That student had misunderstood the assignment, and Holmes reminds the class that they have to listen more carefully. Then the chimes ring, and everyone picks up their backpacks and moves on.

For Friday's multiple-choice test, Bill plans to study only the material on the atom. He figures, correctly, that Holmes' test will concentrate on that topic. Bill knows that Holmes will be on a new topic by Monday.

Bill then goes to band practice, where he plays the tuba. Last week the music teacher handed out new music and asked the players to be ready to play it today. Bill had spent more time than ever learning the music because the tuba part was complicated and had a big solo. He did it over and over, criticizing himself whenever he made a mistake, moving to a new part only after he had mastered the troublesome part. After many hours and a few days, he was pretty sure that he knew the music fairly well. Now, if those darn freshmen had practiced, they all could play the piece today. But the freshmen hadn't practiced, and the music teacher took most of them aside for more work. Before he starts working with the freshmen, the teacher asks Bill:

"Bill, will you take the freshmen tuba section and help them? You have the music down pat, but they need work." Bill is ecstatic and undertakes his tutoring task with glee.

In the meantime, Sara is just finishing up her last class before going to her counselor. The last class is her favorite, an elective English class that has her editing and writing for the school newspaper. Because she is an honor student, Sara has been given free reign to do everything from copy editing, mock up, and other fundamentals to actual serious writing. The only time she checks with the teacher is when she runs into a particularly perplexing situation, which is not often. Sara especially likes the teacher because she works to solve problems with Sara, rather than simply lecturing or giving canned solutions. Sara revels in the freedom and the hard work of doing something on her own.

When Sara gets to the head counselor's office she is ushered into a large office with six other seniors. The counselor, Miss Farnsworth, tells them: "I just wanted to let you know that, as you review your transcripts, be sure that the courses you have taken meet the admission criteria. The state universities have announced that they will take only the top 30% of the graduating class, so you'll want to double-check the computer printout, because sometimes a mistake can happen. If that is the case, make an appointment to see your grade-level counselor to see if any mistakes can be corrected."

Sara finally gets to cheerleading practice. Miss Hennessey is coaching the 15 girls and four boys that make up the cheerleading troupe.

"Millie, look, do it like this," Hennessey instructs a girl how to pirouette in a 360-degree turn. The girl tries again, and Hennessey encourages her: "Keep working at it. You're getting it." She then turns to the other cheerleaders and asks them to run their drills.

As they run drills, Sara has a bright idea. "Miss Hennessey, how about if we tried this?" and she turns and does a flip, landing at Hennessey's feet, perfectly placed for audience viewing.

"That's great, Sara. Let's put that in the routine. Okay, everybody, Sara has something to show us." Sara demonstrates again, and the others begin emulating her moves.

On the bus home, Sara is really excited as she talks to her friends. "Then I showed Miss Hennessey what I'd been practicing all weekend at home, and she liked it and had everyone else learn how to do it! I just love cheerleading . . ." and she goes on bubbling about it and her experience.

Meanwhile, Bill sits with Tim on the way home. "Whoa, was I lucky not to get called on in chemistry. I knew squat about the homework or what he was saying. But I guess I'll do all right as long as I can cram for the test on Friday."

He did and got a B-. Sara took her SATs and scored 650 quantitative and 665 in verbal. Three of her friends, those who were not in honors classes but studied hard anyway, did not score high enough this time for college standards. They will take the SATs again and again to get their scores up.

Bill and Sara's parents go to the basketball game on Monday. Sara's mom pays more attention to the cheerleaders and Bill playing his tuba in the reduced version of the band playing at the game than she does to the game itself. At halftime her husband shoots from the free-throw line to try to win a prize, but he barely loses to his competitor. As they drive home that night after the game, the parents talk about Emerald and how pleased they are.

"What a great school," the mom says. "I hope they know this is the best time of their lives. They seem so happy. Sara was beside herself that Miss Hennessey thought her new move was so great and included it in the routine."

"Yeah," says her husband, "Bill really enjoys band, but I worry a little about his academics. I mean, it won't be long before he applies to college like Sara."

"Oh, he'll be all right. I talked with Dr. Taylor the other day when I was attending her advisory committee, and she feels he is coming around and will get pretty good grades."

"I hope so. I read today that schools are really going downhill. I'm sure glad our kids have Emerald and don't have to go to one of the lousy schools," her husband replies.

The Schools We Have

Sara and Bill's parents are pleased; they worry only about schools in general, not about their own children's school. Their children do what is expected of them in class and find, as Bill did, alternative ways to meet teachers' expectations. Most of the real pleasure Sara and Bill find in school comes from their extracurricular activities — except for Sara's newspaper work. The only real teaching came from Sara's cheerleading coach and newspaper mentor, who modeled what they thought was good and encouraged students to try new things on their own, and from Bill's music teacher, who encouraged teamwork by giving Bill a "first-among-equals" team role.

This tale would sound familiar to any educator who worked in any high school 40 years ago or, unfortunately, in high schools today — they have hardly changed at all in that time except to decrease electives. Because of that, American high schools' curricula are remarkably similar. Almost all now offer only academic core subjects and extracurricular activities, but little fine arts or vocational experiences. Some have tech-prep programs and school-to-work, designed mostly for those students who feel they are not going to college. The standard five- or six-period day still predominates, though a few high schools are experimenting with block schedules.[2] In a typical high school day today, or 30 years ago, students are exposed to one version or the other of science, English literature, mathematics, history or other social studies, physical education, and a limited selection of electives, usually one of the arts, music, foreign language, tech prep, or some other non-core curriculum subject. The goal in high schools also has remained the same over the years: collect sufficient credits for students to graduate and expose students to the content of various watered-down subjects (perhaps with the exception of Advanced Placement college-level courses).

That ritual and rite of passage called high school education actually contributes to the development of a two-tier workforce by narrowing the career potential of some students and perpetuating low/high income inequalities. The myth of high schools as a place where all students are prepared equally for a chance at the good life is just that, a myth. In reality, for most students that chance never materializes. Why is that? Two reasons predominate: 1) the tendency for high schools to sort out what their staffs believe are college-bound from non-college-bound students, and 2) the irrelevance of the high school subject-matter, discipline-based curriculum. In addition, the overwhelming use of the "lecture-test-lecture" form of instruction is totally antithetical to how people come to know something, that is, it is antithetical to real learning.

For more than 40 years, the main job of high schools has been *sorting* students. The diversity of high school students' abilities, backgrounds, language, and ethnicity is dealt with in most schools by various "tracking" systems. Tracking is the process of structuring courses so that they match the perceived abilities and interests of different students, which is a means for sorting students into those who are capable of going to college, those who will need to get a job, and those who are judged incorrigible and sent elsewhere (continuation high school). The ostensible rationale for tracking sounds as if it is rooted in educator concern: "We are tying to meet individual needs" or "We don't want to slow down the brighter students." However, the unspoken reason is to establish a two-tier high school: one tier designed for those who obviously will be going to college, following a path similar to that taken by most of their teachers, and the second for everybody else. In that system, the best teachers teach the upper-tier kids; the average or poor teachers teach the rest.

More than 86% of high schools find a way to differentiate certain classes in terms of content, the intensity of the work, and the level of expectation for students. State and local school boards determine the approach a high school takes to tracking in 59% of the cases. But principals, too, have influence, with 47% of them able to determine how courses will be differentiated. In some cases, even parents may determine how students with different abilities will be taught.[3]

Currently, about 15% of schools follow a traditional policy of strict tracking for differentiated student groups. Thus a college-bound student is counseled into and tracked through a series of "honors" classes. Most schools are more "democratic." They still have differentiated courses; but they allow a student to take any course, provided the student has successfully met the prerequisites. In those classes, there is an opportunity to move from one track to another, depending on performance. Only 14% of high schools offer undifferentiated courses and allow any student access as long as prerequisites have been met.[4]

Rigid tracking does not allow students, even if they have demonstrated their superior abilities, to move from a lower track to a higher track. Less than half the schools (48%) even have some provision for moving students or letting them move of their own self-determination with counselor approval, but only 14% said that happened very often. On the other hand, moving from a high track to a lower track happens often, with 50% of the schools reporting that students are moved to lower-ability courses in math and 39% are moved in English. Only 16% of the schools said they never moved students.[5]

There is only a very slight chance that a student might get into a high-level course on his or her own, regardless of how confident the student may feel. Usually, entrance to a higher-level course is determined by teacher recommendations, the prerequisites taken by the student, and by the student's previous grades. Of course, if a student is being tracked, getting into even the prerequisite courses is nigh onto impossible.

A student who is tracked into the upper-level classes in one subject also is likely to be in upper-level courses in other subjects. For example, more than three-quarters of 10th-graders assigned to higher-level math classes are also in high-ability English classes.[6] The result of this differentiation is that certain students tend to get the best teachers and the more-challenging courses. The students in those classes are those most apt to get into college and most apt to become symbolic analysts in the workplace. Thus the track in which a student is placed greatly determines the life path of that student.

It is no coincidence that the two-tier system feeds right into the economy's two-tier workforce. Counselors help steer students onto the "correct" path. Families from lower socioeconomic backgrounds who do not have enriched environments at home may never make it to honors and AP classes. Indeed, it is a common practice to group minority and poor kids into lower tracks and keep them there. As one analyst puts it:

> The formal ritual of tracking and the informal clustering of cliques . . . inform students of the stratified society and their own comparative worth. . . . Students from lower socioeconomic backgrounds have inferior school experiences. . . . High- and low-income students were segregated in virtually all aspects of daily life. They lived in separate neighborhoods and had attended neighborhood elementary schools. Elementary schools in low-income neighborhoods were more likely to be housed in old buildings with small, poorly equipped playgrounds. Additionally, the most professional principals and competent teachers were assigned to high-income schools, while low-income schools were likely to have part-time principals, part-time ancillary staff . . . and higher pupil-teacher ratios.[7]

The students tracked into the lower-ability classes, typically working-class kids, face at least three deleterious outcomes. First, they are automatically blocked from attending college because they will not have completed the requisite college entrance requirements. Second, as their parents report, the effects of being placed in "second-class" courses, which "everyone knows" are second-class, damages children's confidence and vitality.[8] And, third, the instruction is of inferior quality because teachers fail to build on the students' *prior experiences*, as they do for college-bound students. That is because most teachers' personal experiences are similar to those of middle-class students; thus they present information and project expectations geared to the middle- and upper-middle-class students who have had the benefit of enriched environments at home and in their communities. In addition, the best teachers are teaching the upper-level courses. So what are other kids getting? How are they to get the educational wherewithal to apply for college, even community college, without the attitudinal and cognitive advantages given to the students from affluent families?

Many teachers are just as frustrated as the students with traditional courses and tracking systems. Teachers feel pressured to teach what is *mandated* and *tested*, and they often doubt the appropriateness of that for the students they teach. Indeed, teachers themselves often are bored with the curriculum they feel they must teach. And the traditional didactic process of instruction is criticized by *all* students, whether college bound or non-college bound. Instead of the boredom of passively listening to lectures, watching films, or writing answers to questions in the textbook or worksheets, students want more active involvement in their own learning, just as Sara did in her newspaper editing course. Experts have confirmed what Sara felt:

> Students express enthusiasm for learning experiences that are complex but understandable, full of rich meaning and discussion of values, require their own action, and learning which they feel about which they have some choice. Students describe the classes they consider the most boring are those that have activities that conform most closely to standardized materials and traditional transmission techniques.

Students want more participation in important choices inside the classroom.[9]

But most of all, high school students and their parents want an education that will help them prepare for an occupation, whether that includes getting further education in community or four-year college or getting a job immediately after graduation.[10]

In spite of that desire, little is happening beyond cosmetic change. Many teachers, administrators, and parents are willing and even eager to change things; but they feel the same hopelessness about schools that the larger society projects. Also, teachers already have a full-time job; they do not have the time for radical change. Even when they want to change, teachers need more time to rethink the curriculum and instruction and to have honest dialogues with one another regarding teaching. They know a good deal of knowledge exists regarding the improvement of teaching and curriculum, but there is little time to learn or share such knowledge.[11] Teachers report that their best experiences are when they are able to connect with students and are able to help them in some way, but they also report that they have precious little time during the day to seek out individual students.

Parents are concerned about safety, drugs, gangs, physical violence — the same fears many students have. Ask any high school student what they want and the answer is clear: clean, aesthetically pleasing and comfortable places to learn; courses that challenge them to think; and learning in which they participate as people.[12] One of the few saving factors may be sports, and that is why millions of high school students participate in them.[13]

So why aren't things changing? Business people are crying for a world-class workforce. Many teachers and high school principals see the boredom and dysfunction of what is happening in curriculum and instruction. Students want to be actively involved with more interesting, challenging, and real education. Parents, especially less-affluent parents, want a better shot at life for their children. Why haven't things changed? That is a question that school reformers are having a hard time figuring out. But some analysts think they have a clue.

252

Stifling Reform

Attempts to reform high schools have been extraordinarily vigorous since the beginning of the 1980s and the publication of *A Nation at Risk*. Many older reform traditions, even those which were beginning to have an effect on the high school curriculum, such as Bruner's structure of the disciplines schema and the EPDA curriculum activities that followed, were tossed out because they did not bring about change rapidly enough to satisfy politicians and business people. What followed were a number of formulaic "reforms": Madeline Hunter's instructional procedures, effective principal criteria, total quality management principles, numerous "accountability" processes, and many others, all relatively ephemeral as various advocates pushed one idea after another on federal and state bureaucrats. Later, more serious reform efforts began to emerge, such as the Coalition of Essential Schools and other ideas stemming from the National Association of Secondary School Principals. Even some ideas initiated by the federal government in partnership with business, such as the New American Schools Development Corporation, were exploring newer ways. Finally, in frustration and perhaps with some ulterior motives, came the push for vouchers, privatization, and direct operation of schools by private businesses. Thus far, none of those reforms has shown any promise. Test scores continue to be stagnant, bilingual kids still fall behind Anglo kids, inner-city kids still do not perform as well as kids from the suburbs, kids in Finland still push American kids out of first place on international tests in math or some other academic area, and business people still yap about kids being unprepared. What could account for such continued "failure"?

Because the "changes" initiated were cosmetic and formulaic rather than substantive and systemic, they were easily displaced by any sensible-sounding new idea. And there were many people for whom education is a business and who were willing to advocate almost anything as a panacea. Political and school district leaders would get excited with an idea for education and would allocate funds for it; but when their terms were up or they were

253

tossed out by the electorate, their ideas also died. For example, of 36 top-ranked district administrators who had initiated serious reform efforts in 1993, only two remained after 1994. That constant stop-and-start process frustrated and exhausted conscientious educators. And as each "reform" effort failed to have its promised impact, those teachers dug deeper and deeper bomb shelters, resisting further impositions. There was no consensus on what to do and where to go, no mission.[14]

But that did not slow down reformers, especially those outside the system. Soon business persons were calling for "restructuring," "re-engineering," and "reinventing" education, all terms that translated to mean increasing competition among schools as if educating children and young adults was the moral equivalent of manufacturing an automobile or a personal computer. As long as those gurus and hucksters avoided looking at the deeper issue — the built-in institutional inertia of schools and the local versus national definition of educational problems — any consensus that existed about educational goals existed only in the minds of those propounding the latest reform notion.

Even when there were half-way decent ideas proposed, such as language experience, concept-based science and math, integrated disciplinary curriculum, and greater use of technology in the classroom, the ideas withered from lack of investment in professional development funds and activities. State policy makers said that they could not help schools because of limited funding. But they went ahead with the easy solution — accountability systems — which showed their "commitment to education" without costing them anything. Of course, when those accountability systems brought little change, anxious politicians turned to other quick fixes, such as establishing national standards, again something that cost little. It seemed that the only way schools got additional funding was when they had already failed and were either about to be or were taken over by the state or some other extra-local body.

When it comes to improving education, we seem to focus on everything but local schools. Only at the local level can there be a dialogue about what the school's mission should be and commitment given to that mission. Political leaders write national goals, and state-level policy makers draft curriculum frameworks and new accountability systems. We do a lot of things to schools and make lots of demands on schools. But rarely do we start off discussions with the question: How can we make schools into more effective learning communities?[15] And that discussion has to start at the local level.

What many people do not realize is that change can take place only at the local level, not from the dictates of state or federal officials nor even from the demands of generalized business needs. As long as the school's mission is defined in the way it is, it is succeeding. Sara and Bill's parents are happy with Sara's grades and feel proud of her participation in honors classes and even more proud seeing her leadership in cheerleading and newspaper work. They feel confident about Bill's progress because they know he will stick to it, just as he does with his music. As involved parents, they feel themselves part of the establishment, empowered; and they take credit for its successes. Is it any wonder that American parents, like the Jacobsons, always find that their own schools are wonderful, even though they have doubts about the schools other Americans have?[16] These parents "know" that other high schools have problems, but their children's high school is a success. If anything, many citizens want a return to old nostrums. If the old ways worked, why did we need radical and expensive new solutions? Why change?

Change Is Needed

We need to change high school and college curriculum and instruction because the demands, challenges, and opportunities of the 21st century will demand new competencies from our graduates. That New Economy, as we have seen, is having a profound effect on society, especially on the prospects that high school and college graduates have for getting a decent job. And while schools continue to dabble with peripheral adaptations, the organization and management of work and the kinds of decent jobs available in America's economy have changed dramatically. The American workplace has evolved from a system where work is broken into simple tasks and is controlled, systematic, and highly authoritarian to one where high-performance organizations use advanced technology and where workers are seen as thinking and creative human beings. Schools have not yet made that shift.

Today's curricula and assessments still mirror the model of the industrial society of the 1950s; each subject is treated as independent of the others. Furthermore, we continue to see students as passive recipients of teacher/disseminators' knowledge, rather than viewing students as learners in their own right and teachers as facilitators of the learning process. As one expert correctly points out, within the last decade, skills on the job changed at a rate four to five times faster than curriculum and organizational changes in our schools, leaving a gap between what students were learning in the high school and community college classrooms and what was expected of them in the workplace.[17]

Work today does not require simply more of the traditional skills, regardless of their sophistication; it requires entirely new and different skills. Higher-order language and thinking skills are required. Craftworkers must use statistical numerical controls and understand other advanced technological applications involving knowledge of statistics, logic, probability, measurement systems, and applied physics. Because they need to communicate with their work teams and customers on a regular basis, workers' literacy and communication skills must be finely honed. And they must be technologically literate, not just with computers but with the theory and systems of computer-based technology. They will be responsible for setting and constantly resetting the work flow, must operate and monitor quality control systems, and must be familiar with wide-area network systems. However, despite 14 years of high school reform, many experts tell us that we now have the greatest gap in our nation's history between the skills young people possess when they leave high school and the skills they need for employment. The reason for that situation should be apparent:

We assumed that simply providing higher standards in the traditional basics would rectify the problem.

The job demands for today's craftworkers are so complex that the job of high schools now is to lay a foundation for extended training and career development in community colleges and the universities. High schools need to help students build higher-order thinking and communication skills. They need to teach students how to apply mathematical concepts and how to attend to the investigation of meaningful problems from a multidisciplinary perspective. High schools must give their students technological literacy through active learning so they can complete their basic education before locking into career paths and specific occupational training. High school education should take upon itself the traditional functions that elementary schools have performed so well: education for fundamental civic and personal responsibility for all students. Economic competence will build on those.

Even so, it is still important to identify how those high school experiences will relate to subsequent educational experiences. Before we can narrow the gap between the preparation of high school graduates, adult learners, and the requirements of the workplace, we must define precisely the skills demanded of entry-level craftworkers (the discussion of the education of symbolic analysts will come later). Until recently, educators had little to go on, because we never identified the specific skills, knowledge, and behaviors demanded of craftworkers. But by 1996 sufficient effort had been expended to clarify in what direction schools and community colleges — or extended vocational training and apprenticeships — should proceed. A central topic in American education for the past several years, in that regard, has been the need to raise standards to a level that enables high school graduates and community college graduates to function effectively in the increasingly sophisticated work world.

Much of the problem was confusion with what is expected of craftworkers. Small-business people asked for what they have always asked for from graduates, which were the same needs as in the old mass-production companies: a good work attitude, punctuality, and responsibility. Now there is a more precise and consistent picture of what is needed to compete in the global economy of the 21st century. Several research projects addressing this issue have been conducted by various groups across the nation. Essentially, the new knowledge, skills, behaviors, and attitudes called for are reflected in the in-depth work done by the SCANS group. Here is what it said would be needed by individual craftworkers in the future workforce:

- Resources: Identifies, organizes, plans, and allocates resources.
- Interpersonal: Works well with others.
- Information: Acquires and uses information.
- Systems: Understands complex interrelationships.
- Technology: Works with a variety of technologies.[18]

The very first thing that the reviewer is struck with is the emphasis on process, rather than content. Students are expected to *do* things, not simply *know* things. The process skills include higher-order thinking, problem identification and resolution, understanding how a total system works, and the ability to fit changes and improvements into those systems. Equally essential is to be able to work effectively in groups, which means good personal and interpersonal communication skills.

Other researchers have identified similar skills. A massive field study of work skills done by the state of New York, the Career Preparation Validation Study, attempted to identify more specifically the skills needed by a modern workforce. The final report corroborated the SCANS material. The skills identified by the New York State researchers also emphasize higher-order abilities. Like SCANS, they do not dismiss such "basic" skills as good reading ability and the ability to *apply* mathematics; but they suggest that the basic skills are merely foundational for applying higher-order skills.[19]

Together, the lists identify the actual level of skills and kinds of knowledge, behaviors, and personal attributes that graduates need to succeed in today's changing workplace. Those skills lists can be used to define more clearly the competencies that community college graduates should have, which in turn can guide changes in curricula, programs, and instructional practices in high school. Indeed, both the New York and SCANS reports focus on skills that should be acquired *now* by high school and community college students. Right now students are not learning those skills in school. And students will not even begin to learn those skills in school until schools abandon their traditional curricula and teaching and create a new educational model, one designed specifically to prepare our students for the 21st century.

The Failure of Reform

With all their faults measured by contemporary standards, perhaps high schools being organized like factories was an effective means for coping with the huge influx of new students into the school system as America became increasingly urban. Before World War II, educators became so enamored of the success of the mass-production process and the organization structure on which it depended — Taylorist hierarchy and exact division of labor — that it was not long before age-dependent grade levels were established (division of labor) and hierarchical command structures became the pattern for school organization (teachers at bottom as workers, superintendents at top as CEOs). That organizational design remained unquestioned until the 1990s.

And what has the Taylor model given us? Student loads of 150 to 160 kids a day. Teachers isolated in their own classrooms with little opportunity to talk with other educators, to collaborate, evaluate programs, build consensus, or do other things it takes to substantively change present practice. Anyone who has taught in a high school knows that it is next to impossible to cope with 150 essays, to evaluate 150 term papers, or to personalize instruction for 150 individual students, much less to get to know the students. In the scenario above, we saw how easily Bill was able to beat the system with his homework assignment. That happens all the time.

Another effect of the Taylorist model in the schools has been the sacrosanct use of subject-matter disciplines as the sole means for organizing classes and courses. In a world as complex as ours, it is difficult to justify the narrow vision students get from such isolated disciplines. Teachers rationalize that it is the students' jobs to put the discrete subject-matter pieces together by themselves. But with new information being discovered every moment, it is not even possible for teachers themselves to deal with such an explosion, much less academically immature students. Can anyone read or watch on television something about the "discovery in Antarctica of microorganisms in pieces of rocks from Mars, which was deduced through chemical and radiological means to be evidence of possible life on Mars" and still maintain that a person can begin to make sense of the world through single-focus disciplines? But, given the Taylorist model, that is what we do.

Even then, we cut short the time for teacher-student dialogue, 42 to 52 minutes a period. By the time attendance and other busy-work are finished, there are about 25 minutes left for substantive stuff. With that many students and so little time, assessment of students is a joke. To cope, teachers use the simplest and quickest processes available — multiple-choice tests that in no way accurately assess what a student can actually *do*.[20]

The logic of Taylorist organization and the supposed efficiency of that teaching practice may well have led to the high school's practice of sorting kids into the good and bad, college and non-college, smart and dumb categories. However, all of those justifications are irrelevant in light of the vast changes in society that have taken place since the Taylorist system was adopted 70 years ago.

Although district-level administrators seem satisfied that the Taylorist structure works, it has become increasingly dysfunctional as we approach the 21st century. Many teachers and principals know that is true. But until now, there has been little agreement regarding what constitutes good schools and teaching. Thus even our most enlightened education intellectuals admit that after 15 years of trying, very little has changed.[21] Why is that?

Education reformers have tried everything to make high schools more responsive to changing realities, even when those efforts were misguided. For example, schools in the 1950s were faulted for letting the Russians get an object into space before America did. In the name of national security, there was a crash effort to increase the amount of science and mathematics students were required to take. During the 1960s the charge was that no one could tell what the schools were teaching kids, that the curriculum was barren of significant knowledge structures. Huge amounts were allocated by the federal government to train teachers in the "structure of knowledge" in various disciplines by involving academic college types to teach science, math, social science, and other disciplines.

Then the charge was made that measurement of student achievement was unrelated to what children had been taught, so there was no way to hold teachers accountable nor a way to use evaluation data to change the curriculum. Some business-oriented types pointed out that the defense industry had a precise way to do those sorts of things, and administrators soon were attempting to transfer programmed project budgeting systems into school curriculum practices, breaking down costs for the most minute components of instructional time and resources. A softer version of the same phenomenon was implementation of "behavioral objectives," in which teachers were required to write out what they expected students to know after a sequence of lessons, then test students by translating behavioral objectives into "criterion measures." A more sophisticated version of performance objectives came from use of taxonomies that showed mental processes ranging from low-level facts through analytical and synthesizing abilities.

In the 1980s, as business people started to see profits erode from loss of market share and increasing competition from other industrialized nations — Japan and Germany in particular — the hue and cry arose again for improving education. Schools were faulted for allowing so many students to drop out. As Japanese business prowess grew, studies compared Japan's schools with ours and found ours wanting. When those studies said Japanese students go to school more hours a day and more days a year, America' education establishment responded by adding 20 days to the traditional 160-day schedule and more minutes in the day.

261

Tight dropout prevention programs were implemented and succeeded in getting more students back in school who did not want to be in school. When the pundits claimed that America's school curriculum was not as rigorous as in German and Japanese schools, educators added more courses and established a finer division between honors and general classes. The result of those "reforms" was merely adding more coverage, rather than intellectual substance and depth.

By the late 1980s and into the 1990s, business had become so frustrated with its weak global competitive position and continued loss of market share (and consequently their profits) that stronger demands were made for education "reform." This time, however, business people went directly to key politicians to change things. From that effort we have *America 2000* from a Republican administration and *Goals 2000* from a Democratic administration. We have gotten a number of panaceas: the effective schools movement, "total quality management," "re-invention" of schools, school-to-work, academic discipline standards, and other attempts to "reform" the schools and make them more responsive to business needs.

Yet even then, school reform was crawling. Frustrated, a number of pundits and analysts, especially those working for such conservative think tanks as the Hudson Institute (the very same that had written much of *America 2000* for the government and had helped Mr. Gerstner write his book), began calling for privatization of public schools. Make them compete with each other and that will get results. The pitch was that those schools that cannot compete will lose money and have to fold, just like any other business. Before long, businesses specializing in running schools and school districts sprang up and several companies were signing contracts with school boards to do just that. Some entrepreneurs got a foot in the door by promising free technology for schools; the only obligation was that kids be required to watch commercials for 15 minutes a day. But many of those businesses found that even they, with their lollypop inducements, could not overcome the inertial forces of poverty-induced student lethargy, boredom, dilapidated buildings, lousy materials, too much TV, working parents, non-English-speaking students, burned-out teachers, frazzled administrators, and the other sorry attributes that pass for urban secondary education today.

Some of those companies finally resorted to cheating, claiming to get results that were not real. As their failures emerged, they lost contracts and have begun to sink into the morass of education's real-world problems, for which they had no better answers than had already been proposed by conscientious professional teachers and administrators.[22]

While all of that was happening, schools found themselves faced with additional demands from mandates and changing demographics. The Supreme Court declared segregation to be unconstitutional. Since then, thousands of schools have become multiracial and multicultural. Teachers, especially in large urban districts, had to provide for a larger, more poverty-stricken group of children than ever before. Parents of special education students complained about the exclusion of their children from the mainstream, and a series of legal steps successfully broadened the inclusion of their children in "regular" classes. With a huge influx of non-English-speaking and immigrant children, schools have been struggling to find the elixir for effective bilingual instruction and multicultural programs. Added to those legitimate needs were mandates that schools take responsibility for the social problems for which no one else had an answer: anti-gang programs, sex education, drug education, childcare, anti-smoking programs, community safety, crime prevention programs, character education, and numerous other programs, all demanding time in the curriculum and the classroom.

Some pundits claimed that the primary culprit for the decline of the schools is their lack of accountability. Tighten up the ways schools and teachers are evaluated, the cry went, and things would get better. As a result, on top of every thing else they were supposed to do, teachers' instructional time became loaded with tests of all sorts. To legitimize disadvantaged programs, standardized tests had to be administered, which usually took two to five days away from instruction time. Then states had their own standard-ized tests, such as the Regents in New York and the Classroom Learning Assessment System (CLAS) in California, which took additional time away from instruction.[23]

The curious thing for many is that school curriculum and instruction changed very little, regardless of all the demands and threats and the challenge of privatization. Even in the past few years, when the push for "reform" has been so exceedingly in-tense, high schools have remained pretty much as they were over a decade ago. In 1984, for instance, John Goodlad and his associ-ates conducted a massive study of the schools and reported it in a book titled *A Place Called School*. Goodlad's team found that all immediate stakeholders — parents, teachers, and students — agreed that there were four essential mandates for schools: intel-lectual growth, personal development, social competence, and vocational preparation.[24] But when the Goodlad team conducted its massive survey and on-site inspections of high schools, it found deadening conditions, even in the best schools. The curriculum was what all of us are still familiar with today: the core disci-plines, art, music, and physical education, along with a desultory vocational education strand. The classroom was dominated by teacher-centered activities — primarily talk and giving assign-ments — and passive students. Teachers spent 75% of the time in a daily class on instruction, 70% of that time on lecture and "telling."[25] Teachers managed to talk three times for every one stu-dent comment.

That students would rather have been more actively engaged in their own learning is beyond question, again as revealed by Good-lad's data. No academic classes received more than 30% "very interesting" responses from students when they were asked about them. Only those classes in which students were actively involved — such as art, music, and physical education and such electives as the school newspaper — were rated high.

Vocational education in 1984 was not well regarded. It was a dumping ground for those not going to college. That judgment could not be made publicly, of course, so "general" classes were defined for all those not gaining admittance to the "college track." General education track students were expected to take their places in the workforce immediately after graduating. That in itself produced ambivalence for high school faculty, who continued to focus instruction on college-bound curricula and standards even when it was watered down for general and vocational courses. As Goodlad said:

> When schools seek to meet both the expectations of higher education, on one hand, and of an assumed job market, on the other, consideration of what constitutes good education for the dual aim of developing individual potential and responsible citizens are relegated to secondary importance.[26]

A decade later in the 1990s after a period of intense pressure to change, what Goodlad's team described as the deadening conditions of high schools had persisted. Theodore R. Sizer laid out the continuing problem in *Horace's School*. He gently but pointedly reminded all of us how far we have yet to go to get high schools into the 21st century. Everything Goodlad's team had reported, Sizer found was unchanged, except that perhaps things had become worse. Student passivity was still rampant. Bell systems still shuttled students between 52-minute classes that had no relationship to each other. Classes were still filled with 30 or so students, and teachers still had difficulty getting to know the students in any real sense. As Sizer described it, many teachers know that high school often is deadly boring for students. They are aware that students, even the good students, have figured out the system and can feed back to teachers what they want to hear, collect their credits, and move on. In those classes, as Sizer says, "passing the test becomes an end in itself. The detailed stuff of schooling is covered in a list of topics to which the students are to be exposed and in courses to be passed. What the kids are to do with all of that material is left vague. How they are actively to use it in their lives is left even vaguer."[27] Other students simply find the line of least resistance, do what they are told, and count the time until they graduate. Everyone knows the game:

The fact that what passes for schooling fails to even met the test of simple common sense counts for little. Critics can argue that few of us at any age do serious intellectual or imaginative work, or that mere exposure to a body of knowledge enhances a student's knowledge. They can easily explain that even a veteran teacher cannot get to know well 120 or 150 or 180 students.[28]

Even though they may know that things are not what they should be, little has been done to change the system. Regardless of how much external pressure is placed on the high schools, they have remained quite imperturbable.

Individual schools respond poorly to detailed commands for reform by distant authorities. Educational authority in America is largely disbursed, usually to local school boards, and many of them are fiercely jealous of their autonomy. . . . Finally, most decisions about children's learning are made at the bottom of the organizational pyramid, by specific teachers; it is they who will decide what will happen and what will not. The heart of the system — the schools and the individual classrooms within them — is difficult to reach. Not surprisingly, change has been slight.[29]

By the 1990s only a handful of enlightened school and university-level educators seriously were looking at the substantive reasons for high school ineffectiveness, such as didactic teaching and narrow discipline-based coursework. Indeed, most investigators concentrated on more juicy, newsworthy issues. As Sizer succinctly notes:

The broad and deep support necessary for consequential school reform is at present far from being attained. Even after all the reform talk of the 1980s and the fresh zeal of the 1990s, the number of those converted to the need for serious educational reform is still small. One reason may be the very case that the 1980s leaders adopted for their crusade, a case that was basically an argument for America rather than one for individual Americans. The leaders worried aloud about the quality of the labor force, the competitiveness of this

266

country in the global economy, the quality of our civic culture. However important these issues are, they do little to allay the concerns encountered in the daily life of schools, such as those of a typical parent: Will my children be safe at school? Does anyone know my children well and care for them? Will there be a future for my child, and is the school helping them to achieve it?. . . Ambitious school reform will come about not because presidents and governors and Fortune 500 executives want it to, but because parents and local communities and teachers and principals want reforms that addresses their appropriate concerns as well as broader ones.[30]

Even though Sizer's observations were well-known factors, local communities did not begin to push for change. Like the Jacobsons, parents liked their high schools. But by the late 1980s and early 1990s, as we have seen, state and federal policy makers and opinion makers rediscovered schools as an issue. They again raised a hue and cry about the schools' ineffectiveness, raising doubts in parents' minds. As we shall see, they had the right message for the wrong reasons.

Successful Failures

In one sense the Jacobsons are right. By any reasonable account, given their historic mission, America's schools *are* the best in the world. And our university system is the envy of the world.[31] The evidence that confirms those statements is overwhelming. For example, the academic effectiveness of America's schools has been documented thoroughly in a series of reports by Gerald W. Bracey in the *Phi Delta Kappan* journal and in his book, *Transforming America's Schools*, and in a recent book by David C. Berliner and Bruce J. Biddle, *The Manufactured Crisis.*[32]

Independent corroboration of the academic effectiveness of America's schools had come much earlier than that in the Sandia Report.[33] Sandia is a national laboratory and a branch of the Department of Energy, not Education, thus it had both academic credibility and independence when it was ordered to investigate the academic condition of America's schools. Sandia's report was straightforward praise for the accomplishment of America's schools, especially under the trying conditions with which they must operate. The federal administration at the time was not looking for an upbeat report about America's school effectiveness, so the Sandia Report was suppressed.[34] Unfortunately, since the upbeat message in the report made no splash in the media, as had more negative opinions about the schools, the positive picture the report painted of the schools never became widely known until years later. Even when it finally was released, it went almost unnoticed until the *Phi Delta Kappan* published its findings as part of the Bracey Reports.

Suppressing the Sandia Report achieved its political goal, since the public was not made aware of the success of its schools. Instead, it was inundated with negative news. Headlines blared, "SAT Tests Show Gains Made in 1980s Eroding" and "Students' Reading Skills Fall Short, NAEP Finds," "Study Finds Johnny Can't Write Too Well," and similar dismal news.[35] The Sandia Report also had cautions for politicians.

> The Sandia researchers questioned the use of the Scholastic Aptitude Test (SAT), a test designed to assess an individual's probable success in college, as a yardstick of public school performance. Among the popular misconceptions they addressed is the belief that SAT scores began declining in the mid-1960s and bottomed out in the late 1970s. Since then, it seems that students have made only modest gains.[36]

Sandia analysts reported that 60% of today's youth attempt postsecondary studies in community colleges, trade schools, and four-year colleges. Thirty percent earn a bachelor's degree, the highest rate in the world. Foreign students flock to American universities. Annually, 50% of engineering Ph.D.s and 25% of science Ph.D.s are awarded to foreigners studying in U.S. universities, and almost half of those new Ph.D. holders stay in the United States after earning their degree.[37] Sandia researchers also discounted comparisons of U.S. students with students of other nations, commenting that such comparisons, given the complex variables, are not open to straightforward interpretations.

Other independent sources also have praised the effectiveness of American schools. In 1995, for example, the RAND Corporation, a think tank that usually does analyses for the Air Force and other government agencies, investigated school academic outcomes. The RAND study was conducted by a research team of sociologists and statisticians, not educators. Their general conclusion was: "In terms of student achievement, our estimates do not support the commonly held perception" that today's schools are less effective than they were in the past.[38] They found that in addition to effective teachers, scores went up because parents were more highly educated, family incomes were more stable, and family size was smaller. When asked by the media, "should we throw in the towel on public education?" RAND's lead researcher replied:

> Not unless we want to give up on a major success story. Reading and math achievement levels are higher today than in 1970, with the greatest gains registered by blacks and Latinos.[39]

Perhaps the most widely held idea was that the Scholastic Achievement Test, or SAT, scores had slid drastically. Although there was a slight drop in the middle of the 1970s, the normal SAT average scores have again been achieved. The amazing thing is that SAT scores continue to rise in spite of the increased numbers of students taking the test. The Sandia Report, for example, pointed out how students with different academic rankings increasingly took the SAT, even if they felt that they would never make it in college:

Table 7.1: Percentage of students taking SAT by class rank, 1975 and 1989.

Rank	1975	1989
Top 5th	49%	45%
Second 5th	28%	27%
Third 5th	22%	25%
Fourth 5th	2%	55%
Bottom 5th	0%	1%

Adapted from Sandia National Laboratories, "Perspectives on Education in America: An Annotated Briefing," *Journal of Educational Research* 86, no. 5 (1993).

Sandia concluded the obvious. If there were a real decline in SAT scores, it could be explained by the increasing number of students with less academic qualification taking the test. The push was on to get everyone into college, so the number of high school students taking the SAT surged. But even then, Sandia said, look more closely at what is being called a "decline." With a 53% increase since 1975 in the number of kids from the middle and lower levels of school achievement taking SATs, the scores have remained relatively stable.[40] Moreover, when comparing the higher-achieving students with past and international results, there actually has been an increase in SAT scores.

Fundamentally, of course, the entire process of using SATs to measure school effectiveness is misguided. As the Sandia Report and others have stated, SATs were not meant to be a measure of school effectiveness at all — even colleges that use SATs know that. The purpose of SATs is to assess an individual student's potential success in college, not what was learned in school.[41]

Interestingly, the use of SAT scores as a whipping post by conservative critics of the schools was thrown an additional curve when the College Board recently "recentered" the test. That revision, which essentially was merely an updating of the norms from the original norm group, resulted in a boost in SAT scores for the current crop of students. Conservative pundits did not like that, because they were losing a major argument for attacking the schools and their raison d'être for advocating vouchers for privatization of schools. Nevertheless, the College Board saw the wisdom of renorming, since the students in 1940 who composed the original norm group were all white, upper-middle-class students, totally unrepresentative of today's student body.[42]

Additional evidence of the effectiveness of American schools came from the National Assessment of Educational Progress (NAEP), which was established in 1969 to give Congress and the Administration a way to monitor educational progress of students. The NAEP was actually much more useful for policy makers and planners than the SATs. The NAEP, in contrast to press and pundit negativism, usually has shown positive results. And since it provides state-by-state data, NAEP information is more useful for strategic planing as well. In the late 1980s the federal government began to publicly distribute state ranking and scores (not all states were participating then), which increased the NAEP's importance to state planners. What the NAEP results have shown is a steady increase in scores on basic skills in the majority of states.[43] Even states with a high number of immigrant and bilingual students have seen their NAEP scores increase. It appears that NAEP assessments confirm that in the basic skills areas, the United States is among the world's educational leaders.

Interestingly, the results of the international version of NAEP, administered by the International Association for the Evaluation of Educational Achievement, also have been used to criticize American schools. At one point, conservative think tanks delighted in comparing U.S. students with those in whatever country happened to be gaining competitive advantage with U.S. businesses. Thus at one time the Japanese schools were praised to high heaven because their math scores "exceeded" those of students in the United States.

Looking at international results for 14-year-olds, the United States ranks in the top 10 of the industrial nations. Those countries scoring higher than the United States all are single-ethnic cultures. The effects of single-ethnic group culture is demonstrated by looking at Switzerland's scores. Although they usually are shown in aggregate, when they are broken down into Switzerland's German, French, and Italian sectors, the students in the German section always score higher than students in the other two sectors. If that happens in a relatively small country like Switzerland, what are the implications for a giant, super-multiethnic, bilingual country such as the United States? In addition, when the tests are written in such a way that the questions mean the same and are testing the same skill, the results are even more complimentary to American education, as shown by the recent re-analysis of the international comparative reading scores, in which the U.S. ranked second after Finland.[44] The biggest interpretation of all this testing that one could make is that the American education system is doing pretty darn well.

There are other measures of the academic effectiveness of America's schools. High school graduation is at an all-time high of 86%; and more than 61% of those graduates are attending some level of college.[45] Even unobtrusive measures show the effects of better schooling. For example, there has been a continuous increase in newspaper readership since the end of World War II. In 1946 there were 94.6 million readers. By 1990, 125 million read newspapers. And that readership is made up of Americans of all classes and educational levels.[46]

Of course, the major judge of America's school are parents. And here again, after decades of negative publicity, cranky books, and pundit scorn, there is consistent support of parents for their children's schools. That is evidenced in more than 29 years of Gallup polls.[47] True, parents express doubts about *other* people's schools, but not their own child's school. It is not that parents do not have some concerns. Lack of discipline and fear of violence are top contenders, but so is concern with the school's lack of financial support.[48] The same patterns found by the Phi Delta Kappa/Gallup polls are replicated by other pollsters. In a Times-Mirror poll taken in California, 57% of the parents rated their children's schools adequate or excellent. When asked why such high regard, 54% said the quality of teaching. Perhaps the best indicator of parent support for schools is judged by their pocketbooks. While many adults in California would continue the funding restrictions imposed by voters in 1978 (Proposition 13), 57% of the *parents* were willing to change the law to make it easier to raise taxes for schools.[49] That new willingness to pay for the schools, in comparison with past practices, is perhaps the best measure of parents' positive feelings for their children's schools.

Going into any further detail regarding the comparative data would be redundant, since excellent empirical studies have been made by many others.[50] But we do have to remind ourselves of some of the things high school critics have not mentioned when they make their comparisons. For example, researchers who became enamored of Japanese schools when Japan was closing the competitive gap with the United States failed to mention the deep cultural tradition in Japan emphasizing a "you can do it" value that often leads to physical punishment by teachers and parents for "slow" children. Or the pressure on students whose school "failure" reflects badly on an entire extended family. Nor do they mention the harshness of a system that drives teenagers to suicide.[51] Would any American family really settle for that pressure?[52] And now that American business is on a roll, are they thanking U.S. schools for a job well done and advising the Japanese that they should emulate us? Of course not. Go figure.

So Are We Ready for Tomorrow?

If American schools have been effective, what is the problem? The problem is that the schools are replicating curricula, instructional practices, and a governance structure that are suitable for the past, not for the challenges of the future. Economic change is accelerating; technology is replacing the need for workers; and the new jobs being generated are low-wage jobs. Not only that, society is changing, becoming more global and more multicultural as national boundary lines become blurred by new information and telecommunications systems. The way high schools are holding on to tradition and their obstinate failure to recognize the demands — personal and social, as well as economic —that will be placed on young Americans in the 21st century is a discredit to American educators. It is in that sense that the schools are failing, not in what pundits and conservative analysts point to as failure.

> It is not hyperbole to say that today's school reform debate is critical to our national destiny. The challenge is a thrilling one: to make every child the possessor of a kind of intellectual competence once available to only a small minority. This inspiring — and new — task means granting all young citizens the conviction that they can have wonderful ideas, invent theories, analyze evidence and make their personal mark on this most complex world. Such a transformation of the idea of why children go to school would in turn transform the American workplace, as well as the very nature of American democratic life.[53]

The key factor in that transformation is to find ways to get parents, teachers, and other stakeholders who are directly responsible for the education health and welfare of young people to work together. Too often, stakeholders get so put off by external demands from governmental officials, pundits, business executives, and soothsayers that they dismiss their own values regarding educational processes and outcomes. Real school transformation will come only when key stakeholders realize that it must begin with them.[54] Already some educators have not let external forces deflect their drive to transform education; and they, along with parents, are testing better ways to serve our young people, as we shall see.

Some innovations are actually taking root in some of the nation's high schools, but wholesale change is occurring slowly and haphazardly, if at all, in many others. In a recent study based on a survey of 3,380 high school principals, the most comprehensive survey in decades, the progress of reforms in public high schools was examined. It found that hundreds of schools are using some new ideas, such as cooperative-learning techniques, incorporating new national standards for teaching mathematics, and giving more decision-making authority to teachers and parents. But those efforts are spotty, and few schools are attempting systemic reform by taking on and integrating several changes at once.[55] The reason for that spottiness, according to the National Association of Secondary School Principals, is the lack of consensus about how to restructure high schools. There is a lot of activity, the NASSP says, but there is no clear vision as to what is necessary to restructure the schools.

The high school study found that some technological innovations, but not many, have been incorporated into high schools. For example, the survey found that only 64% of the schools regularly use video-instructional materials, while 60% routinely offer their students opportunities to practice word-processing skills on computers. More sophisticated technological innovations, such as computer modems enabling students to obtain information from outside databases and networks, are rare.[56] There are some who question whether teachers will use even that limited technology.[57]

The study also suggests that the trend toward site-based decision making — which the survey defined as "a system in which individual schools take responsibility for the teaching that goes on inside them" — may have gone as far as it is going to go without further pressure. While 66% of the schools have fully or partially implemented such programs, only an additional 4% plan to do so next year.[58]

Such resistance to modern technology and governance, with their proven capability to help students learn, is a real indicator to how far high school transformation has to go. The roots of the resistance are deep and profound. If high schools are to become more significant institutions in the lives of students, a focus on systemic reform is essential. But that is not happening.

The survey had some other bits of data that do not augur well for how effectively high schools are helping students develop workplace skills. For example, while higher-order thinking is a high priority for business, only 30% of high schools have established a thinking-skills curriculum and instruction programs; but many of them (48%) want one. Teamwork will be an important expectation in high-performance work organizations, and almost 50% of the high schools reported having implemented cooperative learning. But since only 32% of the high schools have implemented a comprehensive professional development program that includes new teaching strategies, it is reasonable to conclude that many of the changes that have been implemented deal more with organization than with curriculum or instruction. When asked to analyze this plodding change, the survey authors thought they knew why:

> High schools have long been considered the most resistant to change of all the levels of schooling. High schools frequently are more complex and bureaucratic than smaller elementary and middle schools [the study] suggests and have faculties that tend to be more protective of their "turfs." As a result high schools have received relatively little attention in the reform movement [Perhaps the study's] findings will place high schools squarely in the reform spotlight.[59]

The authors of the high school survey have identified important data. However, they missed perhaps the most critical factor stifling high school transformation: Carnegie units.[60] The Carnegie unit was established in 1908 as a device for promoting college teaching careers. The Carnegie Foundation for the Advancement of Teaching had established, as one criterion for successful application, the establishment of 14 "standards" that would guide admission to college. These standards became what are now called Carnegie units, which now are used in more than 3,000 colleges in the United States. Because Carnegie units have become almost universally adopted by institutions of higher education, most high schools have adopted the process and have based graduation on the successful completion of a required number of Carnegie units. Alternative admission techniques — such as actual demonstration of knowledge or performance of skill — are eschewed. Today, almost all American high schools conform to the same Carnegie standards, which are earned through discipline-based coursework, course credits, and grades.

It is not that colleges have had no empirical evidence that alternative admission standards work, because they have had such evidence for some time. Many educators are aware of the compelling research of Ralph Tyler, the late University of Chicago scholar, whose Eight-Year Study tested the idea of alternative admission standards for college attendance. Students demonstrated mastery in several academic areas to demonstrate their readiness for college work, rather than just accumulate credits. That study, most of us know, showed that students who went through a profoundly "different" high school experience succeeded in college at a higher rate than did those who attended traditional schools. Unfortunately, high school educators let the ball drop; and they must share some of the blame for not using Tyler's work to change a meaningless system.

Today, therefore, if a high school wishes to change to an integrated curriculum based on a thematic approach, in which the discipline areas have no distinct identity, colleges may not recognize the credits earned by students as valid. And most high school educators are aware of how hard it is to change.

276

In a study conducted by the University of Minnesota's Center for School Change, 22 high schools in 12 states that tried to change their graduation requirements found they were stymied by traditional admission standards. Most still "retained the 50-60 minute courses and the usual system of credits because of convenience and concern from teachers, administrators, and parents that acting otherwise would endanger graduates' chances of being admitted to college."[61]

Sizer sums up the frustration: College admissions "drive the kind of high school programs millions of students attend. Changing admission standards is one of the central issues of high school reform."[62] If business really expects high schools to prepare a world-class workforce, they will find it happening a lot faster if they jump in and push for alternative criteria for college admission.

Another contributor to the snail pace of high school change includes those most closely associated with the schools: teachers, administrators, parents, and others. As Goodlad and others have found, teachers tend to teach the way they were taught, especially if they had teachers in their own schooling that they admired and liked. Teachers also get comfortable with the way they have been teaching for years; they usually have been evaluated positively by their principal, even recognized for their efforts, and are willing to help socialize newcomers to adopt these standard ways.

Administrators also get trapped into familiar ways. Many principals feel they are not competent to judge ideas about integrated disciplines, collaborative teaching, demonstrated learning assessment, and other pedagogical changes, especially if those ideas are out of their own subject specialties. And district-level administrators find themselves isolated or too far removed from the high school to judge ideas for improvement. They also have to be particularly cautious because school boards and parents are quick to complain when any change in routine is suggested, especially if it has any potential of making it more difficult for their children to get into college or to get a good job. Even if boards and parents accept reasonable changes recommended by administrators, they expect quick results and have little tolerance for anything that can not be measured soon after implementation, which most substantive changes cannot.

Faddish changes have made teachers jaded and wary of new ideas, especially when presented as panaceas. In addition, they know that school districts often fall prey to a cycle of innovation that leaves teachers and parents displeased.

> Top administrators . . . tend to ride into office on the promise of bringing something better, which usually means advocating a "new" idea about the way school should "keep." This approach, almost by definition, means overthrowing the predecessor's plan, by fiat if necessary, even though some parts of the former plan might have been beginning to show results. This administrative paradox of density-through-advocacy (to get the job) and conservatism (to keep the job) can leave faculty members feeling that their safest response is to stand quietly on the sidelines regarding any new promises as something akin to New England weather: Wait a minute and it will change.[63]

Parents can be the most conservative when it comes to changing the high school. As pointed out in the Jacobson scenario, many parents relive their own high school days through their children's experiences and have idealized the "way it was," even when the reality was deadening for them, as well. And just like the teachers who have difficulty imagining other ways to teach, parents have a hard time seeing how learning might be different. Thus when different schemes are proposed by administrators, parents are naturally skeptical.

Finally, certain government and organizational policies themselves inhibit high school change. They range from such simple factors as athletic league scheduling to the legally defined number of subjects and credits needed for graduation. A high school faculty that wishes to implement block scheduling, for example, can accommodate league schedules with a little bit of creativity. And the state could draw regulations that recognize multiple credit for integrated disciplinary and project-based studies. But those bureaucratically driven encumbrances to reform take a little extra work to overcome. They break the mold of tradition and, in some situations, may threaten people's jobs, so a lot of inertia is built into any attempt at change.

What is needed to begin the process of change has been clear for some time. But we need a model of what the new school should look like. What schools do we need to meet the personal, social, and economic needs of America's youth? That is to be considered next.

Notes

1. Linda Darling-Hammond, "Reframing the School Reform Agenda: Developing Capacity for School Transformation," *Phi Delta Kappan* 74 (June 1993): 757.
2. "Impact of Reform Said to Be Spotty and Not Systemic," *Education Week*, 9 February 1994, pp. 1, 12.
3. National Center for Education Statistics, *Curricular Differentiation in Public High Schools* (Washington, D.C.: U.S. Department of Education, December 1994), pp. 5-31.
4. Ibid.
5. Ibid.
6. Ibid., pp. 28-29.
7. Ellen Brantlinger, "Social Class in Schools: Students' Perspectives," *Phi Delta Kappa Research Bulletin No. 14* (March 1995): 1.
8. Institute for Education in Transformation, *Voices from the Inside: A Report on Schooling from Inside the Classroom* (Claremont, Calif.: Claremont Graduate School, November 1992), pp. 1-68.
9. Ibid.
10. John I. Goodlad, *A Place Called School: Prospects for the Future* (New York: McGraw-Hill, 1984), pp. 38-39.
11. Institute for Education in Transformation, op. cit., pp. 1-68.
12. Ibid.
13. "By the Numbers: Games Students Play," *Education Week*, 5 October 1994, p. 4.
14. "Rapid Turnover in Leadership Impedes Reform, Study Finds," *Education Week*, 11 January 1995, p. 6.
15. Paul Hill, James W. Guthrie, and Larry Pierce, "Whatever Happened to the Local School?" *Education Week*, 10 January 1996, pp. 56, 33.

16. See, for example, the historical support for local schools in Stanley M. Elam, ed., *The Gallup/Phi Delta Kappa Polls of Attitudes Toward The Public Schools, 1969-1988* (Bloomington, Ind.: Phi Delta Kappa, 1989).
17. Willard Daggett, "The Skills Students Need for Success in the Workplace," *California Catalyst* (Fall 1993): 4-13.
18. Secretary's Commission on Achieving Necessary Skills, *What Work Requires of Schools: A SCANS Report for America 2000* (Washington, D.C.: U.S. Department of Labor, 1991).
19. Daggett, op. cit., pp. 4-13.
20. Elaine Woo, "Theodore Sizer: Selling Education Reform to Tradition-Bound High Schools," *Los Angeles Times*, 18 August 1996, p. M3.
21. Ibid.
22. Peter Schrag, " 'F' Is for Fizzle: The Faltering School Privatization Movement," *American Prospect* (May-June 1996): 67-71.
23. CLAS came under attack by religious right conservatives. It was first withdrawn, then redesigned to satisfy their complaints.
24. Goodlad, op. cit., pp. 38-39.
25. Ibid., p. 232.
26. Ibid., p. 203.
27. Theodore R. Sizer, *Horace's School: Redesigning the American High School* (Boston: Houghton Mifflin, 1992), p. 10.
28. Ibid.
29. Ibid.
30. Ibid., pp. 14-15.
31. Michael W. Kirst, "Strengths and Weakness of American Education," in *The State of the Nation's Public Schools*, edited by Stanley Elam (Bloomington, Ind.: Phi Delta Kappa, 1993), pp. 3-12.
32. The Bracey reports have spanned several years. See especially, Gerald W. Bracey, "Why Can't They Be Like We Were," *Phi Delta Kappan* 73 (October 1991): 104-17; "The Second Bracey Report on the Condition of Public Education," *Phi Delta Kappan* 74 (October 1992): 104-17; and "The Third Bracey Report on the Condition of Public Education," *Phi Delta Kappan* 75 (October 1993): 104-17. Gerald W. Bracey, *Transforming America's Schools: An Rx for Getting Past Blame* (Alexandria, Va.: American Association of School Administrators, 1994). David C. Berliner and Bruce J. Biddle, *The Manufactured Crisis: Myths, Fraud, and the Attack on America's Public Schools* (Reading, Mass.: Addison-Wesley, 1995).

33. Sandia National Laboratories, "Perspective on Education in America: An Annotated Briefing," *Journal of Educational Research* 86, no. 5 (1993): 259-310.

34. Daniel Tanner, "A Nation 'Truly' at Risk," *Phi Delta Kappan* 75 (December 1993): 288-97.

35. *Los Angeles Times*, 25 August 1994, p. A3; *Education Week*, 22 September 1993, pp. 1, 16; *Los Angeles Times*, 8 June 1994, p. A22.

36. Mary McClellan, "Why Blame the Schools," *Phi Delta Kappa Research Bulletin*, No. 12 (March 1994): 2.

37. "Sandia Study, Our Study, Our Slandered Schools," *I.D.E.A. Reporter* (Spring 1993): 1-5.

38. David W. Grissmer, Sheila Nattaraj Kirby, Mark Berends, and Stephanie Williamson, *Student Achievement and the Changing American Family* (Santa Monica, Calif.: RAND, 1994): 105-109.

39. "Perspective on the Schools: Sinking Scores? Not in the Numbers," *Los Angeles Times*, 28 May 1995, p. M5.

40. Sandia National Laboratories, op. cit., pp. 259-310.

41. McClellan, op. cit., p. 2.

42. *Los Angeles Times*, 24 August 1995, p. A25; Gregory J. Cizen, "S.A.T. 'Recentering': Baby Boomers Get a Break," *Education Week*, 21 September 1994.

43. U.S. Department of Commerce, *Statistical Abstract of the United States, 1995* (115th Edition), p. 44.

44. The newspapers reported it as a negative. See "U.S. Students Ranked No. 2 in Literacy," *Los Angeles Times*, 18 June 1996, p. A12.

45. U.S. Department of Commerce, *Statistical Abstract of the United States, 1995* (115th Edition); and Gerald W. Bracey, *Transforming America's Schools: An Rx for Getting Past Blame* (Alexandria, Va.: American Association of School Administrators, 1994), pp. 9-27.

46. James Flanigan, "N.Y. Times Leaves Imprint with Offer," *Los Angeles Times*, 2 June 1993, p. D1.

47. Elam, *The Gallup/Phi Delta Kappa Polls*, op. cit.

48. "Lack of Discipline Tops Public's Concerns About Schools," *Education Week*, 6 September 1995, p. 16.

49. Ibid. Proposition 13 requires a two-thirds vote to raise taxes or pass bond measures. Interestingly, the total population's attitude toward revising Proposition 13 restrictions to allow the schools a simple majority vote to raise taxes was split, 48% in favor, 45% opposed,

and 7% undecided. Many analysts consider even that split affirmation of support for the schools.

50. Berliner, op. cit., pp. 13-64; and the Bracey Reports cited above are the best summaries.

51. Robert L. Baker, "Japanese and U.S. Education: Compared and Contrasted," Paper delivered at 1993 Superintendent Symposium, Monterey, Calif., January 1993. Negative reports about Japan are rare, but sometimes do emerge. See "Teen-Age Suicide Shed Light on Brutal Bullying in Japan," *Los Angeles Times*, 23 December 1994, p. A5.

52. It is not my intent to disparage Japan nor its education system. What it has is what it wants; and if they wish to change it, that is their responsibility. My comments are to describe more sharply what kind of things go on so that American educators and parents can more fully understand that appeals to test scores as the only measure of schooling do not give the entire picture.

53. Deborah W. Meier, "Get the Story Straight: Myths, Lies and the Public Schools," *The Nation* 21 September 1992, pp. 271-72.

54. Hanna Shatter, "Developing New Traditions in Secondary Schools: A Working Model for Organizational and Instructional Change," *Teachers College Record* (Summer 1996): 549-68.

55. "Impact of Reform Said to Be Spotty and Not Systemic," *Education Week*, 9 February 1994, pp. 1, 12. The poll was conducted by Gordon Cawelti, the executive director of the Alliance for Curriculum Reform, for the Educational Research Service, an organization that serves as a research arm for seven national education groups.

56. Ibid.

57. Gary Chapman, "Are Schools Ready for the Net?" *Los Angeles Times*, 9 November 1995, pp. D1, D11.

58. "Impact of Reform," op. cit., pp. 1, 12.

59. Ibid.

60. Joe Nathan, "To Improve High Schools, Change College Admissions Policies," *Education Week*, 15 February 1995, p. 30.

61. Ronald D. Thrope, "Schools, Colleges, and Mending Reform," *Education Week*, 8 March 1995, p. 31.

62. Ibid.

63. Ibid.

Chapter Eight

The Schools We Need

The vast majority of today's high schools and colleges have a long way to go before they can prepare young adults for the 21st century. And time is growing short. If America's schools and colleges cannot meet the exigent demands of the economy for highly skilled craftworkers and for a larger cadre of high-level service workers, Corporate America will begin looking elsewhere. Already several American corporations are hiring technicians and symbolic analysts from foreign countries. Already much work, especially that which can be done electronically, is shipped out to foreign countries for processing before being sent back to the United States for sale and distribution. Thus far, that phenomenon has been relatively unorganized and limited to just a few companies. But it easily could grow. For example, if businesses and the government are convinced that the public will be better served by implementing job-expansion policies and if educators do not increase the supply of American craftworkers and symbolic analysts to keep up with the new demand, there will be even further erosion of income and benefits and standard of living for almost all Americans as foreigners take American work. Some say that if reform does not occur within the next ten years, especially at the high school level, it will be too late; privatizers will take control. But getting to reform has not been easy.

The interchangeable terms "reform" and "restructuring" have become commonplace, but they have almost lost their meaning in the competition by various interest groups to gain converts to their own special brand of "reform." Even worse, few of the major government and private interest groups' schemes for "restructuring" actually confront the deep changes in high schools that would produce the kind of effective learning needed in America's technologically advanced society.[1]

It is not that educators do not know what needs to be done. A few high schools have implemented practical reforms, and there are many other sound innovations that could be incorporated easily if teachers and administrators were *prepared* to implement them. However, preparation means more than having inservice workshops or visits from consultants. As Theodore Sizer and others have pointed out, teachers, principals, and other stakeholders must talk through ideas and issues to find their own viable paths to improvement. But huge inertial traditions, such as those described in the last chapter, work against such planning; and so little changes. If students seem satisfied with learning the "hidden" curriculum's rules, rather than engaging in serious study, who cares? If parents are happy that their children are enjoying high school's social life, sports, and other extracurricular activities and show little concern or at least are passive regarding the deadening aspects of high schools, why change? If teachers are burned out or so enraptured of their own subjects that they can see no other ways, why fight it? If principals are so wrapped up in administrative and bureaucratic minutia or traditional Chamber of Commerce public relations, how can they be convinced that they need to become change agents? All of these sentiments conspire to keep high schools as they have been for sixty years. To paraphrase an old saw — while high schools burn, those stakeholders appear to be fiddling.

Yet the need to transform high schools has become exceedingly urgent. Neither the new techno-informational economy nor society in general is waiting for high schools to change. And the students who will move into that world are already in school.

Today's high school students will be facing a vastly different national and global environment.

Technology will reign supreme in every niche of human activity — at home, at work, at play, and in the schools. The Internet will become the major mode of personal communication. However, there already is a wide gap between the affluent and the working poor in owning technology. Only 14% of poor high school students' families have a computer; only 7% of those earning under $20,000 own one. In contrast, more than 82% of affluent families earning $50,000 or more have computers.[2] Access to the Internet shows similar proportions, with 62% of the affluent families having access compared to just 31% of poor families. In one major study, it was reported that "The most affluent students use computers about twenty percent more than the average student, and tend to use them for higher order learning such as writing, analysis, and synthesis."[3] And the wealthier a family is, the more likely it is that the students will have access to computers and the Internet. In independent surveys, 86% of families believe that the computer is the most beneficial technology they could buy for their children. That is why there is steady growth in home computers, increasing from 25% to 39% of households just between 1994 and 1995.

However, the schools seem to be among the poor when it comes to the information superhighway. Almost 50% of America's schools in 1995 had access to the Internet. Unfortunately, that access is not easily available to individual students; only 9% of classrooms are on the Internet. Even public libraries are doing better, with 23% making the Internet available to their clients. It certainly is not the lack of student interest that keeps schools from using the technology. A survey conducted by the National Center for Education Statistics revealed that less than 1% of high school students showed little interest in computers and the Internet. Instead, the NCES identified lack of funds as the most critical barrier to school use of technology. To get all schools up to speed would take about 4% to 5% of the total K-12 budget, compared to the measly 1.3% spent now.[4]

Familiarity with technology is very important for graduates. Workers able to use modern technology earn 10% to 15% more than do workers who cannot. Yet education continues to be underfunded. Each year Americans spend $494 billion on the military and related costs and $340 billion on entertainment and recreation, compared to a paltry $270 billion on education.[5] And education funds are projected to go lower between now and the year 2000, while military costs will continue to expand for a number of years, long after the end of the Cold War.[6]

Access to technology is not the only problem. Too many American high schools are not rethinking curricula, not using recent research on effective pedagogy, not integrating technological innovations in a meaningful way, and not reconsidering budget priorities. That lack of effort is unfortunate, because there are some excellent high schools that are changing and are using different approaches that better prepare students for their future.

We could see profound changes in America's high schools. For example, the National Association of Secondary School Principals and other groups have recommended seven areas of change in high school curriculum and organization:

- Personalization through small size and coherency in clarity of mission and expectations.
- Alignment of assessment and teaching.
- Natural grouping of subject matter around themes.
- Scheduling patterns that will provide greater time for students to conduct in-depth studies and for teachers to jointly plan and develop instruction.
- Comprehensive use of computers, computer peripherals, and other technologies, including telecommunications.
- Professional development, including teachers taking on new roles and responsibilities.
- Leadership, which begins with the development of the principal's instructional and curriculum expertise but also includes leadership development for teachers, students, and others who have an influence on the education of high school students.[7]

All of those changes are necessary to bring today's high schools in line with best practice. However, getting beyond that point will call for a more radical reorientation of schooling, in addition to those changes recommended by NASSP.

The New High School

The high school of the future will have the important challenge of developing in *all* students the necessary cognitive skills, personal awareness, and democratic precepts that will undergird their participation in society as self-reliant adults. On a theoretical level it is quite clear what kind of high school is needed to give young adults that 21st century preparation. We need schools that will consciously and systematically educate students so that their ability to use higher-order thinking and intellectual processes is accelerated, and in which they have an opportunity to actively practice collaborative and healthy interpersonal skills. What they learn in high school should be a *precursor* for helping them prepare for careers and decent occupations in a world-class workforce after attending two- and four-year colleges. But the *primary mission* of the high school should be the development of potential for *all* students.

> Students [are seen] as citizens of tomorrow, and [an active learning strategy] attempts to prepare them to assume that role. . . . Students are not merely the passive recipients of knowledge; they are constantly shaping their lives as they learn, being empowered to develop the best they have within them.[8]

American schools will need to do more than simply "reform" themselves; they will need a complete metamorphosis. Some thoughtful schools across the country already have begun the transformations that will change them into something unique, but even they still have a long way to go before they are entirely new.[9] Still, even in their current condition, those schools are harbingers of what future schools will be.

The broad outlines of the school of the future are beginning to become much clearer as a result of two factors: the combined effects of the pioneering efforts of those "best practice" schools and the knowledge coming from cognitive science and education research.[10] That research and exemplary practice have demonstrated and will continue to demonstrate that there are more effective ways to educate people, even high school students. There will be many changes in high schools over the next decade or two, but the most profound will be changes in the dominant instructional strategies — from didactic to constructivism, from passive to active — and the pervasive use of technology to support those strategies.

The changes expected in high school teaching and curriculum are driven by a number of factors in addition to best practice and research findings. Many of the predicted changes will be beneficial for high-performance work organizations. But that will not be the primary reason that high schools will change.[11] Rather, the need for change is driven by such interrelated antecedents as:

1. The expansion of knowledge has made "coverage" of subject matter physically impossible, not only within the four years of high school but even with four more years of college.
2. Socioeconomic conditions have become so complex that personal experiences, natural phenomena, and sociopolitical events can be understood only from an integrated-disciplinary stance.
3. There is a rapid expansion of non-English-speaking and immigrant students in the schools.
4. Technological innovation in software and hardware have opened new ways for students to interact with each other and the world.
5. The techno-informational expertise needed by teachers is driving demand for greater differentiation of the professional staff.
6. Growing opposition to state and federal government "impositions" (for example, national standards and bureaucratic controls) has led to a demand for expansion of local control mechanisms, most importantly exemplified by independent charter public schools.

7. There is a growing move to integrate school services and social services — such as preventative health care, child care, parenting teaching, worker retraining — into community learning/social centers.
8. There is a continuing — and potentially accelerating — demand for highly educated craftworkers and symbolic analysts.[12]

Those major factors and others associated with them are the real forces acting on schools and will be discussed in more detail. For now it is important to realize that, as those factors come together, high school education in the first quarter of the 21st century will be unrecognizable to those of us familiar only with today's traditional model.

The new high school will center student instruction on "authentic challenging tasks," in keeping with a constructivist point of view.[13] In contrast to today's traditional high school, it is not possible to specify — except as a speculative exercise — the coursework or sequences, or even the critical subject matter, that will be involved in the high school of the future. However, by extrapolating from today's best practice, the trends in technology and information systems and emerging learning theory, we can gain a fairly clear picture of the new high school's broad outcomes, dominant teaching strategies, assessment techniques, and technology.[14]

Just what practices can be predicted for the new high school model? There is no question that the new high school's paramount driving force will be student-centered instruction. Student-centered instruction means that students are actively involved in their own learning and that greater attention is given to face-to-face student contacts, more personalized instruction, and facilitative and coaching teacher behaviors. One of the main stumbling blocks to a student-centered high school has always been the huge and too demanding teacher-to-student ratio with which today's high school teachers must cope. Another is the tenacity of individual subjects, which leads to the compartmentalization of abstract information and largely ignores how the real world works.

Both of those conditions — high student ratios and isolated subject matter — can be overcome through the use of technological innovation. With sophisticated hardware systems and appropriate software, there no longer is any reason for not offering personalized, individualized instruction. There is no technical reason schools should not be designed for student-centered instruction at every level. Schools can stop the elitist tracking systems by which they sort students.[15]

The appropriate teaching strategies for personalized learning have been identified; and the way the curriculum is developing, it will encourage such instruction.[16] The curriculum will be structured by themes, which lend themselves most readily to the instructional methodology called "constructivism." Constructivism is a learning strategy that states:

> Learning is not the result of development; learning is development. It requires invention and self-organization on the part of the learner. Thus teachers need to allow learners to raise their own questions, generate their own hypotheses and models as possibilities, and test them for viability.
>
> Disequalibrium facilitates learning. "Errors" need to be perceived as a result of learners' perceptions and therefore not minimized or avoided. Challenging, open-ended investigations in realistic, meaningful contexts need to be offered, thus allowing learners to explore and generate many possibilities, both affirming and contradictory. Contradictions, in particular, need to be illuminated and explored, and discussed.[17]

In contrast to the unbending sequence of courses, class schedules, and subject prerequisites found in most high schools today, curricula will move away from "coverage" to the exploration of a number of broad, meaningful themes.[18] A natural grouping of the disciplines — perhaps science and mathematics or human studies and literature — will become the source of the concepts and processes of inquiry.[19] In that way, each theme will have embedded within it the core concepts of the disciplines. However, the emphasis will be placed on concepts and processes that are useful in situations *beyond* the classroom.[20] Thus they must meet the criterion of applicability.

Active learning will be the driving force for exploring those themes. Students will have opportunities to participate in meaningful projects, research, simulations, productions, exhibitions, community applications of learning, and other activities that challenge them, broaden their experience, and give them direct evidence that what they are learning has utility in the real world. Much of their learning will be project- and problem-based.[21] Problem-based learning allows students to select activities that best match their own learning styles and interests.[22] A project-based environment allows students to demonstrate their knowledge through high-tech presentations and exhibitions combining audiovisual presentations, written stories, reports, and models.

In the new high school, teachers will not be forced to try to cover everything in a subject. Knowledge is increasing so rapidly that no college professor can hope to keep up, much less anticipate what information will be useful; thus it is vain to expect a high school teacher or student to do so. In fact, the traditional disciplines, as we have known them, no longer exist. The rapid growth of information has led to a myriad of subdisciplines that only loosely fall within the subject areas taught in traditional high schools. Thus teaching discrete subjects is irrelevant and misleading. However, the disciplines are a source of intellectual processes by which people can make sense of their worlds; and the inquiry techniques from the disciplines help students process information and make sense of it for themselves.[23]

It is unreal to present a discipline's subject matter in an episodic manner, as a static body of knowledge, because that deludes students into thinking that knowledge is a given, meant merely to be passed on, rather than something constantly being constructed and reconstructed. It also leads high school students to assume that "passing a test" is the true outcome of studies, rather than the development of wisdom and the self-initiating, self-reflective, and self-evaluating skills that lead to constructing meaning for themselves. Students must move away from seeking the "right" answers and begin to learn how to behave when confronted with paradoxical and ambiguous situations. Doing so requires a shift from valuing knowledge acquisition to valuing knowledge production.[24]

Those discrete disciplines will be replaced by in-depth thematic studies that allow students to pursue a topic over longer periods of time and to develop the intellectual *processes* that will carry into real life. However, the new high school curriculum will not be "content-free," as Costa and Lieberman point out:

> We must have something to process, however. Our recommendation is not that content be devalued but, rather, that content be rethought as means, not ends. We must value content because it enhances the development of processes, and judiciously select content because of its generative qualities. Through content we experience the euphoria of knowledge production, the revelation of our own efficacy as continual learners, the application of learning to other settings, and the expansion of our repertoire of response patterns.[25]

The disciplines will play a critical function in the new high school; but rather than the content of the disciplines, it is their investigative processes that will prove most useful. A discipline's formal body of information, which now typically forms the core of courses of study and textbooks, is represented as a fixed body of knowledge to be covered and memorized. The "best" students are able to do that at a level acceptable to traditional teachers, but even those students soon forget most of what they worked so hard to memorize.[26] A discipline's intellectual and investigative processes, on the other hand, are tools that are useful for the investigation of phenomena, paradoxes, and problems.

The curriculum in the 21st century will be what is today called an *emergent curriculum*. That does not mean that all learning activities simply emerge from the students' interests. Instead, teachers do broad planning but build in sufficient flexibility to allow students to respond to unforeseen opportunities and other "emerging" contingencies. Then teachers help students blend new discoveries into a more complete intellectual framework. The curriculum "emerges" because it is different with every class of students; every new group of students will have different levels of prior knowledge, interests, and learning needs.[27]

Foxfire's curriculum exemplifies the emerging curriculum. Following are the seven common ingredients that guide Foxfire's program, as reported by past students and teachers in the program:

1. All the work teachers and students do must flow from student desire, infused with choice, design, revision, execution, reflection, and evaluation. Questions that arise in class go back to the student.
2. Connection of the work to the surrounding community and real world are clear to teachers and students.
3. Work is characterized by student action, rather than passive receipt of processed information.
4. Emphasis on peer teaching, small-group work, and teamwork.
5. Role of teacher as a collaborator and team leader, rather than boss or the repository of all knowledge.
6. Audience beyond the teacher or school is the focus for student work.
7. Academic integrity of the work must be absolutely clear and meet standards of disciplined inquiry.[28]

Note that the teacher's role is still instrumental to help students make decisions within a larger framework of choices. Since students have significant responsibility to identify themes and activities, the resulting curriculum motivates them to become active participants in their own learning. Indeed, as an emergent curriculum, it remains open-ended and is negotiated continually by the teachers and students. Indeed, teachers often find themselves in the position of co-learner with students, especially when tasks demand sophisticated computer skills, which students often master more quickly than their teachers. Such is the case in the schools involved in Maryland's Virtual High School Project, where students have a wide variety of information available to them technologically.[29]

Within such a setting the idea of collaborative learning will take on new meaning. Cooperative learning as we know it now — with small groups of students working together on a task — will be expanded to incorporate routine collaboration with students in distant places, as well as with scholars, decision makers, and pundits through telecommunication, videoconferencing, and telecommuting. The collaborative teams will conduct research that involves data collection, manipulation, and analysis using sophisticated computer technology and software. Their products will demonstrate their ability to integrate ideas, concepts, and information into meaningful explanations, solutions, and recommendations. Students will communicate their "constructions" to others — students, experts, and their teacher-facilitators — for confirmation or reconstruction and elaboration. Interestingly, all those collaborative team skills and processes are the very sort that Corporate America seeks.

However, there are other elements of the new high school that may confuse Corporate America's pragmatism. For example, many students will pursue their goals through the arts. Eisner has demonstrated very clearly how the arts can be strong vehicles for developing higher-level thinking and reasoning, and they have the added benefit of a higher level of creativity.[30] Almost all students in the new high school will become actively engaged in the arts as a way to experience the joy of personal creativity, as well as for demonstrating their knowledge. Art gives students a chance to express their feelings and their thoughts in different modalities, ones that often can be more meaningful than written reports or findings. The arts contribute to what has been called a "metacurriculum" consisting of thinking skills, imagination, and oral and written expression.[31] Here is how one school summarizes the importance of the arts in the curriculum:

> As educators learn more about how children make sense of ideas and of their world, the arts provide schools with a powerful alternative model of teaching and learning. . . . Whether one focuses on conceptual understanding, on equity issues, or on utilitarian concerns of the workplace, their intellectual aims and pedagogical means make sense.
>
> In evaluating higher-order thinking . . . teachers . . . [will] assess students' perceptions, their productivity, and their reflection.[32]

Therefore, art will become an essential vehicle for developing not only creativity but also high-level thinking skills. Arts education is active learning and a way students have to construct meaning. Aside from its own intrinsic values, art is a marvelous vehicle for educating symbolic analysts and craftworkers in the precepts and processes involved with creativity.

Although the new high school will not attempt to train students for direct entrance into the workforce, the curriculum will include more work-related skills and attitudes. Those might come from traditional, but improved, cooperative education programs (which now involve about 8% of the high school population) that give students more meaningful work than the "hamburger slinging" jobs they experience today. Or schools might establish career academies or schools-within-a-school organized around occupational domains (now found within about 150 programs spread across the United States) where generic skills and processes are taught in academic courses through vocationally oriented simulations and projects. Or tech-prep, which links high schools with two-year community colleges in a supposed seamless development of career and craftwork occupational skills and knowledges, can tie high school and community college experiences more tightly.[33]

Apprentice programs, the last major way in which schools could become involved in the world of work, have generally not worked as well in the United States as they have in Europe, and less than 1% of America's youth are involved in them. That probably stems from the lack of cooperation from business in providing real work for apprentices and a lack of enthusiasm for those programs from unions fearful of member displacement. However, post-high school apprenticeships have proven to be an effective means of training craftworkers, judging by European successes, especially when governments assist smaller businesses to offset the program's costs.[34]

Three Fundamental Changes

The new high school's curriculum goals described above will set the tone for other changes. Those changes will reflect several important modifications in the high school's organizational pattern: staffing, governance structure, and relationship with the community and central administration. But there are three changes much more substantive than even those, innovations that will change the basic way instruction is delivered and assessed in the new high school:

1. A sophisticated technological infrastructure,
2. Constructivist pedagogy and authentic learning, and
3. Performance assessment.

Each of those three substantive changes has been foreshadowed by practices in some of today's progressive schools, but they will become commonplace as the United States enters the 21st century. The outcomes from those powerful changes in teaching and assessment will be students prepared with the fundamental intellectual processes and affective values needed to pursue further education and eventually craftworker and symbolic analyst jobs. The first of those changes will be the tremendous impact of technology.

Technology: As computer-based technology becomes the predominant mode of work and play, educators are aware that the mission of effective schooling in the age of information needs to be defined more clearly. They are asking: What technological vision will prepare students for an electronically linked worldwide society in which international computer networks and instantaneous communication will make American students members of a global society?[35] Howard Mehlinger, former dean of the Indiana University School of Education, puts it this way:

> The use of the new technologies will profoundly affect the schools. The very relationship between students and teachers will be challenged because the technologies enable learners to gain control of their own learning. . . . The new technologies provide students access to information that was once under the control of teachers.[36]

The potential of the new high school is to create a "community of learners" through technology, which could mean that a high school would not be confined to a single physical location. Rather, learning could go on in the home, the library, or anywhere through the use of electronic networks. In such a situation, not only students would be affected. As "schooling" becomes more broadly defined, there will be adults who will need retraining for new jobs that demand high-tech skills. Other adults interested in learning skills for hobbies, parenting, and other interests will become part of that community of learners. But that condition still lies somewhere in the dimmer future in which only futurists have confidence. A more grounded extrapolation is more cautious and emphasizes a phased development of the technological capacity of schools.

The new high school will need an infrastructure to handle a wide array of technology. By the year 2000, a computer-based interactive delivery system will provide a huge worldwide database for student exploration and self-discovery. Single sources, such as textbooks, will become antiques as learners scan vast electronic resources to find the information they need. Indeed, as Perelman maintains, if schools do not use computer-based technology wisely, they may soon become obsolete themselves.[37]

The question is whether schools *will* be able to transform themselves sufficiently to capitalize on that technological prowess. Currently, there is only one computer for every nine students in the United States, and many of those computers are out-of-date machines that cannot support important peripherals. In addition, the few available computers often are placed in computer labs where they have the least amount of accessibility to students and teachers. Other components of effective technology — CD-ROMs, Internet, modems, fax machines, and so forth — typically are unavailable in the classroom. The state of technology in the schools is so bad, concludes the Office of Technology Assessment, that the "majority of K-12 schools are ill-equipped to participate in the opportunities presented by telecommunication networks."[38] With the current push by businesses for high-tech workers and as the federal and state governments respond with increased funding, that dismal picture is changing. Connectivity is just around the corner.

The key to classroom accessibility is "networking," the digital interconnectedness of computers, other technologies (for example, telephones, modems, faxes, and the like), and fiber-optic cables and satellites. Networking expands the student's universe and, in that sense, will be a major factor for transforming schools.[39] Networks will increase the quality of information available to all classrooms. But networking also promotes a decentralized and an essentially democratic learning environment.

Technological competence will develop in these new high schools because students will learn to see technology as a tool, not merely as something for playing games. Many of today's students already are so comfortable with computers and related equipment they use them easily when given the opportunity. But technological competence goes beyond merely using a computer. Competence involves being able to evaluate the most appropriate and effective technology. Competence means being able to explore and to critique inappropriate uses of technology and to make judgments about the social consequences of technology. It also means dealing with ethical issues. Such issues are appropriate topics for the problem-based, integrated curriculum the new high school will have.

Some of the technology needed to accomplish technological competence is available to high schools right now; but much more will be needed, though it is unaffordable under current funding formulas.[40] The schools in which private investors have taken an interest show what can be done. For example, the now quite famous Apple Classrooms of Tomorrow project (ACOT), sponsored by Apple Corporation and some public agencies, has not only demonstrated the power of technology's use in education but also has taught educational designers some interesting lessons. As summarized by Apple's project director, David Dwyer, these were important in-progress findings:

- Teachers interacted differently with students. They became guides and mentors, rather than lecturers, because technology made access to huge databases so easy.

- Teachers began teaming, working across disciplines and altering schedules to accommodate ambitious student projects.
- Teachers altered the physical setup of the classrooms to accommodate collaborative student projects.
- Students often took leadership in the classroom, some organizing collaborative groups and some becoming tutors.
- Teachers became more student-centered in their planning and execution of curriculum themes.
- Students were systematically engaged in higher-order cognitive tasks.[41]

In ACOT schools, student activities were organized around themes with concepts from the disciplines embedded within them. Inquiry and process skills were highly valued outcomes. Collaborative student activities were the primary classroom organizational pattern.[42] All those efforts are paying off. After a four-year longitudinal study, the ACOT schools found important differences in student academic behavior. Students routinely used inquiry, collaborative, technological, and problem-solving skills. All those skills were very consonant with the SCANS skills for a world-class workforce. Perhaps the most significant finding from the ACOT project was:

> The greatest student advances occurred in classes where teachers were beginning to balance the appropriate use of direct instruction strategies and collaborative, inquiry-driven, knowledge construction strategies. . . . [Students] were seen as learners and expert resources; and [were] challenged by problems that were complex and open-ended. . . . In assessing students' work, teachers looked for evidence of deeper understanding — statements of relationships, synthesis, and generalization of ideas to new domains. And, of course, students had opportunities to use a variety of tools to acquire, explore, and express ideas. . . . [Students were able to] collect information in multiple formats and then organize, play, visualize, link, and discover relationships among facts and events.[43]

While ACOT schools were pioneers, others have begun to follow their lead. Aliso Niguel High School in Orange County, California, is just such a school. It has been hailed as a "cutting edge" high school for its extensive technology and curriculum innovations.

> Each classroom . . . features a Macintosh computer and a remote control linking a twenty-seven inch television monitor via fiber optic cable to a library nerve center filled with racks of laser disc players, CD ROMs, and other state of the art gadgets. At the stroke of a computer key, another information network will let students browse through the databanks of the Library of Congress, or look up documents at the United Nations in New York or Geneva.[44]

As with ACOT schools, the payoff for Aliso Niguel is significant, with students showing growth in all areas of academics and in inquiry and creativity. Aliso Niguel and ACOT schools are perhaps the most dramatic demonstrations of the power of technological applications in the classroom; they are showing how implementing technology changes both teacher and student approaches to learning. Computer-based technology goes beyond just the use of electronic tools; it impels teachers to reconsider how and what they do.

As the pervasive influence of technology spreads it will affect schools everywhere.[45] Administrators of high-tech urban and rural schools report that restructuring the schools around technology has revolutionized their ability to reach children with diverse learning styles and to track their progress. Disadvantaged or advantaged, young or older, gifted or remedial, English-speaking or bilingual, all students have an equal chance for success.[46] All students quickly learn to master computers and other technology, since most have begun at home or in elementary school. Thus, by the time students reach high school, their ability to use the technology effectively and independently is impressive.

Technology also has particularly beneficial effects in isolated rural school districts, affecting America's 6.9 million rural students. Distance learning, in particular, has been especially helpful for teaching special subjects for which there usually is no staff —

foreign languages, advanced placement math and science, and the like. Indeed, many of the innovations being sought by urban schools today — multigrade groups, cooperative learning, peer tutoring, close community ties, and the like — were pioneered in rural schools.[47]

But the most important movement will be connecting households with the schools, which will allow the school environment to extend into students' homes. This already is happening experimentally in a number of school districts. Several projects have been funded through the Department of Education's Technology Challenge Grants and the Department of Commerce's efforts to pilot "virtual communities." The federal Telecommunications and Information Infrastructure Assistance program has spent more than $25 million (plus $43 million put up as the matching grant funds by participants) to build pilot telecommunication systems linking households together with communities and schools. For example, teachers in Ogden, Utah, monitor the students enrolled in their classes and interact with them while they are at home with their computers.[48] Other districts, typically rural districts with distance-learning capabilities, use e-mail, the Internet, bulletin boards, the World Wide Web, and other means to communicate with students far from a school room. Whole communities are tied together with telecommunications, often centralized at the local school or similar learning center.[49] It will not be too long before those pilot programs are diffused throughout the country, that is, if the money keeps coming.

And money is the story. The hope in supporting the projects discussed was that computers and other technology would by now be ubiquitous in the schools. Districts predicted they would make heavy investments in stand-alone computers to be used in classrooms, rather than in computer labs. The projection was that by the 1990s, hardware and software purchases would be at an all-time high for schools.[50] In spite of the rhetoric, schools currently are about 10 years behind the technology used in the workplace and other areas. Many schools are not yet using personal computers as tools, let alone taking advantage of newer technologies.[51]

301

Interestingly, according to the National Center for Education Statistics in-depth report on technology in the schools, it is not an issue of *not having* technology but, instead, of not using or misusing it.[52] Much of the technology in schools has been reserved for administrative applications or has been placed in "computer labs" that are not routinely accessible to students.

Because of that misuse of technology, there are some who would give up on public high schools. Technophiles, such as Lewis J. Perelman, for example, believe that technological innovations will make schools unnecessary in the future. And no doubt, many of the innovations Perelman and others discuss will modify school practices merely by their implementation, even if they are met at first with resistance. But those who put their entire faith in the capability of technology to educate children and adults fail to understand the functions schools perform that go beyond simple absorption of information. Individual learning is more complex than that. And yet, Perelman has a point. There is a danger that computer-based networks could be used to transmit and amplify traditional and outmoded elements of schooling. It would be stupid to use the power of computers simply as electronic books; but if technology is looked on merely as a way to better transmit information, "school would be out."

That is why many thoughtful education leaders realize that creating more authentic and engaging curricula is as important as integrating the latest technological developments in schools. The promise of new technology will come only when practitioners realize how sophisticated technologies empower more effective models of teaching and learning and then act on that knowledge.[53] Existing technologies already are playing an important supporting role in promoting authentic learning.

Constructivist Teaching, Authentic Learning: Student-centered instruction and active learning will dominate in the new high school. Both strategies are needed to help students develop the self-reliant competencies discussed previously. Cognitive studies quite clearly have demonstrated for a decade or so that students learn better when they are actively involved in solving real-life problems, rather then being involved in decontextualized studies.[54] Until recently, however, it has been difficult to personalize and individualize the classroom sufficiently to put those findings into practice.

Classrooms will become more student-centered, collaborative, and interactive as they become increasingly involved with computer technology and telecommunication networks. With student-centered pedagogy, teachers plan for individualized and personalized learning, infusing technological assets where appropriate. For example, they can teach for multiple intelligences by making sure that students have multiple ways of attending to a problem or doing a project. They can structure learning environments or call attention to real-world concerns as a means for developing student curiosity. In other words, the pedagogy used by teachers should clearly focus on one major goal: the construction of knowledge through inquiry and reflection, or what others call higher-order thinking.

The substantive differences between traditional practices and the student-centered, active learning practices that will be seen in the future high school almost certainly will come from *constructivist pedagogy*. Cognitive science tells us quite clearly that people do not learn simply by accumulating more and more information into their brains, but by processing raw information into schema and concepts that have functional applications and that can provide feedback when used in creative ways. Because each person perceives and experiences reality slightly differently than does any other person, the learning process ensures the unique development of each person. Constructivist pedagogy capitalizes on that principle by creating situations that challenge students' naive or ill-formed schema. It allows them to confront their own paradoxes and anomalies and, through a process of inquiry and metacognitive reflection, facilitates their development toward expertise. The latter happens when, after they have gathered information and explored ideas related to a problem, they interact with their teachers and fellow students to discover the fit between what they have learned and a broader conceptual framework. Thus there is also a process of social construction. Together, as a result of that data, dialogue, negotiation, reflection, and consensus, students develop an understanding of the problems, paradoxes, phenomena, and conundrums they confront. The processes translates into real-world intellectual activity because the problems themselves are based in the real world.

The experiences of teachers who already are using constructivist teaching and the findings from empirical research have revealed several reliable ideas for effective constructivist teaching. Interestingly, the basic components of a constructivist pedagogy that will be found in the new high school also fit Corporate America's demand for an informed, creative workforce. Five elements characterize constructivist classrooms: 1) complex learning environments, 2) social negotiations, 3) juxtaposition of academic disciplines, 4) nurturance of reflexivity, and 5) student-centered instruction.

Complex Learning Environments: The classroom environment in the new high school will be a complex "generative learning environment," one that introduces paradox into student assumptions and naive formulations, anomalies in conventional wisdom that will initiate inquiry, research, and problem solving. Simulations are an effective means for introducing such complexity. For example, "Science World," one of the components of the Microworld program, is an interactive video-based world in which students conduct science experiments that usually would not be feasible in a school setting. In one simulation, students manipulate various combinations of an ecological system to discover the most cost-effective economic use for an environment.

As students become more skilled, they may wish to conduct complex studies on topics, many of which are not amenable to a single answer, only a consensus with others about the "best" answer or solution. For those kinds of resolutions, students must come to an affective as well as empirical consensus, called "social construction of reality."

Social Negotiation: Students develop a consensus on reality regarding definitions and solutions of problems through social interaction — reflection, dialogue, working to clarify definitions, quantifying observations, experimentation, and the like — in collaboration with others. It is much the same process that physicians use when attempting to make complex diagnoses and recommend courses of action.

> Collaboration is not just a matter of asking students to work together in groups or to share their individual knowledge with each other. Rather, collaboration enables insights and solutions to arise synergistically . . . that would not otherwise come about. For example, can you recall a situation in which, but for the efforts of a group, some problem would have gone unsolved? No single member of the group would have had the wherewithal to independently generate an effective solution, but the members together had the necessary knowledge.[55]

Collaboration also is important for helping students develop the ability to understand other people's perspectives as they themselves gain insights from their own explorations and electronic interactions.

Juxtaposition of Academic Disciplines: This is the process of examining the same issue or problem from multiple disciplinary perspectives, rather than from a single discipline. Looking at issues of poverty from the perspective of pure economics may lead to only partial understanding. Looking at poverty from a sociological and political perspective, in addition to economics, may broaden students' understanding and help them formulate more reasonable propositions. Looking at problems from all angles helps students construct a newer, *personal* understanding of reality.

Nurturance of Reflexivity: Constructivist classrooms are hotbeds of metacognitive musing. Metacognition is an awareness of one's own thinking and learning processes and the ability to critique their strengths and weaknesses in various contexts. It is a way, Marcy P. Driscoll says, of "Helping students to become more aware of their thinking processes [and] is essential to the development of mindful, strategic behavior or cognitive strategies."[56] Metacognition means more than passive introspection.

Reflexivity means that students become aware of how and what conceptual schema create meaning; and by using that awareness, they are able to invent and explore alternative structures and contexts. It is the process of mulling problems and even proposed solutions through the lens of different schema, by which students learn the habits of mind that Sizer, Meier, and others have suggested are the real outcomes expected of the high school experience.

Student-Centered Instruction: In the constructivist classrooms, the teachers present instruction in a framework of simulated or real situations that give students the opportunity to pose questions and explore anomalies. But it is the students who make judgments as to what, when, and how learning will occur, in contrast to the passive role they play in traditional classrooms. Students must be empowered to make such fundamental decisions in order to become autonomous learners. Teachers, of course, have a critical task in such classrooms as facilitators, coaches, and challengers. However, even though a classroom is student-centered, it is the teacher who provides the intellectual scaffolding and *contextualized* setting that engage student interest.

The aim of constructivist teaching is to move students from intellectual naiveté to higher-order thinking. In the constructivist classroom, learning intellectual *processes* is the goal. Thus teachers focus more on depth and intensity of learning than on breadth of coverage.

The Role of the Teacher: Students need teachers to coach them and to help them integrate their socially constructed new findings into broader intellectual schema. In that regard, the role of the teacher is critical for helping students discover the relationship between their "findings" and the broader conceptual patterns of the disciplines or more general intellectual frameworks.[57] The students' ideas are an important source of an emergent curriculum, but they are only one of many possible sources.

Teachers' facilitative role becomes especially critical with the heavy infusion of computers and other technology as tools for learning. Students will spend much of their time in independent and collaborative group activities, and they even may spend some time working from home. As students explain what they are doing and what they are discovering and as they interact with each other, the teacher must help students expand their range of choices and give examples that challenge too early closure on issues.

As constructivist pedagogy takes hold as the dominant approach to teaching, and as technology provides a world of information and enriched communication, the emergent curriculum will be the vehicle for students to discover ideas and knowledge. However, students, even the bright ones, are still naive, because they use prior experiences as their only guide for making sense out of new and unfamiliar data or events. That is where the facilitative role of teacher becomes critical. Constructivist teachers aim to have students learn that which is significant and meaningful, rather than trivial and ephemeral. The teacher must help students to "aim their work at production of discourse, products, and performances that have value and meaning beyond success in school."[58]

Aside from the personal growth students will experience in the new high school, there will be economic benefits for them and their future work. Taken together, education that focuses on the use of technology as a tool and constructivist pedagogy to help students develop higher-order thinking skills are exactly the world-class abilities that business wants for high-performance work organizations. As the new high school focuses on constructivist teaching aided by computer-based technology, it will accomplish two goals simultaneously: it will prepare young adults for the challenges of the 21st century and it will prepare them for high-performance work. However, that also will demand elaborate and effective assessment practices. Fortunately, the new high school will have a solid foundation in the assessment practices that are used now in today's forward-looking high schools.

Assessing Active Learning: Assessment of student progress and the effectiveness of school programs has always been an important aspect of public education. However, there now are at least three competitors, each with a different motive for controlling assessment. The state and federal governments want assessment data to rank and compare school districts and schools for political capital. Business wants evaluative data to confront schools and teachers with their weaknesses, hoping thereby to motivate them to do better in preparing the national workforce. Finally, there are principals and teachers who want assessment data in order to improve instruction and keep parents informed.

On the massive scale that the government wants, the only practicable way to get data is through standardized, multiple-choice tests. For business, any kind of "objective" test data — SATs, basic skills tests, national assessment tests, international comparative tests, even dropout statistics — is considered sufficient for what they need, which is merely evidence to show that schools are doing well or poorly.

Only at the level of the school and community is assessment seen as instrumental in changing the lives, behaviors, and habits of children. Teachers and parents want to know what children can *do*. That is something that standardized tests cannot do. Thus, a significant portion of the assessment process does not support teachers, students, and parents. In addition, when assessment is considered some other institution's responsibility — business or central government, rather than the schools — the results of assessment are not taken as seriously by students and teachers, as anyone who has worked in the schools knows.

What goes on inside the high school classroom rarely changes because some outside agency or a business charges that schools are not performing up to standards.[59] That is one reason that the decades in which state and federal governments inflicted inauthentic assessment on school districts has not brought change.

As Linda Darling-Hammond has said, the engine for school change — the catalyst for a community's political and educational development — must reside in the local school arena if it is to be effective:

308

The foundation of genuine accountability — one of the most frequently used words in the school reform lexicon — is the capacity of individual schools: 1) to organize themselves to prevent students from falling through the cracks, 2) to create means for continual collegial inquiry (in which hard questions are posed regarding what needs to change in order for individuals and groups of students to succeed), and 3) to use authority responsibly to make the changes necessary. No testing program can produce this kind of accountability. It will occur only if we find ways to empower, encourage, and allow schools to build an inquiry ethic, a community of discourse in the school, that is focused on students and their needs, rather than on the implementation of rules and procedures.[60]

As long as measurement of student learning depends on standardized measures — which focus on facts and formulas, rather than thinking — Bracey and Berliner are right: Our schools are doing great given their diversity. But standardized tests are not the measure of life abilities; they do not assess the ability to apply knowledge, to create, to innovate, or to do reflective thinking and logical analysis of real-world problems. Indeed, when standardized tests merely ask a student to choose an answer from a list of possible answers, the teacher cannot tell whether even the students who made the "correct" choices really knew the answers. In addition, the factual information that is learned in schools and assessed in tests is forgotten quickly. For example, a recent survey conducted by the National Science Foundation found that only 25% of those asked simple, factual, science questions — such as "What travels faster, light or sound?" or "True or false, the center of the earth is very hot" — gave correct answers.[61]

In the new high school, assessments must measure student cognitive understandings and developmental growth, that is, whether they can actually do something with their information. Performance assessments in which students must actually do something, make something, or otherwise demonstrate they can apply what they have learned will give teachers empirical knowledge of what their students are capable of doing and will lead to more focused instruction.[62] Those performance assessments are called "authentic."

Performance-based assessment will be the essential way of assessing high school students in the future. Indeed, performance assessment is gaining great credibility and use in schools today. There are many reasons for that growth. In particular, performance assessments: 1) provide for a more relevant and comprehensive evaluation of achievement, including students' strengths and weaknesses; 2) help focus curricula on critical thinking and multi-disciplinary understanding; and 3) encourage the use of effective instructional practices in the classroom.[63]

One of the more powerful performance assessments in use today — especially among the high schools participating in Theodore Sizer's Coalition of Essential Schools — is called the "exhibition." Exhibitions are presentations — verbal, written, graphic, models, computer simulations, or a combination — based on criteria set by teachers. But there are still other types of performance assessment being used, for example:

- *Portfolios* that consist of selections of student work. These might range from drafts of student work to finished products.
- *On-demand tasks* that require students to respond to a prompt or to a problem within a short period of time. The student usually does not have too much leeway in task definition.
- *Projects*, which are more complicated tasks and involve integrated disciplines to achieve. Projects last longer than on-demand tasks, and they might require group effort. The products of these projects may be included in portfolios.

Portfolios are a particularly interesting means for assessing students' developmental progress. The teacher and the students set out their expectations collaboratively, and the students collect evidence of their progress to establish benchmarks of progress several times over the course of a project or theme. A recent variation on portfolios — student-centered assessment — asks students to participate in their own assessment. The students help design the portfolio, develop it, and use it to make periodic self-assessments and self-corrections. The process motivates students, because they can see their own progress and can recognize gaps that need filling and because teachers can use information from the collaborative assessment process to coach students. Students take responsibility for telling at least part of the story of their own achievements to their families, a link that makes assessments real and motivating.

Performance assessments are having a positive effect on curricula and instruction. For example, project-based authentic assessments encourage greater integration of the disciplines; they also motivate students to use a variety of communication techniques, such as video, multimedia, and computer-based presentations.[64]

Some parents and pundits are reluctant to see performance assessments implemented more widely.[65] They are concerned that universities will not accept performance assessment results as valid for admissions. Many teachers, students, and parents worry that doing away with "objective criteria" — as if teacher grades and SATs could ever be considered objective — will leave little means by which colleges can distinguish college material from non-college material. However, if educators had a better understanding of their own history, such anxiety about college entrance requirements would be unnecessary. A look at the famous Eight-Year Study demonstrates that there are other, perhaps more valid, ways to determine a student's potential for college potential.

The Eight-Year Study, inspired by the Progressive Education Association in the 1930s, involved a group of 30 experimental schools that had put into place many of the reforms high schools are once again talking about — block schedules, integrated disciplines, continuous progress, nongradedness, assessment by demonstration, and others. Three hundred colleges and universities agreed to accept students from these schools based on teacher recommendations and student products, rather than on test scores and Carnegie units. The results of the study were spectacular and more than confirmed the strength of progressive methods. From its evaluation of nearly 1,500 matched pairs of students from experimental and non-experimental schools, the study demonstrated that, on virtually any dimension of student development and performance — from academic honors to civic and social responsibility, according to the judgments of professors, teachers, sociologists, and others —

the students from experimental schools outperformed those from traditional schools. Sociologic follow-up studies also showed that those positive outcomes continued far into the adult behavior of the participating students, who had less divorce, better jobs, and generally more successful lives than the comparison groups.[66]

When students are able to demonstrate what they have learned, rather than merely parroting back what they have heard from a lecture or read in a text, they can become self-reliant, effective citizens and participants in a world-class workforce. They can demonstrate their knowledge and creativity in actual situations.

Thus the new high school will be characterized by a student-centered curriculum with multidisciplinary themes and a focus on students' intellectual and personal growth. The amassing of more and more "information" will be replaced by a thematic, problem-based, constructivist approach to learning. The function of that approach is to help students develop *generative competencies*.

Generative Competencies

Generative competencies are knowledges and intellectual processes that enable students to apply their learning to new situations and new problems, thereby expanding their conceptual schema. As such, they have the greatest potential for transfer from classroom settings to real-world problems and situations. Generative competencies include *instrumental*, *personal*, and *technological*.[67]

Instrumental Competencies are the knowledges and skills that enable a person to accomplish specific tasks in a variety of situations. The essential aim of instrumental competencies is to make students self-reliant. They include basic literacies in reading, writing, mathematics, listening, and speaking. But they also involve more complex cognitive functions, such as higher-order and critical thinking and problem solving, as well as the creation of innovative or novel ideas. In the process of learning instrumental competencies, students also master essential concepts and structures that become, in turn, further instruments. The Coalition of Essential

Schools and a few secondary schools, such as Central Park East in New York, have what they call "Habits of Mind" that guide curriculum decisions. These Habits of Mind include:

- How do we know what we think we know? What's our evidence? How credible is it?
- Whose viewpoint are we hearing, reading, seeing? What other viewpoints might there be if we changed our position — our perspective?
- How is one thing connected to another? Is there a pattern here?
- How else might it have been? What if? Supposing that?
- What differences does it make? Who cares?[68]

Instrumental competencies are the basic rational and intellectual capabilities an educated person should be expected to have acquired on graduation from the new high school. They will form the foundation for that person's further life experiences.

Personal Competencies are those a person needs for satisfactory and fulfilling interpersonal relationships with family and friends and for effective social and civic involvement with people in their wider communities. One very real indicator of the failure of American education is the collapse of civic responsibility and a motive for altruism in the United States.[69] Therefore the critical issue in American education is having young adults address and become directly involved in human relations issues and problems, especially as they relate to common areas: values and ethics, solving problems, building consensus, team spirit, work ethic, attitudes of self-caring, interpersonal communication skills, tact, and others.[70] Those things are learned best by involvement and action, not as abstract ideas that keep people remote from one another's feelings or, worse, by mastering the content recommended in the new national civics standards.[71] They are learned in classrooms and schools that practice democratic behavior and processes, teamwork, collaborative learning, and consensus formation strategies.

The active learning of personal and social competence calls for community involvement and service projects. The community should see these service activities as generous acts by the students, who are giving back to their communities services that are needed, wanted, and appreciated.[72] Students, in turn, come to experience the personal rewards of altruism.

Such service is very much akin to the older "project-method," in which students became involved in real-life activities as a culmination of a unit of study. The modern adaptation of that involvement also is designed to give students experiences that add to their classroom studies, but these service activities also are more activist and include a high concern for civic duty. The activist model emphasizes what William Kilpatrick called "social reconstruction" and is aimed at enabling students to gain a sense of civic empowerment, an outcome that is more closely related to constructivist pedagogy.[73]

Service learning has been controversial; some conservative groups and parents have been critical. But the core idea is to let students do something with their newly acquired knowledge that will give them a sense that they can influence the course of events. Civic learning will be one way in which students can demonstrate what they have learned by engaging in a highly personal activity, one that their parents should be involved in helping them decide. What better way to show one has mature personal competence?

Technological Competencies are knowing how to use a wide array of tools — computers, modems, fax machines, scanners, the Internet, etc. — to access and manipulate data and to communicate ideas.

At both the high and low ends of use, technology is a fact of life in a modern industrialized economy. For high school students, gaining technological competency will be as basic as learning to read and write. Students will need to master these skills both for work and for active involvement in society. But in order to develop those skills, students must apply them in a variety of ways while in school — for example, writing, planning, using graphics in reports, conducting investigations through worldwide sources, telecommunicating, videoconferencing, and hundreds of other things.

The substantive changes in curriculum organization and instructional outcomes and in how education is delivered and assessed form the heart of the new high school. But further changes are in the cards — changes in size, staffing, and community involvement — that will affect the systemic focus of school transformation.

Organizing for Success

Even though emergent curricula, intense use of technology, authentic learning, and performance assessment all represent substantive changes in the future high school, they still represent a continuity from today's best practice in exemplary high schools. They have developed through a natural progression of education research and experience from the 1920s through today. However, there are other changes that must be made in order to accommodate those substantive changes, and they will profoundly alter the delivery of instruction in the new high school. Those changes include: 1) smaller schools with better scheduling, 2) differentiated staffing patterns, 3) changed governance processes, and 4) expanded community social and health services.

Smaller High Schools: The traditional assembly-line model of high school education — characterized by rigid class periods, teacher-led courses, large class sizes, passive students, and huge student bodies — has long ceased to work anywhere. It makes no difference if those traditional high schools are in the inner cities or suburbs — bigness makes the high school experiences too impersonal for students. Even worse, large, impersonal high schools slow student progress and help students develop attitudes antithetical to learning. Those attitudes are not found in small high schools.

The National Association of Secondary School Principals advocates an ideal size for a school of 600 to 900 students. That size high school has been found to correlate quite directly with improved achievement and reduced disruptive behavior.[74] In addition, small size leads to more attentive staff and more personalized instruction. Indeed, all aspects of a school become more personalized in a small school; just consider a cafeteria that is no longer crowded by 2,000 or 3,000 students waiting to eat.[75]

A small school has distinct advantages. First, teachers can get to know their students. Also, instruction can be more personalized and individualized.[76] That individualization will be strengthened as more schools adopt two of the strongest features of small high schools: assigning teachers as "personal adult advocates," which expands the counselor role to more active involvement with the students' lives, and the completion of a "personal plan for progress," by which each student's development can be mapped and remediated. None of these can be used in the large high schools we now have; it is physically impossible to do so.[77]

Fortunately, large high schools can be converted into small high schools through scheduling techniques and timing to organize schools-within-schools. That technique allows a large school to gain some, though not all, of the advantages of a small school.

Small high schools can enhance instructional effectiveness through scheduling innovations, such as block scheduling, that are proving to be very useful for both students and teachers. Block scheduling allows longer periods of time for in-depth exploration of themes and problems and for the completion of hands-on projects. It also enables teachers to have smaller classes and more personal contacts with students. Teacher loads in schools with block scheduling often are reduced from 150 students a term to 90 students, which allows teachers to work more closely with individual students. Block scheduling also frees up time for teacher planning and professional development activities by gaining anywhere from 50 to 90 minutes a day from direct instruction.[78]

Differentiated Staffing: Teachers should focus their teaching almost exclusively on facilitating student understanding and application of higher-order thinking processes. The capacity of modern technology to store and disseminate information from all over the world and from all kinds of expert sources will make didactic teaching even more archaic than it is today. Saying that, however, does not do justice to the complexity of teaching in the future.

316

Teachers in the 21st century will need to master effective cognitive strategies and facilitative and coaching techniques. They will need a full, working understanding of how humans learn and the implications of neuroscience and cognitive science for education. In addition, teachers will need to master other critical instructional techniques. That means learning how to apply the fundamental processes of constructivist and responsive teaching. Teachers will need to become cooperative planners working with other teachers, parents, and administrative support personnel, as well as with students. On top of all that, all teachers must learn the intricacies of applied technology, the use of computers, word processing, videos, CD ROMs, scanners, printers, the Internet, World Wide Web, and a host of software applications.

With those expanded responsibilities, teachers soon will realize that organizational encumbrances get in the way of effective learning. Thus teachers and their support personnel will need to master skills that help eliminate or reduce organizational impediments to continuous school improvement. That means learning about organizations and applying "organization development skills" and "interpersonal and small-group communication skills." Some teachers will even need community organization skills to help bring communities together for common purposes.

There is little hope that any one teacher can master all those challenges and do them equally well. Those complex tasks will need to be differentiated and divided among specialists, and that means the professional staff will be organized differently.[79]

In some ways, the new staff division of responsibilities will be similar to the differentiated staffing innovations in the early 1970s; but the essential basis for differentiation will be specialization, just as physicians have specialized.[80] Since the 1970s, a new interest in differentiated staffing has emerged. Certain districts in New York (such as Rochester's Career in Teaching program) and many states in the South have established differentiated teaching positions, defined by responsibility instead of simply by training. California took the lead in establishing the Mentor Teacher Program that has been emulated in several other states.[81] As education moves further in that direction, it is possible to envision what further differentiation may look like.

For example, there may need to be "education designers" who put together master lessons that kick off simulations that initiate student problem- and project-based investigations and then monitor the programs along the way. They might design and deliver electronic educational packets to schools and other learning centers. Education designers will need to know how to do database searches and organize data into a variety of modalities to meet students' multiple intelligences. Those same designers will have a strong role in developing and presenting professional development activities through telecommunication, teleconferencing, and teleworkshops. And they also could perform the same service for retraining parents or workers or anyone interested in expanding their knowledge or preparing for a new career.

There would be a variety of specialties, from teachers who are responsible for dealing with organizational and extra-organizational problems to paraeducators who work with small groups of students. There would be no ranks, but certain teachers would be assigned administrative roles, perhaps on a rotating basis.

Differentiated staffing is not a far-fetched idea; it was piloted very successfully in the early 1970s.[82] Even more recently, at least one district tried to associate differentiated staffing with other reforms. That experiment did not last, partly because the reform was a top-down decision that angered teachers who traditionally identify themselves as professional equals. That need not happen when the differentiation is based on widely accepted professional standards and arises from prolonged dialogue and consensus, as more successful differentiated staffing programs had been.[83] The point is that the professional challenges educators will face in the high-tech world of the 21st century will be beyond the capacity of generalist teachers, making differentiation of responsibilities a necessity. And just as the new role of frontline craftworkers are changing how decisions are made in high-performance work organizations, the new roles for teachers will necessitate changes in the ways schools and school districts are governed.

Governance: At the turn of the century, America's schools were inundated with students who had moved off the farm to the cities and with waves of immigrants. As America's education institutions became larger and the social and economic conditions of modern lives ever more complicated, Americans increasingly relied on bureaucratic procedures to ensure that schools met public expectations. Finance and governance systems were centralized, and 120,000 local school districts were consolidated into what is now 15,000. Soon schools were being held accountable for adhering to *centrally* issued operational rules, not for achieving parentally or socially desired outcomes.[84] That is why the traditional high school is governed by a school board that establishes policies for all schools, sometimes ignoring the unique needs or characteristics of specific schools. Leadership was ceded to district-level administrators; and that, in turn, caused centralized bureaucracies to grow exponentially. That governance process is similar to the Taylor model of control in industry. Today, as a result of that centralization movement, almost one-half of our public school population is enrolled in only 1% of our school districts.

The centralization of decision making has run its course, and the sense of trust that originally led to centralization has been lost. Local communities are beginning to demand more control of their own schools, with as little interference or direction from larger governing bodies as possible, especially from the federal government. That sentiment is exhibited most clearly in the fight over national standards. For many years state frameworks set guidelines for curriculum and, mostly in the Western states, determined what was written in state-adopted textbooks. As long as state curriculum frameworks were relatively innocuous, they stirred few local protests. On the other hand, the attempt to develop national standards and to use them to mold programs funded by the federal government caused a firestorm.[85] Ultraconservatives were the first to object, but it was not too long before more liberal Americans voiced similar concerns. The opposition to federal and even state control of local community schools has led to the emergence of alternative governing patterns for schools.[86]

Charter schools, site-based management, and other local control techniques are demonstrating the direction of change today; but even more profound changes can be expected into the future. With state governments increasingly moving to charter schools as a way out of the hot-potato issue of vouchers and privatization, it is likely that school boards' legal authority will give way, at least in major metropolitan areas, to school-level advisory councils.[87]

Future governance changes probably will continue to weaken the control of the district office and school board over individual schools. The role of the district office will switch from that of authoritarian, Taylorist control to a place where services are available and may be purchased by high schools for a fee.[88] That will include not only classified services but also bookkeeping and auditing, and perhaps even data-processing and personnel tracking services. But none of those services will ever again become a means to control the schools.

A high school organized to fulfill a public trust has to bring together community stakeholders to develop consensus about the school's mission.[89] Principles and the goals of educational programs needed to accomplish that mission must be clearly specified. Such a school must be an energized organization, with consistent ways to actively involve parents and other stakeholders with the school's functions. The school must have appropriate control of its funds and resources; it must be able to invest in its own future by hiring, training, and developing teachers to work effectively in light of student needs and school strategies. It also must create differentiated staffing patterns that reflect the realities of 21st century technology and pedagogy.

Expanded Community Services: One of the features of the new high school will grow out of its stronger relationship with its community. It will become a site where expanded services can be delivered to people in that community. Those services will include community health services; technology centers for those unable to afford the complex technology and the software needed to take advantage of it; parenting and childcare services that provide a safe educational setting for working parents; an elder-care center for the amusement, avocational pursuits, and education of retired citizens; and a re-education center for the retraining of deskilled workers and the special-order training of workers for particular organizations.[90] Finally, the "school" will be used as a general gathering place for community meetings and other events.

Preparations already are being made for such functions. At the University of Washington and Ohio State University, for instance, there are programs specifically designed to cross-train social service workers who could be housed in community centers, such as high schools.[91]

Some groups have resisted making the schools centers of community activities, fearing that it will divide communities, rather than unify them. But those groups are looking at current practices, not at the potential described in this chapter. Schools as community centers are necessary for a synergistic organization of social, training, and educational activities for both young people and adults.[92]

Can Corporations Run the Schools?

Before ending this chapter on the new high school, it is necessary to divert for a moment to consider the move toward privatization and increased financial control of America's public schools by corporations. Some people support those efforts because they have given up on public schools. Others do so because they have personal agendas or vested interests in privatization. But would it make any difference? Could public schools be handed over to private businesses and run better in a market-driven system? The evidence thus far does not support such optimism.

As we have seen, Corporate America's executives think they should be able to control the schools' agenda. Does business have the answer? Most independent authorities say no, Corporate America's goals are too narrow and self-serving for a school system that is mandated to develop the competencies of all American youth.

321

Businesses that have attempted to run school districts either directly through contracting or indirectly through "altruistic" and fiscal influence — such as the New American Schools Development Corporation's (NASDC) support for schools that adopt a business-like point of view — have uniformly not met the goals they set for themselves. Either they fell prey to the same fiscal and organizational limits that professional educators had faced or they were forced to admit that the education of children is not susceptible to the same processes by which one makes automobiles or personal computers. In some cases, apparently, the interests of business executives associated with the "reform" movement were more too push their own corporate agenda than those of schools.[93]

In his excellent, if icon-blasting, *Kappan* article, James Moffett questions both the efficacy and ethics of corporate executives' involvement in education reform. Moffett's article identifies some of those executives and the "hidden" agenda they may be bringing to their reform effort. Our old "benefactor" Louis Gerstner, then CEO of a huge tobacco company (RJR Nabisco), apparently pushed for increased sale of cigarettes to white working-class females and poor black school-age kids at the same time his corporation was funneling $30 million into NASDC activities. Other executives fought against taxes that would be used to improve schools, associated with anti-teacher state activities, and otherwise engaged in questionable activities. It appears to some that corporate executives have been taking away tax funds for schools with one hand and then doling out meager amounts to the schools they impoverished in a bare-faced attempt to gain greater influence for their agenda.[94]

Business, of course, has a legitimate concern with the education of young people in America. But its concerns necessarily must take a back seat to the desires of parents and society in general. Business now seems to be coming around to that point of view. They are beginning to sense the complexity of changing schools and to recognize the larger mission schools have, now and in the future.

The New High School Mission

Business thinks it knows what it wants, but it is backing the wrong horse. Corporate America's goals for schools were narrow and self-serving. Executives suggested that schools are failing at least in part because of the reforms proposed by educators. But business is beginning to see that when schools are used for narrowly focused or special-interest goals, they will not be effective. Business needs high-tech workers; student-centered teaching can provide that and still meet the personal and social needs of students. Constructivist and computer-based pedagogy is a way to prepare high school students for their future, including work. And assessment that demonstrates competence to both businesses and universities is the means for keeping students aware that their efforts are focused on that future.

Corporate America now sees that we are entering the "fourth wave" of reform, the wave that will center on young people first. A leading business think tank boastfully summarized this new view:

> The first wave, consisting of business "rolling up its sleeves" and getting involved in schools, occurred largely in response to publication of *A Nation at Risk*. . . . The second wave of reform focused on the application of sound management principles in schools [by bringing] strategic planning and other management seminars to school personnel. . . . The third wave emphasized advocacy for a variety of public initiatives . . . school choice and higher national standards of performance. But business leaders [finally?] were rapidly discovering that the problems were much too complex and interrelated for any single or simple solution to apply. . . . As the mid-1990s approach . . . a new wave of business involvement is beginning . . . collaborative alliances for systemic change.[95]

Schools should be centers for democracy and centers for integrity. And schools should be the center of inquiry for students, as well as places for teachers to continue to broaden their practice. All of that will happen as the new high school develops.

323

Even though the attributes of the new high school can be rough-ly identified, current reform efforts most likely will fail to change high schools sufficiently to bring them up to speed. Too much inertial force is built into today's high school practices: outmoded administration, unwilling and burned out teachers, fearful district officials, parents who want merely to have their own children replicate the "fun" they themselves had in high school, college admission requirements based on Carnegie units, antiquated state laws, and the whole panoply of traditions from sports activities to bands, all work very well to keep high schools the way they have been for the past eighty years.

So is there a solution? Can the reform movement do anything about inertia? Will high schools continue to be effective only for the small minority of advantaged kids whose parents and family life has been rich enough to make them "naturals" for college? Will high schools continue to leave the remaining majority of stu-dents floundering — most of them fully capable of a better edu-cation but denied it due to sorting, poor teaching, and the other dysfunctional attributes of today's high school? Will high schools become privatized and the exclusive schools for the rich and upper-middle classes, or will they be able to change and continue to perform their role in a democratic society?

The pundits' pessimistic response to those questions is that "nothing will change." But they misjudge the resilience of consci-entious educators. Change will happen. As more schools become professional development schools, affiliating with university col-leagues, senior staffs will enhance their skills. And as an entirely new crop of teachers — skilled in the new pedagogy and with new understanding of organizational dynamics — move into their pro-fessional roles, change processes will accelerate. Getting those teachers is the topic of our next chapter.

Notes

1. David L. Clark and Terry A. Astuto, "Redirecting Reform: Chal-lenges to Popular Assumptions About Teachers and Students," *Phi Delta Kappan* 75 (March 1994): 512-20.

2. The Children's Partnership, *America's Children & the Information Superhighway: An Update* (Santa Monica, Calif.: Children's Partnership, May 1996), pp. 3-7.
3. Ibid.
4. Ibid.
5. "Educators Seek Equal Access to Computers," *Tribune Newspapers*, 2 June 1995, p. A8.
6. U.S. General Accounting Office, "School Finance: Three States' Experiences with Equity in School Funding," HEHS 96-39 (December 1965): 3-10.
7. National Association of Secondary School Principals, *Breaking Ranks: Changing an American Institution, A Report of the National Association of Secondary School Principals in Partnership with the Carnegie Foundation for the Advancement of Teaching on the High School of the 21st Century* (Reston, Va., 1996), passim; "Report Calls for Personal Touch in High School," *Education Week*, 28 February 1996, p. 9; and "High School Reform Plan in the Works," *Education Week*, 2 March 1994, p. 5. It is interesting to see the continuous progression of the National Association of Secondary School Principals in this regard. Compare Herbert J. Walberg and John J. Lane, *Organizing for Learning: Toward the 21st Century* (Reston, Va.: National Association of Secondary School Principals, 1989) with *Breaking Ranks*.
8. Merrill Harmin, *Inspiring Active Learning: A Handbook for Teachers* (Alexandria, Va.: Association for Supervision and Curriculum Development, 1994), p. iv.
9. R.G. Des Dixon, "Future Schools: How to Get There from Here," *Phi Delta Kappan* 75 (January 1994): 361-65.
10. Sandra R. Miller, "A Delphi Study of the Trends or Events that Will Influence the Content of Curriculum and the Technological Delivery of Instruction in the Public Elementary School in the Year 2005," Doctoral dissertation, University of Michigan, Ann Arbor, 1995.
11. David Pearce Snyder, "What's Happening to Our Jobs?" *The Futurist* (March-April 1996): 8-13.
12. David Elkind, "School and Family in the Postmodern World," *Phi Delta Kappan* 77 (September 1995): 8-14.
13. Barbara Means et al., *Using Technology to Support Education Reform* (Washington, D.C.: U.S. Department of Education, 1993), p. 4.

14. National Association of Secondary School Principals, op. cit., passim.
15. Dominic J. Brewer, Daniel L. Rees, and Laura M. Argys, "Detracking America's Schools," *Phi Delta Kappan* 77 (November 1995): 210-15.
16. National Association of Secondary School Principals, op. cit., pp. 21-29.
17. Catherine Twomey Fosnot, ed., *Constructivism: Theory, Perspectives, and Practice* (New York: Teachers College Press, 1996), p. 29.
18. Nel Noddings, "A Morally Defensible Mission for Schools in the 21st Century," *Phi Delta Kappan* 76 (January 1995): 365-68.
19. National Association of Secondary School Principals, op. cit., pp. 11-21.
20. Sylvia Weir, "The Computer in Schools: Machines as Humanizers," *Harvard Educational Review* (February 1989): 61-72.
21. Harmin, op. cit., pp. 2-10. Harmin suggests the specific plans and possible activities that teachers may wish to introduce into their classes to actively engage students in their learning.
22. William Stephen and Shelagh Gallagher, "Problem-Based Learning: As Authentic as It Gets," *Educational Leadership* (April 1993): 25-28.
23. Clinton E. Boutwell, *Getting It All Together: The New Social Studies* (San Francisco: Leswing Press, 1972), pp. 13-33.
24. Arthur L. Costa and Rosemarie Lieberman, "Process Is as Important as Content," *Educational Leadership* (March 1995): 23-24.
25. Ibid., p. 23.
26. Boutwell, op. cit.; see also Costa and Lieberman, op. cit., pp. 23-24.
27. Even though the concept of emerging curriculum began in the early childhood educational setting, it still is, as Deborah Meier said, "Good enough for all of us." See Elizabeth Jones and John Nimmo, *Emergent Curriculum* (Washington, D.C.: National Association for the Education of Young Children, 1994), p. 1; and Joyce McDonald, ed., *Open Education as a Component of Restructuring*, Hot Topics Series (Bloomington, Ind.: Phi Delta Kappa, 1993), passim.

28. Eliot Wigginton, "Foxfire Grows Up," *Harvard Educational Review* 59 (February 1989): 26-27.

29. Weir, op. cit., pp. 61-72.

30. Elliot W. Eisner, *Cognition and Curriculum Reconsidered*, 2nd ed. (New York: Teachers College Press, 1994), passim.

31. Craig Sautter, "An Arts Education School Reform Strategy," *Phi Delta Kappan* 75 (February 1994): 433-37.

32. "The Arts and Other Languages: From Elective to Essential," *Horace No. 5* (Coalition for Essential Schools: May 1996): 1-7.

33. Paul Osterman and Maria Iannozzi, "Youth Apprenticeships and School-to-Work Transition: Current Knowledge and Legislative Strategy," *EQW Working Papers* (Philadelphia: University of Pennsylvania, Center on the Educational Quality of the Workforce, 1993), p. 7.

34. Lisa M. Lynch, *Strategies for Workplace Training: Lessons from Abroad* (Washington, D.C.: Economic Policy Institute, 1993), pp. 2-3, 41-46.

35. The University of Oklahoma Continuing Education Community Programs and the Center for Educational Leadership and Technology are leading the way in this endeavor. See "Visions of Schooling in 'Information Age' Sought," *Education Week*, 24 November 1993, p. 5.

36. Howard D. Mehlinger, "School Reform in the Information Age," *Phi Delta Kappan* 77 (February 1996): 402.

37. Lewis J. Perelman, *School's Out* (New York: Avon, 1992).

38. Office of Technology Assessment, *Teachers & Technology: Making the Connection* (Washington, D.C.: U.S. Government Printing Office, April 1995), p. 20.

39. Fred M. Newmann and Gary G. Wehlage, "Five Standards of Authentic Instruction," *Educational Leadership* (April 1993): 8-12.

40. U.S. General Accounting Office, *School Facilities: America's Schools Not Designed or Equipped for 21st Century* (Washington, D.C., April 1995), pp. 1-66; and National Center for Education Statistics, *Advanced Telecommunications in U.S. Public Schools, K-12* (Washington, D.C.: U.S. Department of Education, February 1995), pp. 3-5.

41. David Dwyer, "Apple Classroom of Tomorrow: What We've Learned," *Educational Leadership* (April 1994): 4-10.

42. "With Computers, Apple Project Finds Less May Be More," *Education Week*, 15 November 1995, pp. 6-7.

43. Dwyer, op. cit., p. 9.

44. Anna Cekola, "High-Tech High," *Los Angeles Times*, 8 September 1993, pp. A1, A3.

45. For example, Los Angeles Unified School District, which has not built a new high school in twenty years, is now about to build the most technologically sophisticated high school in California, and perhaps the country. It will house a business and technology academy and a media and communication academy appropriate for Southern California's major industries. See "Plans Jell for 'Futuristic' High School," *Los Angeles Times*, 21 August 1995, pp. B1, B3.

46. Deborah L. Cohen, "From Cradle to Computer," *Education Week*, 12 January 1994, p. 33.

47. "Demonstration Sites Seek to Help Schools Make Technological Leap," *Education Week*, 16 November 1995, p. 6; "E.D. Report Hails Rural Schools as 'a Model of Strength'," *Education Week*, 3 August 1994, p. 3.

48. Peter West, "Homeward Bound," *Education Week*, 10 January 1996, pp. 3-7.

49. Megan Drennan, "Home Improvement," *Education Week*, 10 January 1996, pp. 23-24.

50. "Districts Plan to Buy More Computer Equipment," *Education Week*, 1 December 1993, p. 4.

51. U.S. General Accounting Office, op. cit., pp. 1-7.

52. National Center for Education Statistics, op. cit., pp. 3-5.

53. John O'Neil, "On Technology and Schools: A Conversation with Chris Dede," *Educational Leadership* (October 1995): 6-12; Paul Resta, "Preservice Education," *The American School Board Journal Special Supplement, "The Electronic School,"* (September 1993): A27-A29.

54. Marcy P. Driscoll, *Psychology of Learning for Instruction* (Boston: Allyn and Bacon, 1994), pp. 205-38.

55. Ibid., p. 368.

56. Ibid., p. 370.

57. Weir, op. cit., pp. 61-72.

58. Newmann and Wehlage, op. cit.

59. Paul E. Barton and Richard J. Coley, *Testing in America's Schools: Policy Information Report* (Princeton, N.J.: Educational Testing Service, 1994), pp. 2-37.

60. Linda Darling-Hammond, "Reframing the School Reform Agenda: Developing Capacity for School Transformation," *Phi Delta Kappan* 74 (June 1993): 760.

61. "Only 25% of American Adults Get Passing Grades in Science Survey," *Los Angeles Times*, 24 May 1996, pp. A22.

62. Rick Stiggins, "Assessment Reform: We're Still Not Getting It," *Forward, California Association for Supervision and Curriculum Development Newsletter* (May 1996): 1, 10.

63. Michael B. Kane and Nidhi Khattri, "Assessment Reform: A Work in Progress," *Phi Delta Kappan* 77 (September 1995): 30-32.

64. For more on this, see Kevin Bushweller, "The High-Tech Portfolio," *Executive Educator* (July 1995): 19-22; Paul E. Barton and Richard J. Coley, *Testing in America's Schools: Policy Information Report* (Princeton, N.J.: Educational Testing Service, 1994), pp. 2-37; and Association for Supervision and Curriculum Development, "On the Cutting Edge of Assessment," *Education Update* (June 1996): 4-7.

65. "Even as Popularity Soars, Portfolios Encounter Roadblocks," *Education Week*, 5 April 1995, pp. 8-9.

66. Lawrence A. Cremin, *The Transformation of the School* (New York: Alfred A. Knopf, 1961).

67. These descriptors are taken from a number of sources, chiefly, Marcy P. Driscoll, op. cit., Chapter 11; Office of Educational Research and Improvement, *Issues of Curriculum Reform in Science, Mathematics, and Higher Order Thinking Across Disciplines* (Washington, D.C.: U.S. Department of Education, January 1994); and Jeang-im Chi and Michael Hannafin, "Situated Cognition and Learning Environments: Role, Structures, and Implications for Design," *Educational Technology Research and Development* 43, no. 2 (1995).

68. Deborah Meier, "How Our Schools Could Be," *Phi Delta Kappan* 76 (January 1995): 371.

69. R. Freeman Butts, "Antidote for Antipolitics: A New 'Text of Civic Instruction'," *Education Week*, 18 January 1995, pp. 48, 38; and "Teaching Democracy," *Education Week*, 19 April 1995, pp. 33-37.

70. David Elkind, "School and Family in the Postmodern World," *Phi Delta Kappan* 75 (February 1994): 8-14.

71. "Panel Unveils Standards for Civics Classes," *Education Week*, 23 November 1994, pp. 1, 11.

72. Jessica Parker, "At Your Service," *Education Week*, 23 November 1994, pp. 19-26.

73. Joseph Kahne and Joel Westheimer, "In Service of What: The Politics of Service Learning," *Phi Delta Kappan* 77 (May 1996) 592-99.

74. "By the Numbers: Ideal High School Size Found to Be 600 to 900," *Education Week*, 24 April 1996, p. 11. This conclusion was drawn from a study involving 789 high schools using data from the federally supported National Education Longitudinal Study.

75. Ann Bradley, "Thinking Small," *Education Week*, 22 March 1995, pp. 27-29; Meg Sommerfeld, "Curtain Goes Up on the Life of a New School," *Education Week*, 20 September 1995, pp. 12, 14.

76. Diana Oxley, "Organizing Schools into Small Units: Alternatives to Homogeneous Grouping," *Phi Delta Kappan* 75 (March 1994): 521-26.

77. "Report Calls for Personal Touch in High School," *Education Week*, 26 February 1996, p. 9.

78. More time is gained by reducing travel time between classes and time wasted taking attendance and other business before students get on task. See "More and More Schools Putting Block Scheduling to Test of Time," *Education Week*, 22 May 1996, pp. 1, 14-15, 17.

79. One idea of how teacher ranks will be organized in the future is presented in Dixon, op. cit.

80. Clinton E. Boutwell, Dean R. Berry, and Robert E. Lundgren, "Differentiated Staffing: Problems and Prospects," in *Differentiated Staffing*, edited by Mary-Ann Scobey and A. John Fiorino (Washington, D.C.: Association for Supervision and Curriculum Development, 1973), pp. 9-22; M. John Rand, "A Case for Differentiated Staffing," in *Differentiated Staffing*, edited by James A. Cooper (Philadelphia: W.E.B. Saunders, 1972), pp. 45-53.

81. Southern Regional Education Board, *Career Ladder Clearinghouse* (April 1994), passim.

82. Boutwell, Berry, and Lundgren, op. cit., pp. 9-22.

83. Jack Rand, Robert Lundgren, and Clint Boutwell, "Differentiated Staffing and Problem Solving: Beyond the Naysayers," *Collective Negotiations in the Public Sector*, no. 3 (August 1972): 219-31. Dr.

J. Rand, Temple City's superintendent, was deeply committed to human sensitivities and had spent several years in dialogue with teachers and their unions before proposing staff differentiation changes to his board.

84. Paul Hill, James W. Guthrie, and Larry Pierce, "Whatever Happened to the Local School?" *Education Week*, 10 January 1996, pp. 56, 33.
85. Peter Schrag, "The New School Wars: How Outcome-Based Education Blew-Up," *American Prospect* (Winter 1995): 53-62.
86. Jacqueline P. Danzberger, Michael W. Kirst, and Michael D. Usdan, *Governing Public Schools: New Time, New Requirements* (Washington, D.C.: Institute for Educational Leadership, 1992), pp. 7-9.
87. See, for example, Cross City Campaign for Urban School Reform, *Reinventing the Central Office: A Primer for Successful Schools* (Chicago, 1995), pp. 6-8.
88. Ibid.
89. Paul Schwarz, "Needed: School-Set Standards," *Education Week*, 23 November 1994, pp. 44, 34.
90. BMW and Mercedes manufacturers are asking school districts in various Southern states to undertake such training. They want to bring Americans up-to-speed on German advanced auto technology. The participating schools receive technical and financial support, as well as capital equipment that can be used for other purposes after the initial purpose has been served.
91. Deborah L. Cohen, "A Working Relationship," *Education Week*, 28 February 1996, pp. 29-32.
92. "Report Urges Family Strategy Broader than School Centers," *Education Week*, 3 April 1996, p. 6.
93. James Moffett, "On to the Past: Wrong-Headed School Reform," *Phi Delta Kappan* 75 (April 1994): 584-90.
94. Ibid.
95. Sandra Waddock, *Business and Education Reform: The Fourth Wave* (New York: Conference Board, 1994), pp. 11-14.

Chapter Nine

From Here to There

Thoughtful educators have shifted from talk of "reform" to consideration of a more fundamental "transformation" of the schools.[1] The influences of technology and a changing economy are too substantial merely to freshen up familiar education practices by wedging in new ideas. Americans will be dealing with new personal, political, and economic complexities. Workers must be able to learn new technologies, frame problems, design their own tasks, plan, construct, evaluate, and cooperate. These changes signal a new mission for education. Tinkering and patchwork are insufficient. The only way to meet that challenge is to make deep changes in the purpose of schooling, teaching, school organization, and policy.

> This changed mission for education requires a new model for school reform, one in which policy makers shift their efforts from *designing controls* intended to direct the system to *developing the capacity* of schools and teachers to be responsible for student learning and responsive to student and community needs, interests, and concerns. Capacity-building requires different policy tools and different approaches to producing, sharing, and using knowledge than those traditionally used throughout this century.[2]

There now are three contending views that attempt to influence the metamorphosis of education. The first, usually held by business and government officials, is a top-down view that sees the function of education as supplying the economy with workers in a cost-effective manner. The second, usually held by parents, is the bottom-up view that sees the function of the schools as the preparation of children for equal opportunities by providing them with the credentials necessary for gaining advantage in the real world. Both of those views are utilitarian economic views of education. They fit with a behaviorist view of education. That view defines "learning" as the management of stimulus and response, something easily controlled from outside the classroom by identifying exactly what is to be learned and breaking it into small, sequential bits for teachers to transmit to students. Advocates of both of those notions focus on tightening the controls: more courses, more tests, more directive curricula, more standards enforced by more rewards and more sanctions.

> One of the most extreme versions of this [behaviorist] viewpoint has been implemented in one of the nation's largest urban school districts, in which teachers are supplied with a K-12 standardized curriculum outlining the scope and sequence for instruction in each subject in each grade, complete with a pacing schedule showing how much time teachers should spend on each topic as well as lesson plans for each day of the school year. Grading standards are also prescribed, showing how much weight teachers should give to each type of assignment (the assignments are also specified) and how they should calculate grades. Promotion standards are determined by standardized tests, which were developed to match the curriculum. The assumption is that marching the students through these procedures is all that is necessary to ensure learning.[3]

In *Roots of Reform: Challenging the Assumptions that Control Change in Education*, the authors summarize the effects on school reform of the behaviorist/utilitarian view with this astute observation:

> The current, dominant assumptions controlling education reform are a complex nest of beliefs, practices, political pre-

dispositions, actions, and compromises of expediency and advantage. . . . The very organization of schools is indebted to the link between school and industry, seen as a model of bureaucratic efficiency during the first decade of this century. A meritocratic view of schooling derives from a meritocratic view of American society. . . . The Horatio Alger myth, the low status of teaching, the sanitized curriculum of whiteness and maleness, the high school schedule, ability tracking, the inevitability of school failure and retention — all are practices and beliefs to which we have become accustomed. . . .

More recent shifts in policies have increased the obstacles to school reform. . . . The shifts from equity concerns to standards of performance, from access to selectivity, and from social concerns to economic concerns have introduced a new and threatening level of school failure for millions of students.[4]

The third view, called developmental, is usually held by educators and is broader in scope than the economic viewpoints of the top-down "social efficiency" or bottom-up "social mobility" advocates.[5] The third view of teaching and learning, the view that underpins school transformation, starts from the assumptions that students are not standardized and that teaching is not routine. That position focuses on building the capacities of teachers and on developing schools as inquiring, collaborative, learning organizations. Consonant with recent research on teaching and learning, this view acknowledges that *effective* teaching should respond to students with different learning styles, with differently developed intelligences, or at different stages of cognitive and psychological development. Thinking about teaching and learning along these lines suggests a very different approach to education transformation than has occurred so far.

From this perspective the primary means to transform schools is to strengthen teaching. That can be done by improving teacher education, licensing, and certification processes; creating knowledge-building institutions, such as professional development schools; enhancing the on-the-job professional development experiences

335

of teachers; involving teachers substantively in school decision making; rethinking teacher assessment practices; and creating self-help networks of teachers and schools. This third view, which we will possessively call the "professional" or developmental view, maintains that the purpose of education is to establish a learning community, one based on shared educational experiences that prepare people for full participation as citizens in a democratic society and a technology-driven economy.[6]

As long as educators, especially administrators, continue to react to the wide variety of utilitarian demands for "reforming" the schools, they can almost guarantee constantly shifting priorities and dispersed funding. Worse, simple-minded utilitarian reforms actually change very little in schools.

> When the launch of Sputnik worried America's military-industrial complex, James B. Conant and other cold warriors demanded an emphasis on "basics," especially more rigorous science and math instruction. Today, as globalization calls all economic certainties into question, IBM's Louis Gerstner and other CEOs seek tougher educational standards. . . . Public schools are often called upon to deal with cultural conflicts over race, religion, ethnicity, moral values, sexuality, and environment problems, among other issues.
>
> In nearly every case, educators have responded by reforming schools according to the demands of the strongest political constituencies (usually corporate interests). And in nearly every case, education is defined as an agency of cultural, social, and economic discipline, so the basic structures and procedures found in most public schools — from curriculum planning to standardized-test-driven instruction to the herding of students down the hall at the sound of a bell — are rarely changed. Reform means refining and perhaps supplementing these basic features with timid and limited innovations; the routines of schooling are seldom thoroughly overhauled. As long as our culture views education as essentially a process of mass producing citizens, workers, and consumers for the existing economic system, we can expect no more fundamental changes.[7]

During these waves of vicious criticism and panicked reaction, education researchers quietly were gathering the empirical evidence that demonstrated the efficacy of Deweyan ideas. Such scholars as Jerome Bruner, Vygotsky, Chomsky, and Gardner added to education's understanding of the function of disciplined logic, language, discovery, and intelligence. Neurobiologists contributed insight into brain functioning. But utilitarian demands keep rising.

As social problems emerged — drugs, crime, broken families — citizens demanded more from their schools. It was not long before the essential mission of schooling was blurred in an ever-expanding array of special interests, each demanding its own piece of the action. The business community is part of that horde with its own demands and its own agenda. Of course, the difference between the business community and the parents' community is clout; business executives are able to influence education policy at the state and federal levels.

Most of the time, the more developmental view of schooling held by educators is subdued by the "economic" utilitarian forces. But the New Economy has changed the rules. To get a decent job now, a person has to be able to think, to apply knowledge, to solve problems, and to be inventive and creative — the same outcomes expected in a "progressive" education. There now is an historic confluence of two formally separate themes: what business wants in its workforce is what thoughtful educators will be able to provide.

While the professional educators may have won the intellectual contest with the utilitarians, they certainly have not been able to transfer their ideas into reality. To get schools to be able to do all that society expects of them, they will have to change profoundly.

> These tasks suggest a radically different approach to educational improvement. Rather than seek to make the current system of schooling perform more efficiently by standardizing practice, school reform efforts must focus on building the capacity of schools and teachers to undertake tasks they have never before been called upon to accomplish. Schools and teachers must work to ensure that *all* students learn to

think critically, to invent, to produce, and to solve problems. Because this goal requires responding to students' nonstandardized needs, it far exceeds what teacher-proof curricula or administrator-proof management processes could ever accomplish.[8]

Tougher graduation standards, longer days, more stringent teacher licensing, more "solids," and other so-called reforms of the 1980s did little to substantively reform high schools because those "reforms" did little to change the basic dynamics of high schools. Some analysts assumed that more coursework and more rigor means more quality. But without changes in teaching strategies, class size, better resources, and curriculum organization, the students in those courses merely find themselves with longer lists of facts and heavier textbooks. Simplistic add-ons and heavier workloads fail to address the underlying issue of why schools need to be reformed in the first place.

The failures of reform stem from the attempts by state governors and federal politicians to find quick, easy solutions to the demands of business for a "world-class workforce." With every recommendation, standard, or goal that is pushed, there is a predictable counter-reaction from other vested interests pushing for their own vision of schooling.

We need to rethink our assumptions about the meaning and purpose of education in a changing world. Schools must serve human needs, not just economic and political agendas; they need to focus first on the healthy development of young people's innate and multifaceted potential. We must stop looking at young Americans as cultural capital, merely as raw material for building a more efficient and competitive economy. Looking only at the economic person deflects schools from their fundamental mission. But that is what we continue to do.

Why Reforms Fail

There are many reasons that "reforms" fail. The primary reason, of course, is that such reform proposals do not follow certain well-known principles that affect the diffusion of knowledge and especially the rules that govern adult learning.[9] Stanley Pogrow has identified a number of myths about change, all of which have guided failed reforms. One of those myths is that rational argument and persuasive techniques, by themselves, are sufficient and effective for generating reform.[10] As Everett Rogers confirmed years ago, using rational arguments to encourage change usually works only with those people who are predisposed to adopt new practices anyway — the "innovators," he called them.[11] Everyone else takes the position of "show me."

Demonstration and personal experiment are the most effective routes to innovation. The least effective techniques are persuasion and top-down mandates. The cumulative research from organization development studies since the late 1930s shows conclusively that for adults to be willing to take the risk and perform the work of change, they must be involved not only in identifying what changes will take place, but also in first identifying the need for change.[12] Trying to use only rational argument to persuade adults to change — attempting to persuade by showing that the facts are on the side of righteousness — simply will not work for either large- or small-scale change.[13]

Thus the innovations that are adopted successfully by high schools today are those that have demonstrated their usefulness for solving problems that teachers and administrators have identified for themselves — for example, block scheduling, integrated disciplines, student-centered curricula, and others.

Successful attempts to modernize the high school have actively involved both education professionals and the people of their community — parents, business people, local government officials, professionals serving in other social agencies, senior citizens, and a host of others. These are the stakeholders in the education of young Americans; and if the high school is to be transformed, these stakeholders must forge a consensus on how the high school should go about accomplishing its mission. While much can be learned from best-practice schools and from research, the "new" school must be the product of community consensus, not some authoritative initiative from state or federal levels.[14]

When the stakeholders begin to consider the characteristics they want in their new school, there is one essential question that needs to be asked:

> Just what kind of high school would be needed if the expected student outcomes were higher-order thinking, teamwork, effective interpersonal skills, self-reliance, problem solving, self-confidence, self-direction, and application of disciplined knowledge to creative problem solving — and yes, fun and joy?[15]

There are other questions that must follow, and a number of those questions concern values. Schools and school districts are social systems, composed of common and potentially conflicting values, views, beliefs, politics, and practices. However, if the school is to meet the criteria described above and is to be effective in preparing young adults for 21st century society, there needs to be a change in the institutional values of the school. Terry Astuto and her colleagues described that change as a shift in values from:

- Individual to institutional responsibility for achievement.
- Instrumentality to entitlement.
- Institutional to personalized outcomes.
- Bureaucracy to democracy.
- Commonality to diversity.
- Narrowly defined to broadly defined social mission.
- Competition to collaboration.
- Intervention to facilitation.[16]

More specific questions narrow the task: What would the curriculum look like? How would instruction be delivered? What pedagogy would predominate? What relationship would students have with the wider social, political, and economic life of the community? How would student progress be assessed? How would the school be organized? What would be its relationship to the district office and state? How would parents be involved? All of those questions need to be addressed by participants — teachers, principals, parents, students, and others.

Note that the object of change is the *individual* high school. That is the school that parents trust. Education is transformed one school at a time. Thus solutions will grow from the bottom up. That also means reducing any influence from federal "voluntary" standards, state frameworks or curricula, or even district office or school board mandates. As far as parents and teachers and principals care, those agencies and mandates do not mean a thing — except to the extent that they must be avoided.

Although federal standards become things to resist, that does not mean that standards are difficult to determine on the "bottom." The people involved in developing those standards — teachers, parents, principals, and other staff — know their communities and know their children's needs. In addition, there seems to be remarkable agreement among Americans on a number of values. In an extensive study of American values conducted by Phi Delta Kappa International, there was a much higher than expected agreement among respondents on what values should be taught in school. The PDK group found levels of agreement ranging from a low of 60% to a high of about 90%. Even when focus groups and interviews were conducted, both educators and noneducators were able to agree on a rank order of the purposes of education.[17]

Parents are a large political block and could become potential allies to professionals as they work to redefine their school goals and communicate them to a wider audience. Parents want to be actively involved in their child's education and in decisions about certain substantive issues. For example, when asked if they should be involved in curricular matters, 61% of the parents said they should. And employers increasingly are letting parents take time from work to attend school activities; 35% do so without penalty, and 42% more can take the time by using vacation time. However, parents are reluctant to participate because they feel that teachers do not want them.[18]

A major problem in getting parents involved in school is the drop in involvement as their children move into the secondary grades. This happens even though the evidence shows that when parents are involved with their sixth- through 12th-graders, their children get better grades, are more likely participate in extra-curricular activities, and are less likely to repeat a grade or be discipline problems. Obviously, involvement is such a positive experience for parents that planners need to make a concerted effort to keep parents engaged. Educators need to use techniques to get parents involved in establishing curriculum goals, discipline policies, and other substantive activities. In that way, parents will develop a sense of working with school people for the betterment of their children and will be more willing to be an ally for change than a resister.[19]

Unfortunately, the gulf between parents and teachers remains too wide. Teachers must learn better ways to encourage more active parental involvement; but education schools and policy makers have *failed* to show teachers how they can do that. In a recent survey by the University of Minnesota's Center for School Change, about 1,800 teachers nationwide were asked about where training fell short and how they would like to see parents play a greater role. Most teachers agreed that more parent involvement is needed. But they defined parents' roles much too narrowly. Three-fourths of the teachers said attending parent-teacher conferences was the most important way for parents to get involved. About two-thirds said parents' general encouragement and help on home-work would make a difference in student performance.[20] Such limited parent participation will not build the loyalty and commitment needed to transform high schools. Building stronger relations means involvement in substantive planning, engaging in work that parents and other stakeholders feel is important and in their interest.

When educators, parents, and the community work together, there is no end to the accomplishment that can be made. One excellent example is the Industrial Areas Foundation organization in Texas. The IAF's aim is to improve the quality of life of people, including improving schools and health facilities. The IAF leadership brings leading educators, such as Theodore Sizer and Howard Gardner, to talk and plan with parents and teachers. But participants do not just sit and listen to those ideas; they become actively engaged in developing and implementing programs based on those ideas. The result is strengthened ownership of the schools and the process.

> That kind of interaction of a united school reformer and a group of parents and activists is often something that is missing from the school reform effort. Too often the movement does not engage parents and community members in meaningful ways. . . . Without the involvement of these groups, schools may make some temporary improvements but not the type of long-term permanent changes that are needed. . . . One [major] element of success [for IAF] that we've identified is that they have enlarged the number of individuals who have ownership in the success of their schools.[21]

As a collegial team of planners, teachers, principals, students, and parents each have a separate purpose. Teachers and principals have the critical function of introducing parents to the evidence supporting best practice. Reviewing those best practices, interacting with leading high school educators, and even visiting exemplary schools with other stakeholders will give everyone a vision of what high school could be like in the 21st century. Parents, on the other hand, need to help professionals understand clearly the concerns and wishes parents have for their children. And students need to react to proposals and test them against their own realities. Team members will disagree; however, conflict resolution is much easier at the school level because there are higher levels of trust.[22]

Another important stakeholder group within the greater community, of course, is business, both large and small. Any number of suggestions, recommendations, and even support has been offered to the school reform effort by businesses; and they will continue to do so. But Corporate America has only recently adopted a more altruistic and long-term view of school transformation. Business leaders first had to realize that quick fixes do not work for education reform. When that insight sunk home, at least for some business leaders, they began to realize the difficulty involved in trying to change an institution like the high school.

343

That is when talk of the "fourth wave" of business cooperation began to take shape. The fourth wave represents the most thoughtful and most potent of the recent business plans for schools; it certainly is more thoughtful than the first three waves and the quick fixes of the 1980s and early 1990s. A new understanding is growing among business people that will make it easier for them to work with educators. Business people involved in the transformation of high schools are learning about the complexities of education change; many now view it more correctly as a large-scale social system and political change effort. They are learning what elements work and what do not work. They also are beginning to listen to some of their own agencies' research, which has been informing them about more effective means of encouraging and influencing change. For example, the business organization research arm, the Conference Board, has advised business people that "after ten years of businesses working 'on' education . . . [the business community is now] working *within* education and *with*" educators. The new business attitude is that "In order to succeed, long-term change efforts that keep all parties working together must be developed."[23]

Part of that message has already paid off. Businesses announced a new council that would work with the Labor Department to get companies to participate in school-to-work programs at a higher level then previously, and they now are willing to involve their own firms to demonstrate their commitment to working cooperatively with educators.[24]

With a new community consensus and a new sense of collegiality with business, major roadblocks to redesigning the high school can be removed. Obviously, moving from the high schools we have now to the high schools of the future will take time, money, hard work, and involvement from all the key players. But the transformation will *not* happen merely by adding innovations. The fact is that no amount of change will affect student learning if *teaching* practices do not change.

If teachers do not change, then nothing changes. If teachers are good, innovations work; if they are bad, then boredom and busy-work deaden students' attention and interest. The only hope for the public high school is improvement of teaching. And that improvement will come only through massive investment in professional development.

It is more important than ever for teachers to develop the capacity to appraise their actions, evaluate their work, anticipate and control consequences, and incorporate new theory and research into practice. Teachers must possess the skills and understanding needed to explain their work to other teachers and to students and their parents. They must become reflective practitioners. In other words, teachers must become true professionals.

Developing Professional Teachers

Exhortations to improve students' higher-order thinking will accomplish little without able teachers who know how to engender such thinking and who teach in an environment that supports, rather than undermines, such learning. To accomplish that goal, we need to concentrate on *capacity building*, that is, to develop the knowledge, skills, and reflective processes of educators in order to enable them to improve instruction through a continuous cycle of self-analysis and learning. And we must do so in such a way as to make schools into true learning organizations for both teachers and students.[25]

A number of policy makers and pundits have argued that anyone with a college degree can be an effective teacher. They frequently argue that alternate routes to teaching can substitute on-the-job supervision for traditional preservice courses. They naively think they know how to teach and just need a few "tricks of the trade" to be successful. These policy makers advocate using alternative means for certifying teachers because they accept schools as they now exist.

Such arguments are wrong-headed and ignore the evidence. The evidence demonstrates that teacher interns who are involved in a combination of college coursework in education and well-designed supervision by college supervisors and mentor teachers far outshine those who have just a liberal arts degree or only coursework experience but have not had clinical supervision in public schools.[26]

Colleges and public schools need to find ways to build a sense of strong identification with professionalism. As part of that effort, a new professional (nonunion) organization should be formed — like the American Medical Association and other professional associations — to establish standards of ethical behavior and to certify members for professional practice. All of those moves will help build teaching as a profession.

Building professional capacity will require a dual strategy. There must be professional development for those teachers already in the schools. And we must redesign preservice education to build the profession.

Professional Development on the Job: Teachers now are expected to educate all students to a level once reached by only 20% of the students and to do so in a highly multicultural, multilinguistic, multiethnic society that is faced with rapid technological change and economic disarray. Teachers also are being asked to participate in making more schoolwide, and sometimes districtwide, decisions. However, instead of enhancing teachers' professional skills to cope with those changes, what they get too often is more prescriptive guidelines that attempt to narrow, rather than expand, their professional judgments.

Teachers want to do the best for their students. That is the primary motive driving them to become better and the key to engaging them in a dialogue with fellow professionals. But that motive is undermined when change efforts do not invest in developing teachers' professional knowledge. That underinvestment is characterized by short-term workshops with limited goals. Teachers continue to complain, rightly, that inservice programs generally are superficial, inadequate, off-target, and foisted on teachers by district administrators. Principals also complain that the same happens to them; their inservice programs usually focus on law, finance, and personnel issues instead of investigating substantive issues in curriculum and instruction or how to develop skills that are important for school leadership.

Some university programs, teacher networks, and collaboratives are helping to develop new models for professional development. The key to change is long-term, consistent development activities that help teachers become reflective practitioners capable of using pedagogical knowledge and organization-development practices for improving schools and student outcomes.[27] In other words, effective teaching is an art that is based on sound cognitive principles. To develop that art, teachers must be given the time to think about and refine their practice.

Typically, teachers have very little time; and like many other time-deprived professionals, they are interested in practical applications, not abstractions. They prefer to know about things that work, and they have little patience for things that do not work. Thus they miss out on discussions of the underlying theory and rationale for new practices. Such things seem to have so little relevance for the reality of their own classrooms.

There is a growing realization that there is a lack of synchronization between current professional development efforts and the aims of high school transformation. That is why professional development has been given high priority by the national and state departments of education. That increasing interest also is shown by other agencies, such as the National Commission on Teaching and America's Future (funded by the Rockefeller and Carnegie Foundations), which has made a number of recommendations for strengthening professional development over the life of a teacher's entire career.[28] The guidelines from that commission, as well as the insights learned by teachers' organizations from past experiences, have led to a better understanding of how to plan and conduct professional development programs. Following is a sample of the guidelines for professional development issued by national organizations:

- Effective staff development provides appropriate knowledge, skills, and attitudes regarding organization development and systems thinking.

- Effective school staff development is based on knowledge about human learning and development.
- Effective school staff development provides for the four phases of the change process: initiation, trial, implementation, and institutionalization.
- Effective school staff development bases priorities on a careful analysis of disaggregated student data regarding goals for student learning.
- Effective school staff development uses content that has proven value in increasing student learning, problem solving, and development.
- Effective school staff development provides a framework for integrating innovations and relating those innovations to the mission of the organization.
- Effective school staff development requires an evaluation process that is ongoing, includes multiple sources of information, and focuses on all levels of the organization.
- Effective school staff development uses a variety of staff development approaches to accomplish the goals of improving instruction and student success.
- Effective school staff development provides the follow up necessary to ensure improvement.
- Effective school staff development requires knowledge and use of the stages of group development to build effective, productive collegial teams.[29]

Those policy groups agree that the job of teaching teachers has to be redefined to focus on continuous learning. There are three principles that should underpin such professional development:

1. Teachers and principals should be intimately involved in planning their own experiences, not just passive recipients of information or someone else's decisions.
2. Teachers and principals should be linked to a "community of learners" who can bring their experience and ideas to complement their work.

3. There must be a balance between meeting the needs of individual groups of teachers and the advancement of school and district goals.[30]

Teachers also need to learn tasks that once were considered the domain only of administrators: organization analysis to identify structural and bureaucratic blocks to transformation; interpersonal and small-group communication skills for serving on decision-making bodies; new assessment techniques; research skills, especially action research within their classrooms; and peer coaching to help their colleagues hone their practice.

However, even with well-designed professional development, it will not be easy to convince teachers who already have a lot of experience to adopt new ideas and new practices. One technique used in the Renaissance Project in California is to have teachers volunteer to try "replacement units," small "chunks" of curriculum rather than an entirely new curriculum. The "chunking" approach also gives teachers the opportunity to keep using their traditional program while still experimenting with new ideas.[31]

Successful professional development efforts are dependent on interaction among teachers and between teachers and other professionals. That interaction is accommodated with the development of professional networks. Professional networks bring together diverse groups of teachers to share and learn from one another. That can be done through professional associations that meet informally, in consortia of schools within a defined area, in county offices of education, or in college-centered clusters.[32] Networks are professional support groups that motivate and help teachers use better methods. Many networks are organized around content areas, such as math, science, reading, literature, social science, etc. Networks have been sponsored by national foundations, states, universities, professional organizations, and local groups.

Networks usually involve face-to-face meetings and seminars, but increasingly they are being conducted through teleconferences and the Internet. Networks produce the same collective strengths that the business networks described in Chapter 6 do for the cor-

349

porate world: they pool resources for cost effectiveness, reach a wider consumer base, and most important, use peoples' different strengths to explore problems and ideas about teaching.[33] In addition, networks provide teachers with needed support to go about the risky business of changing their teaching.

Even with solid networks of professionals, no substantial on-the-job professional development can occur without teachers and principals gaining the time to change. In a recent survey of 178 principals in urban high schools undertaking major transformation efforts, 88% indicated that lack of time and energy were the major problems, even more than lack of funds. On average, high school teachers in those innovating schools devoted 70 days to implementing a project, and the more successful schools used 50 additional days a year for external assistance in training, coaching, and capacity building. The staff of the Effective Schools Network reports that it takes 10 to 20 teacher days per month to develop and implement improvement plans. To learn even a moderately difficult teaching strategy can require 20 to 30 hours of instruction in theory, 15 to 20 classroom demonstrations, and 10 to 15 coaching sessions before mastering the technique and incorporating it into routine classroom practice.[34]

Rather than weaving professional development into the teacher's job, it is squeezed in after school or in short-term summer work. If policy makers are really committed to "reforming" schools, they must fund a better approach. They must rethink the use of time to bring it more in balance, just as other countries do with their teachers.

Professional Development Schools: The massive changes needed in schools to meet the 21st century cannot be made by only re-training current teachers. There simply is too much institutional inertia for that to work. Aside from the personal changes demanded, recalcitrant parents, central office administrators, teacher and classified employee unions, inconsistent school boards, and state and federal government regulations form a mighty barrier to massive change.

The only hope for transforming high schools throughout the country is to get new teachers who already are prepared with the best pedagogical and organization-development insights. In other words, the process of transformation needs the infusion of millions of new, highly trained, professional teachers.

The Bureau of Labor Statistics estimates that more than 5 million new teachers will be hired in the United States between 1996 and 2005.[35] That gives the United States a significant opportunity, because those teachers could be the key to transforming high schools. If the country does it right, those new teachers will come from colleges that have adopted effective teaching strategies for teaching teachers. And the most effective way to educate teachers is a professional development school.

Professional development schools (PDS) are partnerships between a local school or school district and a college of education. They both benefit from that collaboration. The college has a place where preservice teachers can gain experience and where it can place intern teachers. The district benefits by being able to tap into college expertise and gain support for its professional development program. Thus, in true collaborative fashion, the PDS arrangement focuses not only on preservice education of teachers but also on professional development with schools and groups of schools.

Tying the local school to a forward-looking college of education gives both institutions the best of all worlds. Preservice teachers get to practice the latest and best pedagogy in a real-world setting. The university gets to work closely with the school, providing the school with professional development services that the teachers have determined. That relationship makes for a real learning community.

The PDS fosters the learning of prospective and beginning teachers by creating settings in which novices enter professional practice by working with expert practitioners and college faculty. Veteran teachers, by joining in partnership with colleges, can renew their own professional knowledge and skills and can assume new roles as mentors, university adjuncts, and teacher leaders. In addition, both school and university educators can engage jointly in research and rethinking of practice, thus creating an opportunity for the profession to expand its knowledge base by, as Linda Darling-Hammond puts it, "putting research into practice, as well as practice into research."[36]

Professional development schools are modeled on the teaching hospitals that support medical internships and clinical research. Thus the PDS not only supports the learning of individual school staff members, it also aims to redesign university programs for the preparation of educators and to transform the teaching profession.[37] All prospective teachers would undertake an intensive internship in professional development schools. There they would encounter state-of-the-art practice and a range of diverse experiences under intensive supervision. In that way, they would learn to teach effectively, rather than bumble along for a year or more or get so discouraged they leave the profession entirely, as often happens now.

In addition, the PDS would be a place for developing the knowledge base for teaching by carrying on practice-based and practice-sensitive research through the collaborative efforts of teachers, teacher educators, and researchers. That collaborative approach to research would allow teachers and teacher educators to test out and invent new models for teaching and teacher development. Together those at the college and those at the school form a symbiotic relationship, feeding off each other's unique capabilities and experiences to develop a new intersection of preservice education and inservice teaching. The PDS, with its emphasis on developing teaching as a full profession, will most likely develop the future cadre of educators who are aware and knowledgeable enough to redesign and transform the schools.

Technology and Professional Development

Most thoughtful education leaders agree that the successful integration of technology into the curriculum will require a transformation in education philosophy, classroom management, and curricular goals. Learning will not improve automatically just because teachers are taught how to use technology and given the necessary hardware and software.

> For technology to be used optimally, teachers must be comfortable with a constructivist or project-based approach to learning; they must be willing to tolerate students' progressing independently and at widely varying paces; they must trust students to know more than they do about certain subjects and techniques, and in fact take on the role of expert teacher at various times; they must be comfortable about not having complete control over what resources the student accesses or what the student learns, and they must be flexible enough to change directions when technical glitches occur. . . . We are asking teachers to integrate dramatically new philosophies of education, curricular goals, classroom management techniques and new ideas about interdisciplinary and individualized education into their practice.[38]

Technology makes staff development more complex, but technology also holds the answer to many professional development goals. The Office of Technology Assessment, for example, says that professional development by satellite or video-link, which now incorporates two-way communication connections, will allow networks of teachers to talk with each other, presenters to be questioned live, and classroom interactions to be simulated. That practice will become more widespread.

At best, only 50% of today's teachers can claim technological literacy. Even if there were a concerted push to place more sophisticated technology into classrooms, teachers would still need to experiment with it, share experiences with other professionals, and collaboratively plan to incorporate the technology into meaning-centered curricula.[39]

Even when teachers have the technological literacy, they often find it difficult to gain access to the technology. In addition to limited hardware and software, other factors affect access:

- Costs are high for purchasing, connecting, and training to use new technologies.

353

- Technologies may not be located in or near the classroom. Much of the early purchases of computers were for only administrative uses, not for classrooms.
- Hardware in schools today is old and cannot handle many newer applications. For example, the ratio of students to computers capable of multimedia work is 35 to 1.
- New or additional wiring or phone lines are necessary for telecommunications networks.[40]

These problems can be overcome with the proper funding levels. But despite politicians' rhetoric about the importance of technology, the federal government will not pay for the technological infrastructure. Indeed, the national government may be moving away from the concept of technological equity. If it is up to the states and local districts to take the initiative to finance the technology, it will only perpetuate the pattern of winners in affluent locations and losers in poorer regions. Already there are huge discrepancies between states, with some states having a ratio of 15.4 students to one multimedia capable computer (South Dakota, which has a high need for distance learning) down as low as 52 to one (California, whose Proposition 13 limits make it the stingiest state in the nation, falling below even such rural states as Mississippi).[41]

No one denies that the schools are in need. But just like the federal government, no one knows how to pay for what the schools need. Those local communities that are making "massive investments" in technology and training for teachers have achieved positive results. But for most communities, the investment will be prohibitively expensive. The Office of Technology Assessment estimates that the cost of providing up-to-date technology (including a computer for every seven students) and training for classrooms ranges from $10 billion to $12 billion a year over five years, more than triple what was spent in 1996. Compared with the $300 billion the nation spends on K-12 education, $10 billion is not very much; but for strapped school districts, it is next to impossible to dig up the extra dollars.

Unfortunately, many of the pundits' suggestions for solving this problem have been, at best, naive. For example, some conservative analysts have suggested that schools could pay for new technology if they would only redirect money from other activities. In fact, one conservative analyst suggested that California students could explore the Smithsonian Institution in Washington via the Internet with the savings from they would make by eliminating field trips![42]

Regardless of the staggering costs, American students will find it very difficult to compete in the workplace or to participate in community college and university programs without a massive infusion of technology into the schools. And the longer it is put off, the worse it will get.

Some have suggested that businesses could fund significant portions of getting schools online. There were expectations, at least among school people, that schools would receive a basic package of Internet services at a free or low-cost education rate, or "E-rate." But except for some highly publicized activity for the benefit of the Federal Communications Commission before passage of the Telecommunications Act of 1996, nothing much has happened with business "contributions" to schools.

Of course, no politician dares mention the huge defense budget as a potential source of funds. One less B-1 bomber could mean more than a billion dollars for education technology, and it would produce a much greater benefit for the country than the bomber would.

Regardless of how it is funded, technology will become increasingly important in the schools. But it is important to remember that technology is not an end in itself. Rather, the teacher's goal, just as it was with older technologies, is to empower students to use technology to extend their reach and to engage in inquiries that have meaning for them as learners. The combination of technological power and exquisite pedagogy will revolutionize high schools.

The Prospects for Long-Term Change

It appears that by 1996 business leaders and thoughtful educators had reached the same conclusion: To accomplish the goal of school reform, it is necessary to completely redesign the purposes and functions of schools and the preparation of teachers. The Conference Board, a research arm of major corporations and business associations that often is identified as the intellectual mouthpiece for corporate executives, clearly has come out on the side of complexity. It now is advising top executives that their commitment should be to "subordinate 'individual' interests to the greater good of children" and that "all children can learn, though at different rates and in different ways."[43] These epiphanies emerged from the lessons Corporate America and thoughtful educators both learned during the decade in which business was involved in school reform:

- There are no quick fixes to needed systemic change.
- Redesigning the school should begin with clear goals on which all can agree, with global ends met through local means.
- Redesigning school curricula, content, and structure are necessary steps.
- A coalition of key stakeholders must be built to achieve reform.
- School redesign is essentially political, and bringing together the key players is essential for redesigning the schools.
- Always focus redesign goals on children.
- Create a new community infrastructure.
- Make schools learning organizations.

Schools will change if for no other reason than that the nature of jobs will change. That will happen even without job-expansion programs, but it will happen twice as fast if such programs are implemented.[44]

However, educators must not be seduced into a "new vocationalism."[45] Redesigning high schools strictly along more vocational lines — such as career academies or additional cooperative programs or premature expansion of tech-prep programs — to the exclusion of a generic higher-order thinking curriculum would just repeat the mistakes of the past.

Even so, with all the controversy over privatization, with all the divisiveness among rich and poor, privileged and unprivileged, ethnic groups, and the other tribalisms of a myriad interest groups, a legitimate question can be asked: Do we even need public schools anymore? Why not just let each class and each ethnic group, each tribe, educate its own children using computer-based technology?

Building a nation means to develop a common core of values. That has been one of the historic missions of the schools. Every group of immigrants to the United States, including the most recent immigrants, has used the schools to learn those core values, to learn the language, and to prosper. As long as people see the need to build the nation, education will continue to be central to that effort.

It is possible that Americans will become so fractured, so divided by wealth or race or ethnicity or even by region, that they will no longer value public education. In that case, the country will be quite unrecognizable for most of us. One supposes it could happen; but to prevent it, the schools must change so that all children can meet the demands of the next century.

Educators, government officials, and even many business executives have come to realize that the function of the public schools is not to prepare students for specific occupations, nor even for large occupational categories. Instead, schools must provide the fundamental learning and processes of learning that all citizens need. The role of the schools is to attend to the whole child, not merely the economic child.

Deborah Meier neatly summarizes the challenge facing educators and the business community:

> The challenge [of school transformation] is a thrilling one: to make every child the possessor of a kind of intellectual competence once available to only a small minority. This inspiring — and new — task means granting all young citizens the conviction that they can have wonderful ideas, invent theories, analyze evidence and make their personal mark on this most complex world. Such a transformation of the idea of why children go to school would in turn transform the American workplace, as well as the very nature of American democratic life.[46]

If we can avoid political posturing and the diatribe coming from certain business executives, and if we insist on job expansion from Corporate America, then together concerned parents and educators can bring about the changes needed for education in the 21st century. At the same time, they can resolve the jobs dilemma. Then everyone will be winners of the shell game.

Notes

1. Ron Miller, "Reform versus Transformation," in *Great Ideas in Education* (Brandon, Vt.: Resource Center for Redesigning Education, Spring 1996), pp. 1-2.
2. Linda Darling-Hammond, "Reframing the School Reform Agenda: Developing Capacity for School Transformation," *Phi Delta Kappan* 74 (June 1993): 754.
3. Ibid., p. 757.
4. Terry A. Astuto, David L. Clark, Anne-Marie Read, Kathleen McGree, and L. deKoven Pelton Fernandez, *Roots of Reform: Challenging the Assumptions that Control Change in Education* (Bloomington, Ind.: Phi Delta Kappa Educational Foundation, 1994), p. 86.
5. David F. Labaree, "An Unlovely Legacy: The Disabling Impact of the Market on American Teacher Education," *Phi Delta Kappan* 75 (April 1994): 591-95.
6. Ibid.
7. Miller, op. cit., pp. 1-2.
8. Darling-Hammond, op. cit., p. 754.
9. Everett M. Rogers, *Diffusion of Innovations*, 3rd ed. (New York: Free Press, 1983), pp. 241-66.
10. Stanley Pogrow, "Reforming the Wannabe Reformers," *Phi Delta Kappan* 77 (June 1996): 656-63. Pogrow offers another "myth" that is not as adequately supported and is actually contradicted by more recent evidence from organization development — that "top-down programs cannot work." See Hanna Shachar, "Developing New Traditions in Secondary Schools: A Working Model for Organizational and Instructional Change," *Teachers College Record* 97 (Summer 1996): 549-68.
11. Rogers, op. cit.

12. Henry L. Tosi, John R. Rizzo, and Stephen J. Carroll, *Managing Organizational Behavior*, 2nd ed. (San Francisco: Harper & Row, 1990).

13. Jerry L. Patterson, Stewart C. Purkey, and Jackson V. Parker, *Productive School Systems for a Nonrational World* (Alexandria, Va.: Association for Supervision and Curriculum Development, 1986).

14. Joe Nathan, "Activist School Reform," *Education Week*, 21 February 1996, pp. 40, 43.

15. The point about "fun and joy" is to remind us that there is more to both life and learning than just rationality. See Marcella Spruce, "To Build Places of Joy: Re-Creating High Schools," *Education Week*, 28 September 1994, p. 42. Spruce is a former high school teacher and now a middle school specialist.

16. Astuto et al., op. cit., p. 86.

17. Jack Frymier, Luvern Cunningham, Willard Duckett, Bruce Gansneder, Frances Link, Julie Rimmer, and James Scholz, *Values on Which We Agree* (Bloomington, Ind.: Phi Delta Kappa International, 1995).

18. Joe Nathan and Betty Radcliffe, *It's Apparent: We Can and Should Have More Parent/Educator Partnerships* (Minneapolis: Center for School Change, University of Minnesota, October 1994), p. 112; "Teachers," *Education Week*, 9 November 1994, p. 9; William Snider, "Parents as Partners," *Education Week Special Supplement*, 21 November 1990, pp. 28-36; and Lisa Jennings, "Parents as Partners," *Education Week Special Supplement*, 1 August 1990, pp. 18-26.

19. "Parent Involvement Drops Off After the Early Grades," *Education Week*, 7, February 1994, p. 6.

20. "Teachers," *Education Week*, 9 November 1994, p. 9.

21. Meg Sommerfeld, "Ordinary People," *Education Week*, 25 January 1995, p. 19.

22. "When Parents Object to Classroom Practice," *Education Update* (January 1995): 1-6.

23. Sandra Waddock, *Business and Education Reform: The Fourth Wave* (New York: Conference Board, 1994), pp. 11-15.

24. "Leading Business Executives Create Council to Promote School-to-Work Programs," *Education Week*, 14 December 1994, p. 19. Large companies such as Ford Motors, Bell South, and American

Express, plus many others, are participating. Mr. Gerstner of IBM chose not to participate.

25. Ann Bradley, "The Long Haul," *Education Week Special Supplement*, 17 April 1996, pp. 41-49.

26. Linda Darling-Hammond, ed., *Professional Development Schools: Schools for Developing Professionals* (New York: Teachers College Press, 1994), pp. 7-8.

27. Donald A. Schon, *Educating the Reflective Practitioner* (San Francisco: Jossey-Bass, 1987), pp. 22-40.

28. Ann Bradley, "The Missing Link," *Education Week Special Supplement*, 17 April 1996, pp. 7-12.

29. These statements are adapted from the work of two national groups. See: "NSDC and NAESP Publish Elementary School Staff Development Standards," *Education Week*, 15 March 1995, p. 7.

30. Bradley, op. cit., pp. 7-12.

31. Kris Acquarelli and Judith Mumme, "A Renaissance in Mathematics Education Reform," *Phi Delta Kappan* 77 (March 1996): 478-84.

32. Robert E. Floden, Margaret E. Goertz, and Jennifer O'Day, "Capacity Building in Systemic Reform," *Phi Delta Kappan* 77 (September 1995): 19-21.

33. Joanna Richardson, "Teacher to Teacher," *Education Week Special Supplement*, 17 April 1996, 25-35.

34. Susanna Purnell and Paul Hill, *Time for Reform* (Santa Monica, Calif.: RAND, 1992), pp. 3-43.

35. George T. Silvestri, "Occupational Employment: Wide Variations in Growth," *Monthly Labor Review* (November 1993): 58-86.

36. Linda Darling-Hammond, ed., *Professional Development Schools*, op. cit., pp. 4-10.

37. John I. Goodlad, *Educational Renewal: Better Teachers, Better Schools* (San Francisco: Jossey-Bass, 1994).

38. Lin Foa, Richard L. Schweb, and Michael Johnson, "Upgrading School Technology," *Education Week*, 1 May 1996, pp. 52, 40-41.

39. Office of Technology Assessment, *Teachers & Technology: Making the Connection* (Washington, D.C.: Congress of the United States, April 1995), pp. 18-24.

40. Ibid.

41. *Los Angeles Times*, 22 August 1996, p. D1.

42. Ibid.

43. Waddock, op. cit., pp. 32-41.

44. Arthur G. Wirth, "Education and Work: The Choices We Face," *Phi Delta Kappan* 74 (January 1993): 361-66.

45. W. Norton Grubb, "The New Vocationalism," *Phi Delta Kappan* 77 (April 1996): 535-46.

46. Deborah W. Meier, "Get the Story Straight: Myths, Lies and the Public Schools," *The Nation*, 21 September 1992, pp. 271-72.